FREAK-OUT

FREAK-OUT

THE
2016 ELECTION
AND THE
DAWN
OF THE
AMERICAN
DEMOCALYPSE

IAN GURVITZ

ISBN-13: 978-1541297500
ISBN-10: 1541297504
Copyright: 2017 Ian Gurvitz
Cover image: Shutterstock/copyright Argus
Cover design: Victoria Gapin

CONTENTS

PROLOGUE...11

INTRODUCTION...17

CHAPTER ONE – FLASHBACK...22

CHAPTER TWO – WHAT THE FUCK HAPPENED?! THE GREAT AMERICAN FREAK-OUT...28

CHAPTER THREE – HOW THE FUCK DID THIS HAPPEN? CABLE NEWS – DR. FRANKENTRUMP... 76

CHAPTER FOUR – WHAT THE FUCK DID HE DO? TACTICS...86

CHAPTER FIVE – WHY DID IT WORK ON US? WELCOME TO DUMBFUCKISTAN...108

CHAPTER SIX – WHAT IF...WHAT COULD HAVE GONE DIFFERENTLY. WHY IT DOESN'T MATTER. AND WHY IT DOES...128

CHAPTER SEVEN – SURVIVING THE TRUMPOCALYPSE... 150

CHAPTER EIGHT – RESISTANCE. THE PEOPLE ARE REVOLTING...186

CHAPTER NINE – DIGGING FOR THE TRUTH IN THE FOG OF NEWS... 202

CHAPTER TEN – THE 2020 ELECTION. GET READY TO RUMBLE!...224

CHAPTER ELEVEN — THE 2020 ZEITGEIST. AMERICA — SHINING CITY ON A HILL OR TRUMPIAN DYSTOPIA?...260

CHAPTER TWELVE — DON'T GIVE IN TO CYNICISM OR DESPAIR...270

No one ever lost power underestimating
the intelligence of the American public.

I'm paraphrasing H.L. Mencken.
If he were alive today I wouldn't have to.

PROLOGUE

There's always been an element of idiocy in American political life. Unfortunately it's now become a valid intellectual stance. Our dumbed-down culture, enabled by a polarized, profit-driven news media, has created a virtual whirlpool of stupidity that has sucked down our national dialogue, our politics and our lives. That was the premise of a book I published entitled *Welcome to Dumbfuckistan – The Dumbed-Down, Disinformed, Dysfunctional, Disunited States of America.*

It came out in April 2016, though the catalyst for writing it was the 2008 election and the rise of Sarah Palin. The fact that someone so remarkably unqualified and profoundly ignorant could have become Vice President of the United States should have sent shockwaves through the body politic. Her candidacy represented more than just a danger to our national security; it threatened our national sanity. Yet the public and press response was relatively measured. It was as if people were walking past a flaming building, casually remarking that there seemed to be somewhat of a conflagration going on instead of screaming "FIRE!"

Right up until Election Day Palin was, technically, one malfunctioning defibrillator away from possessing the nuclear launch codes. And there was no provision in the rules of succession set forth in the 25th Amendment for skipping over the Vice President based on blatant stupidity.

Ultimately the election results assuaged my fears. Despite getting momentarily dope-drunk, the country sobered up, realizing, or perhaps remembering what can happen when we put fools in charge of government. And I breathed a sigh of relief, confident that this clear and present danger was behind us.

Even though Republicans dug in and chose a path of obstruction as the road to regaining power, it still fell under the heading of political gamesmanship. Yes, there were real world consequences to their actions but despite their opposition, under President Obama the economy was rescued from the brink of collapse, Bin Laden was killed, the ACA passed and there wasn't another 9/11-level attack. His presidency was a reaffirmation of the standards for holding high office: intelligence, experience, compassion, and most of all, basic human decency.

Then, in early 2011, Trump began popping up on TV, making his political bones with his birther campaign—the springboard for his pseudo run for the presidency. The claims were absurd. They were also dark, cynical and intentionally racist. He wasn't simply flouting political correctness, he was mooning civilized society, along with the accepted norms of American democracy. Still, he remained on the lunatic fringe and when he withdrew from the race and retreated to the alternate reality of his reality show, I assumed his cartoonish flirtation with politics was over.

But then came the 2011 White House Correspondents' Association Dinner, where he was excoriated by Seth Meyers and publically humiliated by President Obama. It was a cathartic moment for anyone who detested him, yet it was simultaneously chilling because of the expression on his face. Cold. Stoic. White hot. This guy was enraged at being ridiculed in public. Like many, I couldn't escape the feeling that he not only wanted payback, he wanted revenge.

June 16, 2015. Trump's escalator descent—his metaphorical trip to the bottom—in which he carried himself with all the humility of a Roman Emperor. The only thing missing was a garland on his head and Melania tossing grapes in his mouth. Then he took the stage and kicked off his run for the presidency by spinning tales of Mexican rapists stampeding over the border. It was our first stop on the seemingly endless tour of the dark recesses of his mind.

Ejecting a reporter from a press conference. Mocking a journalist with a disability. Raining down juvenile insults on his opponents. Stirring up violence at his rallies. Stacking a pile of meat on a table after a primary victory. I mean, really. Meat. Who does that?

Still, it was all just a big joke. A media shit-show. Until it wasn't. I watched in horror as Trump continued his national pussy-grab and full-frontal assault on the electoral process, using my book to get out my anger, and my fears.

I finished writing around the end of the primaries, when Cruz and Trump were battling it out for the nomination. One, an arrogant, Harvard-trained lawyer and monomaniacal culture warrior with a face that looked like his wife gave him a dog-turd necklace for his birthday; the other, an allegedly crooked, power mad, pathological liar with the guile of a street fighter and the class of a street pimp. The kind of arrogant dope who thinks it's classy to say, "I have a ton of class."

Each day brought a new low in our political discourse, like democracy had been chained to a car bumper and was being dragged down a back country road. When it reached the point of Trump insinuating that Cruz's father had been involved in the Kennedy assassination, all based on an article he'd seen in the *National Enquirer*, I was ready to jump out a window. Unfortunately I live in a one-story house, so it wouldn't have eased the pain. Instead, I stopped writing and published.

When my book came out I entered the world of shameless self-promotion. Book signings, radio shows, podcasts. I wrote articles for political websites while talking with anyone who was similarly freaked out. Given that the fate of the country, and the world, seemed to be hanging in the balance, the election was the only subject worth talking about. Everything else was trivial, inconsequential nonsense.

Then, Cruz was gone. And then there was one. Donald J. Trump had successfully blitzkrieged his way to the Republican nomination for President of the United States. The unthinkable had become real. This was getting serious.

Despite a tough primary battle between Hillary and Bernie, she was the presumptive nominee. Once again it was her turn. Given the tone of the primaries and Trump's warning shots, I assumed the general election would get nasty. I never imagined it would get hijacked into a dark hellscape. I couldn't fathom the depth of Trump's ignorance on domestic and foreign policy, the extent of his thuggish depravity, or his talent for blatant mendacity. He treated the electorate like a woman he was trying to talk into bed. "It's going to be fantastic!" "You'll have so many orgasms it'll make your head spin!" He wasn't just your generic all-politicians-lie kind of liar. He was a seasoned propagandist who exhibited not just a flagrant disregard for the truth but a seeming disdain for it. Trump abused the truth like it was one of his ex-wives.

I naively assumed that the media establishment would call him out. Most in the print media did. But to most cable news channels Trump was the ratings gift that kept on giving. From the beginning of the primaries I watched in horror as his rallies were aired in their entirety, without commentary. This not only turned them into virtual infomercials, it simultaneously legitimized both the message and the messenger. After all, he can't be an insane, dangerous maniac; he's on TV. As the President of CBS stated: "It may not be good for America, but it's damn good for CBS."

This led to the Republican convention—a cartoonish hate-circus featuring the incoherent ramblings of D-list celebrities and the ravings of Rudy Giuliani, who stood behind a podium like someone's grandpa who ate the wrong brownies at Thanksgiving and flew into a paranoid rage, screaming that terrorists were coming to kill us! Paul Revere meets Nosferatu.

Then came Trump's acceptance speech—a moment I couldn't have imagined, other than as satire or black comedy. A former reality show host and severely damaged human stood behind a podium as a major party's presidential candidate, his jaw jutting out like Mussolini, declaring that "No one knows the system better than me, which is why I alone can fix it!" This wasn't confidence. This was megalomania. The whole affair was less political convention than fascist theater of the absurd.

Nothing seemed to stop him. Not even attacking the grieving parents of a soldier killed in combat. I wrote that if Trump became the nominee, he would, in his parlance, get "schlonged" in the debates by Hillary. I never imagined he'd end up schlonging himself. Snorting, interrupting, dragging Bill Clinton's girlfriends out for a pre-debate public shaming, stalking Hillary onstage like some deranged psycho killer, then finally descending to the level of infantile name-calling. "No puppet! You're the puppet! You're the puppet!"

Childish petulance. Schoolyard bullying. The man was not only degrading the electoral process, he was demeaning the presidency itself. And that was before Pussygate and a dozen allegations of sexual harassment. Still, I had faith that his behavior would eventually cross a line where no sentient human being could think the man had the intelligence or experience to be president. I assumed that no matter how cynical we got about the political process we ultimately never fall out of love with our institutions.

Although some pundits declared that the cake was demographically baked, as we approached Election Day the polls were tightening, courtesy of the Russian DNC hack and the suspiciously timed Comey letter. The final act in this crazy farce was Trump's grand finale, in which he claimed that the election was rigged, and that he might not accept the results — unless he won. Like most people by this point I was emotionally, intellectually and psychically drained.

That's when I began writing an addendum to my book, incorporating the events of the election. Along the way I discovered some lingering typos and a few stupid mistakes. In one instance, I referred to "We The People" as the opening of the Declaration of Independence instead of the Preamble to the Constitution. That was a dumb one. Slipped by after a hundred proofs. An embarrassing oversight in a book about politics, yet one I rationalized as my version of John Belushi's *Animal House* "Was it over when the Germans bombed Pearl Harbor" moment. I mean, why let a few facts get in the way of the truth.

I mentioned a famous New York newspaper headline, citing the source as *The Daily News* instead of the *New York Post*. I also put in an extra word. It should have read: "Headless Body in Topless Bar." Still, I'm a native New Yorker. I should have known that. I also had the U.S. population at 350 million instead of 325. For that I blame the Internet. I'm not a fucking census taker.

I fixed the mistakes and planned to finish my revisions on Election Day — a day that couldn't come soon enough. Trump said he wanted to bring back torture, and he succeeded. This election was fucking torture. By the end, I had descended into the clichéd behavior of nervously flitting back and forth between my Twitter feed and Nate Silver's *FiveThirtyEight,* staring at the election graph like I was scrutinizing my EKG. Small blips. Big blips. Up, down. Widening, tightening. Still, Hillary was three points ahead. I understood that was a superficial, sports-score analysis of the data, but the stat had a calming effect.

Even though Silver cautioned that her lead was within the margin of error, I thought, "Screw the margin of error. That's just geek-speak for covering your ass." This cake was baked. It was demographics. Done, done, and done. Hillary Clinton would be elected president, sending Trump back to his aerie at Trump Tower and out of the public misery. And our long national nightmare would be over. I had no idea it was only just beginning.

Trump's Electoral College win added a corollary to the adage "You can fool all of the people some of the time and some of the people all of the time, but you cannot fool all of the people all of the time." Trump only had to fool enough of the people, one time. And he did. So, instead of stopping at revisions to my previous book, I began writing this one.

It was either write, or scream, both of which I've been doing non-stop since Election Day.

INTRODUCTION

It's human nature to want to make sense of insanity. Which is what we've been doing since Black Tuesday, as I now think of it. It's not enough to walk in circles muttering "but Hillary got 3 million more votes!" That's right up there on the list of useless statements with "but we were using birth control!" And given that the Electoral College voted and Trump was sworn in, there was no electoral abortion.

From the moment they called Pennsylvania, deconstructing the election became the new Democratic cottage industry. Artisanal hand-wringing. Monday morning quarterbacking where your team didn't just lose the game, your players and coaches were lying dead on the field. All the experts, journalists, political junkies, and pollsters went at it.

The same pundits who had it all so right pondered how they could have gotten it all so wrong. They were on every show, website and podcast, holding forth on the direct and indirect causes. The polls. The superior ground game. The metrics and data analytics. The fact that the Clinton campaign had a profile of every single American voter right down to their polyamorous sexual proclivities and favorite low-fat coffee drink. Non-college educated, college-educated, white, non-white, old, young, men, women, rural, urban. They analyzed the shit out of this election then hit the obligatory notes about our beloved democratic institutions and the peaceful transfer of power. Grasping for the best in us while realizing we'd just elected the worst of us.

It turned out that despite the Pledge of Allegiance, we're not "one nation, indivisible." We're 50 states, fragmented. Trump was the anti-Obama. Some voted for him in spite of his racism, others because of it. Not that it was the first time in history an aspiring dictator played on fear and anger in a rise to power. Whether it's the last remains to be seen.

This book is my semi-organized hysteria. Part analysis and part personal reflection, fueled by one, long primal scream. I'm not a professional pundit, commentator, policy wonk, historian or journalist, just a political junkie and freaked-out American. I'm venting. Raging. Yelling at my screen because it's how I process insanity without losing my fucking mind. Like looking back at a relationship after a breakup and wondering how something so right could have gone so wrong. The things you did. The things you didn't do. The things you said. The things you wish you hadn't said. You have to look back to know what happened, if for no other reason than to fix the problems, even within yourself, and to try to avoid them next time.

This won't be a sober, even-handed analysis of the election. I'm in no mood to be gracious, given my above-mentioned panic. There will be gratuitous insults, snark, and attacks on people, ideas and behavior that to me don't rate nuance. You may find my categorizing certain individuals as "fucking morons who are basically a waste of groceries and too stupid to live, let alone vote" as being judgmental. I accept that. Our new president opened the door for these kinds of attacks; I'm just walking through it.

There will be some personal anecdotes, just for flavor and context. Nothing too self-indulgent or autobiographical. Writing one's autobiography seems like the height of egomania. I can't imagine anyone sitting down to tell their life's story without the universe looking on and thinking, "In the grand scheme of things, do you really think your crappy childhood is that existentially significant?"

Finding a title was difficult. That's the thing with titles; they either come right away or they don't. I flirted with "Stillbirth of a Nation." I hit on "Democrazy," but discovered it was taken by a Republican Congressman who'd written a memoir of his political career, highlighted by a coke bust, and his resignation. (Maybe I'll read it, if for no other reason than the Republican coke bust is high on my list of hypocritical Republican failures, on a par with the Republican hooker bust and the Republican airport bathroom gay assignation.)

There was: "America's Trip to the Dark Side," "It's the

End of the World As We Know It," "America's Governmental Nervous Breakdown," "The Rise of King Donald I," "Hello, Sweden," "We're All Going to Die" or just "AAAAAGHH!!!!!" I liked the last one, but was afraid it might be hard to Google. You can incorporate them all as subtext.

There will be movie references, for the simple reason that real life events often hit a trip wire in my brain and I flash on iconic or obscure film moments. Also because the Trumpian alternate reality has proven to be even stranger than the alternate reality in the movies. I'm all for suspension of disbelief, but this required suspension of belief and disbelief, along with a suspension of decency, morality, civility and traditional American values. But at least in most movies, after a couple hours you're rewarded with an ending that leaves you with a sense of closure, or maybe even a feeling of hope. Reality isn't always as generous. Reality says, "This is the way it is. You can think about it, dwell on it, analyze it or wish it had worked out differently. But when you're done, it's still reality. Tough shit if you don't like it."

Despite Godwin's Law, there will be Hitler references. More than one. Sorry. Under the circumstances, they're hard to avoid. Not that I'm drawing a direct comparison. It's more for tone than content. Trump isn't Hitler. He's more Hitler-Lite — All the flavor, but with 10% less hate.

There will also be "fucks." I tried to mitigate the profanity because it can become a crutch, like when a comic goes "fuck" crazy to compensate for an absence of any real insights. Though "Our democracy is being tested like never before" just doesn't seem to express my fears as accurately as "This fucking maniac is going to kill us!"

Another language note: I've used certain words and phrases with a frequency that might have been adjusted by some careful editing. It's not that I have a limited vocabulary. I don't. I have, like, the best words. Yet I finally had to accept that certain words were evidencing themselves for a reason. I wrote "Trump" around 685 times. "Dumb" 34 times. "Stupid" and "fake" each 45 times. "Bullshit" 49 times. "Pussy" 25 times. "Russia" 74 times. At last count, there were only 3 "assholes," but 102 "lies" and 139 of the abovementioned "fucks." Sorry. It just seems to reflect the world we're in, or maybe just how I see it.

I've screwed with tenses every now and then in an effort to explain what I thought at the time, while folding in current events, incorporating them thematically. Trying to make sense of the past while getting bombarded with crazy new shit in the present. It's become near impossible to keep pace with the mania that's taken over our lives. I'm looking back in order to understand what happened and why. I'm in the present, reacting to the events of the day. And I'm looking forward, wondering whether the future will involve draconian rollbacks in social progress, impeachment, or nuclear winter.

There will be mistakes. I'm getting that out up front. They just happen, no matter how hard you fact check. I tried to do the appropriate research and check multiple sources while judging their political bent. Still, I'm convinced there are gremlins who hack your manuscript while you sleep and fuck things up in ways they know you'll never catch. For the same reason, there will also be typos.

I could spend the next year writing and re-writing, editing, proofing, weaving in events as they happen, but I can't. Analyzing this election and its effect on the country and the world will be the work of journalists, policy experts, political pundits, and historians for years to come.

As noted, this isn't some wonk-fest. It's rage. Emotional history. I'm freaked out and I need get this out now, while we still have a First Amendment. And, because it's good therapy. I'm still reeling from PTSD — Post Trump Stress Disorder.

It's like that moment when you wake up, crack open one eye, and slowly realize that you're on the floor, lying under a musty rug, still in your clothes, and that you reek of vomit. Then, as you slowly come to consciousness, you grab your head in pain and moan, "Ugh, how much did I drink? And who is this person next to me? And why do I itch down there? And why am I covered with tattoos, and what the hell do they mean? I mean, what the fuck happened?!"

So, what the fuck happened? For me, the first stop on this tour involved going back to Election Day. Or as I also now think of it, to quote Don Henley, "the end of the innocence."

CHAPTER ONE

FLASHBACK

"The horror…The horror."

Apocalypse Now

November 8, 2016. A date that will live in infamy. It started innocently enough. A beautiful fall morning. Clear skies. The air smelled sweet. Actually it smelled like shit because I live in L.A., where on most days the smog hangs over the San Fernando Valley like flab over a fat guy's belt. Except when the Santa Ana winds blow, and you gaze out in the distance thinking "Holy shit! There are mountains out there!" This was one of those clear days. I took it metaphorically, as if the winds were blowing away the Trumpian hate-storm. The Jimmy Cliff version of "I Can See Clearly Now" kept running through my head. "Gone are the dark clouds that had me blind. It's gonna be a bright, bright sun-shiny day."

Reports out of Florida stated that Latino turnout was high—a good sign, and further confirmation that, despite a dangerous flirtation with madness, America had sobered up and was going back home. Now we can leave this insanity behind and get on with our lives, restoring what was good and decent in the country and in our democratic process.

I got up and went straight out to vote. Given the ugly rhetoric about rigged elections and monitored polling stations, I was locked and loaded, ready to take on the first dumb thug poll watcher who tried to deny me my constitutional right to vote. There was no one. The polling station was in a church. Although I don't subscribe to the idea that it's a holy place, I chose to give that notion special dispensation for the day. It felt holy to me.

I strolled in. A polite, helpful guy pointed me to the correct room. My name was on the list. No request for a driver's license, passport, fingerprint or blood sample. There wasn't a poll watcher in sight, just an affable senior who handed me a ballot and pointed toward an open booth. It made me smile, something I've been accused of not doing enough. But this was so nice, so pleasant, so civilized.

I slid the ballot into the slot, lined it up, punched in my choices, and returned it to the affable senior, who helped guide it into the machine.

I got my "I voted" sticker and tossed it in my bag. I don't wear stickers, or buttons, or T-shirts with stupid jokes. Honestly, it's an impulse I just don't understand. Either have smarter thoughts, buy a smarter T-shirt, or shut the fuck up. But don't out yourself as an idiot.

Having voted, there was nothing left to do but to go about my day and wait for the inevitable result. At least I tried to tell myself it was inevitable but I couldn't shake this uneasy feeling that I'd been carrying around since the primaries. I didn't think Trump could win. But I was afraid Hillary could lose.

I recalled a column by Michael Tomasky on *The Daily Beast* back in early May. He made the case for why liberals should back her, but included an exhortation to the Clintons: "She can't blow it." All I could think was, why write that if it wasn't a legitimate possibility? As I said to friends during a Sunday softball game, where I try to avoid politics but in an election year it's not always possible, the only thing nagging at me was that with all the shit that poured out of Trump's mouth in the last year and a half, why he was only three points behind? Why didn't it send his campaign into the political garbage dump? Traditionally, this kind of behavior is rejected by civilized society. As well, over that entire time, I'd heard the "I hate him, but I can't stand her" refrain way too often, and from people all across the political spectrum.

My uneasiness built during the day, but it really kicked in around noon when I was in that bastion of Middle America, Beverly Hills. Duck Face Village. I was killing time before a doctor appointment, making a conscious effort to ignore the news, as nothing of any substance would be known so early. After writing about this election for years, I felt I owed myself a break.

I had lunch in a local deli where I'd done a signing for my first book, ten years earlier. Just to pass the time I started scribbling a Facebook post. A final goodbye and fuck off to Trump and his minions for hijacking this election and for the hate they slammed into the veins of the national bloodstream.

Just venting while eating a turkey sandwich. I was looking forward to going home later, turning on my screens and basking in the results. Like a prisoner straightening up his cell on the morning of his parole, I was eagerly anticipating the taste of freedom.

The waitress collected my check and I noticed she was wearing an *I Voted* sticker. She casually asked if I'd been following the election. I said I had and asked if she'd heard anything. She said, "not really" but then noted that one customer mentioned something about a high turnout of white voters. That struck me as odd. Why was that a thing? Then I flashed on Republican pollster Frank Luntz and his focus groups, where he always seemed to be pushing the "secret, angry white electorate" meme — the Caucasian Bradley Effect. At the time, I rejected it as someone trying to stir up a little media controversy by flogging a counter-narrative.

I went to my doctor appointment, a quick in-and-out, not usually accompanied by more than casual chitchat. Then the doctor brought up the election. I wasn't exactly in a position to get into a political discussion, so I tossed off something about looking forward to it being over, as I saw Trump as the devil. He replied, "Yeah, but I don't really care for either of them." Excuse me, what? This wasn't coming from some dumbass at a focus group squeaking out talking points like they were beer farts. This was a Beverly Hills doctor. It was unnerving.

Driving home, I flashed on a dinner I'd had six months earlier, when I took my daughter out for her birthday. She brought a friend who, when the election came up, said "Didn't Hillary have some guy killed?" I thought, "Really? Vince Foster? You believe that shit? What the hell are you reading that would even make you aware of it, let alone believe it?" Still, I put it out of my mind as just another aberration.

I got home, settled in, and turned on my screens. I was done. Time to get this shit over with. Then my screens said, "Uh, not so fast." Florida — too close to call? North Carolina — too early to call? What? What happened to blowout?

Landslide? Arizona going blue? Georgia? Over 400 electoral college votes?! Ronald Reagan was going to rise from the grave wearing an *I'm With Her* T- shirt. Americans were finally coming together and declaring that we're not about racism, sexism and xenophobia. This is not who we are as a people, or as a nation. Don't talk to me about "too close" and "too early." Every voting booth should've been tricked out with a fail-safe device, so that if anyone punched a hole for Trump, a boot would spring up from underneath and kick them in the nuts. I did not like this.

Then time slowed down and everything went full Matrix. Florida — gone. Ohio — gone. North Carolina — gone. Ok, I knew Ohio was lost and Florida was close, but North Carolina?! This was not the story we approved! America's off script and improvising some really crazy shit. I was afraid to keep watching but I couldn't turn it off. I covered my face as Steve Kornacki stood at the giant touchscreen, pointing at rural counties and detailing their demographic makeup.

Suddenly I wasn't watching *MSNBC*. Instead it was one of those hokey World War II documentaries with the ominous drum beat soundtrack and the deep-voiced narrator describing "Nazis on the march," as the graphics portrayed their stampede across Europe with the giant, slow-moving arrows. All I could do was curl up in a fetal ball and rock back and forth intoning, "This is bad. This is very bad." Then shit really got dark. Michigan?! Where's the firewall?! What happened to the firewall?! Pennsylvania?! Pensyl-fucking-vania?!

Suddenly, they're cutting to shots of Trump and his disciples staring up at their screens. And they're smiling. Then they cut to the crowd at the Javits Center, where people looked like they'd just seen a puppy get hit by a truck.

Wisconsin?! Oh, my god, they're calling it. They're fucking calling it! We just elected the racist, sexist, pussy-grabber President of the United States! This is not fucking happening! What the fuck happened?! WHAT THE FUCK HAPPENED?!

CHAPTER TWO

WHAT THE FUCK HAPPENED?!

THE
GREAT
AMERICAN
FREAK-OUT

*"I'm mad as hell, and
I'm not going to take this anymore!"*

Network

I keep flashing back to that moment on *CNN* when Brianna Keilar was interviewing Trump lawyer, Michael Cohen. When she mentioned that his boss was losing, his Clarence Darrow-like response was "Says who?" To which she responded "The polls. All of them. I just told you." Yes, it was funny. Hilarious. And I laughed right along, assuming he was just engaging in the Trump spokesperson's pro forma dickish denial of reality. But it always nagged at me that something could go wrong. Maybe it was my New York Jewish head. Always prepare for disaster. Never assume everything's fine, because you're tempting fate.

Weeks before the election, Michael Moore was on *Real Time with Bill Maher* and made a seemingly outrageous statement: he thought Trump could win. At the time I assumed he was just being provocative, while trying to freak out the base and turn out the vote. Turns out he's Nostradamus.

This was not supposed to happen. But it did. An American presidential election got death rolled into the icy cold depths of depravity based on one man's dark, twisted impulses. This election split open the psyche of the country and the anger, fear, and stupidity just poured out. The unthinkable became real.

This was the shock of 9/11, the horror of the JFK assassination, the double gut punch of Martin Luther King and Bobby Kennedy, plus Altamont, the Challenger disaster, John Lennon's murder, Hurricane Katrina, Michael Jackson, Prince, your first break-up, and your doctor telling you you've got stage IV cancer all rolled into one. It was like the founding fathers rose from the grave, stuck a mini-skirt and stiletto heels on the Statue of Liberty and put her on the street. (Yes, I know they weren't contemporaneous, but I'm freaked out, so I'm searching for images wherever I can find them.)

I'm stuck on an emotional Kübler-Ross Mobius Strip, slipping from denial to anger to bargaining to depression then back again to denial, never quite getting to acceptance. How do you accept the unacceptable?

How do you make sense of insanity? It was like that scene in *The Hangover* where they wake up in a trashed hotel room with a live tiger in the bathroom. All you can do is take in the carnage and think "What the fuck happened?!"

What happened was that 63 million people, most notably 77,759 voters in Michigan, Pennsylvania, and Wisconsin changed the course of American history, world history and very likely civilization—assuming we had the right to call it that before and if we'll still be able to call it that after.

This election still should have been a blowout: An outgoing two-term president with a 58% approval rating. An intelligent, experienced, albeit imperfect candidate who would have continued economic policies that were basically working, particularly when measured against the previous administration, which was, in Trumpian parlance, "a total disaster." The Bush years gave us 9/11, Katrina, and a war costing hundreds of thousands of lives and trillions of dollars, while further destabilizing the Middle East. And for an encore, they tanked the economy and almost sent the country into a depression.

Under President Obama there were no major U.S. terrorist attacks. There was an efficient, compassionate response to Hurricane Sandy. Bin Laden was killed. The economy slowly recovered. The stock market nearly tripled and unemployment fell below 5%. If you simply reversed these two records, Republicans would be carving George Bush's face on Mt. Rushmore. Just imagine their outrage if the country had been attacked and the economy tanked under the last president.

But, even if you insisted that the economy had stalled out due to government over-regulation and punitive corporate tax rates—the standard Republican rap. Even if you thought Hillary hadn't addressed the concerns of the working class. Even if you thought the previous administration was slow in responding to the rise of ISIS, and that the Syrian red line was a major gaffe. Even if you thought that, despite 20 million people getting access to health care, the Affordable Care Act was a job-killing failure. (Remember the job-killing talking point? Haven't heard that one in a while. It must have been rendered inoperative when measured against 15 million new private sector jobs.) Even if you were rock solid in your opinion that the country was headed in the wrong direction, Trump should not have been an acceptable choice.

If it was about returning to traditional Republicanism, voters could have gone with any one of sixteen garden-variety "let's unleash the might of American private enterprise" candidates: A dusty old-school type like John Kasich. Granted, the man doesn't exactly light up a room, but he's intelligent and experienced. If Kasich didn't set their hearts racing, they were lousy with other governors: Perry, Christie, Pataki, Walker, or Jindal. They had a feckless, pandering hypocrite like Rubio. If they felt like a religious nut, they had Ted Cruz, Mike Huckabee and Rick Santorum sitting in the pews. There was Lindsey Graham, who would've brought solid congressional experience to the White House while re-popularizing the mint julep. If they wanted to go outside the box, they had a business-type in Carly Fiorina, a weirdo Libertarian in Rand Paul, or a cryptic, soporific ex-surgeon in Ben Carson. They could've even gone rogue and drafted Randian econo-bot, Paul Ryan—a guy with all the integrity of a prison snitch. Or even if they were just feeling lost and wanted the comfort of another Bush, they had one right there. They had an endless supply of supply-side, tax-cutting, abortion-ending union-killers. So why pick the ignorant, shit-talking pussy-grabber? Something else was going on.

In my previous book I made the case that our national dialogue had been dragged down into the intellectual gutter, and that America could become the first world power to crumble under the weight of its own stupidity. But in this case we didn't just go dumb. We went dark. Demonic. Roiling around in a raging shit-storm of anger. Two minutes on Twitter could have told you that this wasn't an election. It was a *Lord of the Flies* pig roast.

But where was the anger coming from? Were we an adult suffering a mental, or in this case, governmental breakdown or were we just bored and wanted change? It seems we always want change. Well now we've got it. New and Improved America! Now with whiter whites!

Or maybe we just needed therapy. We're still a relatively young democracy. Maybe we were just having a tantrum. Maybe someone needed to take the country aside and calmly ask what was bothering us. We should be happy. We're a young, attractive country with an engaging personality. Everyone wants to hang with us. We have most everything a country could want. We're popular, creative, and resourceful. Industrious, ethical and high-minded. We're not prone to violence. Sure, we have around 30,000 gun deaths a year, but it's not like we're as bad as some other countries I could name.

We're also strong. We've stood up to bullies when necessary. Yes, we've had some military meltdowns, and a few misadventures, but our heart has always been in the right place. So why are we so angry? Do we feel unloved? Unappreciated? Misunderstood? Unsafe? Vulnerable? Abandoned? Do we have founding father issues? Or do we just need some sympathy and understanding? Or maybe antidepressants. We already have an opioid epidemic, so we're obviously self-medicating.

Even though Nate Silver ran billions of election simulations, finally concluding that Trump had as much chance of getting elected president as a flea had of impregnating an elephant, it just didn't matter. Money didn't matter. Ground game didn't matter. None of the usual metrics mattered. So how did Trump pull this off? And what does it say about us that he did?

There's a fascinating three-hour documentary about the '70s band The Eagles. For anyone who lived through the era, it resonated, not just for the music, but for the unusual candor of the interviews along with the sadness over the passing of Glen Frey. There's a moment in the film when guitarist Joe Walsh talks about going to rehab and re-emerging with a renewed sense of purpose. He quotes an author who'd written something to the effect that when you're living your life, it feels like total chaos—random events smashing into each other. But when you look back at it, it seems like a finely crafted novel.

Well there was nothing finely crafted or artistic about this election. Why wasn't this a landslide—a complete and total rejection of amorality and shamelessness? We're always patting ourselves on the back about how noble we are. How could we elect someone so ignoble, leading to such an unholy juxtaposition of man and office?

Looking back, I know that the sick, uneasy feeling I had on Election Day didn't come out of nowhere. There were moments during the campaign when reason, common sense, and common decency seemed to be succumbing to chaos theory; moments that filled me with dread. Yet, I stuck those feelings in the Steve Jobs reality distortion field, convinced they were aberrations, and not indications of anything going on in the zeitgeist. Now, with the benefit of hindsight, they seem less like random events and more like part of a narrative. So what was that narrative?

After putting out my book I continued to write about the election, beginning in June 2016 with an article on *Attn.com*. The following reflects what I thought at the time. I've occasionally added comments to add context based on more recent events and revelations.

CHAOS THEORY
IN THE
2016 ELECTION
(June 2016)

In the words of renowned epistemologist Donald Henry Rumsfeld, "There are known knowns. These are things we know that we know. There are known unknowns — that is to say there are things that we know we don't know. But there are also unknown unknowns. These are things we don't know we don't know." This single epigram essentially sums up the collected wisdom regarding the 2016 election. Some experts say the race is Hillary's to lose, others claim it will be tight, and the guy who created Dilbert insisted on *Real Time with Bill Maher* that Trump is a Jedi mind-fucker who will win in a landslide. So much for the sweet science of politics. Still, utilizing the Rumsfeldian paradigm, what do we actually know?

THE KNOWN KNOWNS

TRADITIONAL VOTING PATTERNS

Many pundits contend that the election will follow the 2012 map, which traditionally gives an Electoral College edge to Democrats. Yet others say it could go Republican based on swing states like Florida, Ohio, Michigan, Wisconsin or North Carolina. A recent article on *The Hill* made the case for a Trump path to victory by turning Pennsylvania — unlikely, though maybe not impossible. Clinton war room vet James Carville described the state as "Philadelphia and Pittsburgh with Alabama in between." And a piece on *FiveThirtyEight* noted that over time it's been trending Republican. Still other experts contend that traditional red states like Arizona could turn blue, particularly given Trump's 72% disapproval rating with Hispanic voters.

VOTER ENTHUSIASM AND TURNOUT

Democrats need 2008 turnout levels although there's hardly Obama-level passion for Hillary. Both she and Trump have high unfavorability ratings, with Hillary's coming from the "untrustworthy" meme that's been beaten into the public consciousness for the last 25 years, whereas Trump's stems from the fact that he's an unfavorable human being who made his bones peddling anger, insults, lies and false hope to an angry white electorate. Still, there may be Trump Democrats who are put off by Hillary, or Clinton Republicans who are repulsed by Trump. The question is: how many, and where are they?

PARTY UNITY

Hillary can't fight a two-front war forever. At some point, she and Bernie will have to sit the kids down and explain that they're in love and want to blend their families. Meanwhile, like a scab forming around a festering wound, the GOP is closing ranks behind Trump. Even Paul Ryan finally coughed up a tepid endorsement, though he had to walk it back a day later when Trump went full racist on the judge presiding over his Trump University lawsuit. Ryan's regret was palpable. But his pained look didn't come close to the revulsion Chris Christie sported, standing on stage with Trump. It was like he'd just professed his undying love for the neighbor who poisoned his dog.

THE KNOWN UNKNOWNS

VP PICKS

Popular wisdom is to follow the Hippocratic oath and "do no harm." Just ask John McCain. Hillary needs more of the white vote to lock down the rust belt, so maybe she'll go with Sherrod Brown. Given that Trump's royally screwed himself with women, Hispanics, Asian-Americans, and anyone with any sense of decency, he needs a pick who might appeal to those he's offended. Maybe Megyn Kelly. Or Bill O'Reilly in a dress. Someone with government experience might help, or at least someone who could find D.C. on a map.

Still, balancing the ticket might not be a candidate's "save shot." According to *FiveThirtyEight*: "There's often a big gap between what we think matters, and what factors seem to influence candidates' choices, and how voters react to them... Experience matters. Female running mates garner media attention, but not all of it is positive. Home-state advantage may exist, but only in certain cases... And ideological balancing, along with other forms of ticket balancing, is a much smaller part of the modern VP selection process than many media accounts would suggest."

VOTER SUPPRESSION

Obama's 2008 victory was a wake-up call for Republicans, who instantly realized that the electorate was changing, and it wasn't getting whiter. The solution: make it tougher for these voters to vote. This brought us the "Acorn scandal" and the newly minted concept of "voter fraud." Seventeen states now have new voting restrictions in place for the first time, thanks to a 2013 Supreme Court ruling gutting key provisions in the 1965 Voting Rights Act. Scalia, RIP.

THIRD-PARTY CANDIDATES

After months of threats, we have a Libertarian ticket with former governors Gary Johnson and William Weld. Some say they could pull a Nader on Trump and swing the election for Hillary. Others claim they could steal votes from her. A *New York Post* article cited a Quinnipiac poll stating that the Libertarian run, along with the addition of Green Party candidate Jill Green could "throw the race into chaos."

SURROGATES

Once again, Bill Clinton is out stumping for Hillary, which was obviously the reason Trump brought up his past indiscretions—anything to neuter the big dog. Elizabeth Warren has been pounding Trump mercilessly, and President Obama went on the attack at a Rutgers commencement speech. Although parties traditionally don't hang on to the White House for three straight terms, the president's high approval rating could help make that happen. A trip to Michigan should remind voters that he saved GM when Republicans were ready to let it go under.

THE CONVENTIONS

Given Trump's reputation for understatement, the GOP gala in Cleveland should be a spectacle combining the subtlety of a Super Bowl Halftime Show with the sophistication of the Miss Universe Pageant, along with a dash of Nuremberg. Perhaps we can look forward to another Sarah Palin schizophasic word salad shriek-fest, or the return of Clint Eastwood's chair. Democrats convene a week later in Pennsylvania, and if by then they've managed to disband the debating society and work up a little showmanship, they could make the public forget the opening act and leave a message of unity hanging in the air.

THE UNKNOWN UNKNOWNS

GAFFES

In 1976, then-candidate Gerald Ford claimed there was "no Soviet domination of eastern Europe." This pushed the meme that he wasn't that smart. More recently we had Howard Dean's rebel yell, Rick Perry's brain fart, Romney's 47 percent dissolution, and "binders full of women" remark. Given Trump's penchant for temper tantrums, along with the absence of any big, beautiful wall between his terrific brain and his extended clip magazine of a mouth, he could easily suffer a debate implosion and self-destruct. (Though during the primaries at least, Trump proved immune to the negative backlash that usually follows a political gaffe.)

SCANDAL

Hillary's fantasy is that Donald ends up on the witness stand in his Trump University trial. Trump's is that the FBI leads Hillary off in shackles over her emails. At the moment, he's trying to stamp out fires about his donations to veterans and his taxes, while attacking the media, essentially biting the hand that suckled him from the time he was a puppy.

It's been said that a week is an eternity in American politics. If so, the next five months will be a timeless black hole into which all opinions and analysis disappear. For all the pundits and polls, statistical analysis of voting patterns, historical precedent and demographic trends, chaos theory is alive and well in 2016. The insults between the candidates have only just started flying. And we haven't even hit the debates or the fusillade of attack ads.

Hillary nailed Trump in a scathing speech in San Diego and his pathetic response was halting and erratic with a sheen of Nixonian flop sweat. For the first time, he looked vulnerable. But the experts have been writing The Rise and Fall of Trump for almost a year and it hasn't happened.

The only certainty in this election is uncertainty. In a world where even the known knowns have an element of unknowability, and the known unknowns are multiplying by the moment, and the unknown unknowns are — well, who knows what the fuck they are — the only truth right now comes from screenwriter William Goldman's "Adventures in the Screen Trade" — "Nobody knows anything."

It's eerie to look back, seeing what people thought at the time and knowing how it all turned out. It's like playing back the events in a busted relationship and admitting there were moments where you had a creepy vibe that it had turned a dark corner, but you just didn't want to accept it.

When I finished my book, Hillary was the presumptive nominee, and Trump and Cruz were still battling it out. Then on May 3, Cruz dropped out. We had a match-up: Trump versus Hillary. As we hit the conventions, this is what I wrote.

HATESTOCK
AND
THE DNC LOVEFEST
(July 2016)

The iconic 1969 Woodstock logo promised 3 Days of Peace & Music, and featured a guitar with a bird perched on the neck. 47 years later we get the eerily similar RNC convention logo, only with an elephant stomping on the guitar neck, seemingly threatening to snap it. Of course, the guitar was supposed to be an homage to Cleveland—site of the convention, and home of the Rock & Roll Hall of Fame.

It was quite a feat of multitasking to shit on democracy and rock 'n' roll simultaneously, but the Republicans pulled it off. Right from the start it was a show in search of a low point. A parade of D-list personalities. A plagiarized speech by the candidate's wife, which turned into a mini-scandal, replete with the usual staunch denials and followed by the obligatory scapegoating. Somebody blew it. The speech was a wasted opportunity, as they obviously just take Melania out of the box for special occasions. There was Rudy Giuliani's paranoid raving and Chris Christie's theatrical courtroom-style indictment of Hillary Clinton—this from the man with Bridgegate hanging over his head. And for the Grand Guignol finale, we were treated to Trump's version of America as a gangsta's paradise.

But of all the ugly, clueless, classless and surreal moments of the RNC conclave none topped the song that kicked in at the end of Trump's 75-minute, fact-challenged, dystopian diatribe. I was sure my ears were screwing with me when the dictator-wannabe began soaking in the adulation to the familiar opening chorus of The Stones' "You Can't Always Get What You Want."

Put aside that they probably took the song without paying for the rights, why would you use it at the Republican National Convention, where the theme is "You Can Always Get What You Want And It's Even More Fun if You Can

Screw The Poor While You're Getting It." In all, the whole affair came off as a mismanaged, pathetically choreographed shit-show. More Hatestock than Woodstock.

A week later, the DNC kicked off its Philadelphia convention. The change in tone was as if someone cleared the children out of the room so the grown-ups could talk. Though it was not without discord. Despite passionate speeches by Senator Cory Booker, Michelle Obama, Senator Elizabeth Warren, Senator Franken, and Senator Sanders himself, along with Sarah Silverman's blunt "you're being ridiculous," the Bernie or Bust people remained unmoved. They were out in full force, and full voice.

I get the passion, along with the rhetoric of revolution. I marched in demonstrations against the Vietnam War with people carrying signs that read "Peace Now!" A noble ideal, yet I always felt an annoying twinge that the message reflected the petulant demands of a generation raised on instant gratification. "Peace eventually" didn't quite have the cadence to chant during a march.

As things turned out, there was no "peace now." There was peace, if you can call it that, about five years later. Now my Gap T-shirts are made in Vietnam. So what was the point? Yes, hindsight is brilliant, but it's tough to make the case for the Domino Theory based on the fact that they now have Domino's Pizza in Ho Chi Minh City. Revolution in thirty minutes or less.

Social change doesn't happen overnight. There's no instant utopia, just a slow turn of the wheel. What Bernie Sanders brought to this election was a movement grounded in a vision of the values this country should stand for. A declaration of how things ought to be: fairness, equal opportunity, universal health care, getting the money out of politics by overturning Citizens United, getting the rich to pay their fair share in taxes and protecting a woman's right to choose. Dismantling our American oligarchy, fighting income inequality and restoring the American dream for everyone. And I agree. It's the way life ought to be. But given the fact that the polar opposite vision exists on the other side, this will always be a tug of war of ideals. Paul Ryan is correct: it's a binary choice. And if you've observed Trump's conduct over the past thirteen months, you realize this is not a debating society, it's a street fight. The timing of the WikiLeaks email dump should give you some idea of the tactics involved.

It took 100 years to get from the Civil War to the Civil Rights movement. And while there has been progress, 50 years later the same struggle rages on, whether it's in the streets or in the courts. Standing proudly with your unshakable ideals, stubbornly insisting on casting a protest vote doesn't turn the wheel of progress. It may make you feel intellectually pure, and protect you from the nagging sensation that you've compromised, but Bernie or Bust is not going to magically make your dreams come true. Given the stakes, it amounts to a political temper tantrum.

To those who insist that it's our way or the highway, I would suggest you look at the career of the man who inspired you. Bernie Sanders has been in public service for 35 years. Fighting for what you believe in is a constant struggle in which you get as much as you can at any given time, and live to fight another day. Senator Sanders was tough during the primaries and graceful in supporting Hillary. He made his presence known at the convention, and in shaping the party platform.

Passion gives someone the strength to fight over time. Patience and pragmatism are not the words of capitulation. They're the language of realism. And it's time to get real. It shouldn't take more than remembering that Ralph Nader's 2000 run bequeathed us George Bush, the Iraq War, Katrina, and almost a second Great Depression. So before you curl up in bed with your ideals, take a breath, look at the past, and then imagine the future beginning next January when Donald Trump takes the oath of office.

At some point this isn't about personalities, it's about policy. And the ability to make policy depends directly on who gets elected. If Hillary wins and the Democrats re-take the Senate, they will go into next year in a position of strength, beginning with a Supreme Court nominee who will instantly change the balance of power.

And that brings me back to The Stones' song and its relevance to the Democratic Convention. The chorus goes: "You can't always get what you want. But if you try sometimes, you might find, you get what you need."

The difference between the lunacy of the GOP convention and the sanity of the Democrats' gathering a week later seemed to exemplify the difference between the candidates. The Republican convention was like being in a hot, crowded grocery store on a rainy Friday night, and suddenly realizing you left your wallet home. Then your kid starts freaking out. You could lose it but instead you take a breath, summon all your resources and tell yourself you'll find a calm, rational way through this nightmare. Then your kid shits his pants, and you think "Ok, maybe I won't. "

But then the Democrats took stage and wiped it all away. Anger, fear, and hysteria were replaced by reason, experience and intelligence. And yes, even compassion. As we hit the end of August, the election was feeling more set. *FiveThirtyEight* had Hillary's odds at around 74-26. But then Trump went to Mexico, Hillary went MIA, and the shit started getting surreal.

TRUMP GOES TO MEXICO
AND PHOENIX.
HILLARY GOES MIA
(August 31, 2016)

Apparently, Trump's advisors told him he needed to take some of the ugly out of his immigration rhetoric and look more presidential, so he flew down to Mexico for a "meeting" and "press conference" with Mexican president Enrique Peña Nieto—a man whose name he'd obviously just learned to pronounce. Yet the media dutifully followed him, covering the trip like it was JFK in Berlin, deconstructing his every word and analyzing his stage presence and appearance, right down to the bobby pin in his hair. It was "Look at me. I can walk on stage with another president, put on my serious 'presidential' face, stand behind a podium, read from a paper, and not say anything racist for five minutes, so it's safe to vote for me." They reported on it as an event instead of calling it out as an obvious campaign stunt.

They gleefully jumped into the swamp of the "wall" narrative, swimming in the intellectual muck of who told whom in public or private that they would or wouldn't pay for a wall. In reality, there was no wall. There never has been a wall. There never will be a wall. The only wall that's ever existed has been the big, beautiful, metaphorical wall in Trump World, which has already been built.

Then, as part of his whirlwind, international tour there was the Phoenix speech that night, where Trump's people claimed the candidate would finally lay out his immigration policy. Set up with concepts like "pivot" and "softening," the media raced to cover it, under the guise of informing the public.

At one point, Mark Halperin wondered if Trump would be able to "tone down the rhetoric," then commented on his "I will be so presidential" Teleprompter address by observing that the candidate was "very focused, very on message." He went on to note that "If the campaign can move more toward organization, people will be, at least, somewhat comforted…"

But there was no message. No policy, just the same inflammatory rhetoric and racist tirades. Trump pandered to swing voters in the morning then threw red meat to the base at night, and it was broadcast without interruption by a media sucked into the centrifugal force of Trump World. It was non-stop Trump TV. Trump team coverage! Trump breaking news! All Trump, all the time. I realize it's not the prescribed role of journalists to editorialize, but at what point are they getting played? At what point does their coverage afford a stunt instant credibility? At what point do they simply become his personal production crew?

And, amidst it all, Hillary was MIA. Gone. Lost in the netherworld of the Hamptons, raising money. It didn't matter if she'd actually vanished; she virtually vanished. All I could think was: Secretary Clinton, what the hell is going on? What aren't you on my TV? Why aren't you on my phone or computer screen? Is this a rope-a-dope strategy, where you let the dope punch himself out? Because I'll be honest, it doesn't seem to be working, for the simple reason that I've momentarily forgotten you're running for President. I only hear your name in reference to FBI email dumps, and AP stories about Clinton Foundation "scandals." I don't care if it was expected that the polls would be tightening. So is the knot in my stomach. I don't care if the pollsters and pundits say the cake is baked. With three debates coming up and *Fox News* anchor Chris "I don't need no stinking fact-checking" Wallace moderating the last one, it doesn't feel baked!

I'm glad you're raising money. I'm glad the plan is to pound Trump into oblivion with TV spots in swing states. And, yes, your surrogates are wonderful. Tim Kaine is a lovely guy. Smart. Experienced. Likeable. A solid Veep choice. Though not exactly a rhetorical maverick. There's no Chris Matthews leg tingle. And yes, Vice President Biden can turn a phrase. He's intelligent, and folksy. A tough trick to pull off, even with the optics of the loosened tie and the rolled-up shirtsleeves. I imagine it plays in the rust belt, but ultimately there's no power in it. And Trump has power. He understands power. The people he's surrounded himself with understand power—how to get it, and how to use it.

I'm sure President Obama will be out on the stump reminding people who saved GM and who wanted to let it go down the tubes. But he's not running. You are. So, run. The media is not going to cover you if you don't say or do anything worth covering. Be on my TV! Get on my screens! And on my Twitter feed!

Then, finally, she re-emerged—just in time to call half his supporters "deplorables." Brilliant. Why not just call them dumb, Bible-thumping, gun-loving redneck dipshits who are a waste of groceries and too stupid to vote. And maybe you could burn the Confederate flag while you're at it. I mean, as long as you're trying to make friends.

Why debase half his supporters? To what end? Was this her way of getting tough? A way of showing she could get down to his level? A way of marginalizing his support? Did no one see the potential for backfire? There's nothing Trump's people love more than having a rallying cry against the elites and wearing it as a badge of honor.

Then, for an encore, she bolted from a 9/11 tribute and passed out getting into a van at the exact moment Trump was pushing the "stamina" story. Fantastic. What's next? Showing up at a rally with a rolling oxygen tank and a day nurse? The optics sucked.

Right up until that first debate Trump was on a roll. The polls were tightening. Suddenly, she was losing ground. Liberals were freaking out. Sales of Cabernet, Xanax and adult diapers were going through the roof.

Even if it was just pneumonia, it didn't matter if she was having a real collapse. She was having an optical collapse, and Trump's "I'm winning" bullshit started to seem frighteningly real. The bar for the first debate was set so low, as long as he didn't expose himself on stage some in the media seemed ready to declare him Emperor Donald the First.

But before we could even get to the debates, there was still the gauntlet of network shows, hotel launch press conferences, and pre-debate damage control.

THE
COMMANDER-IN-CHIEF
FORUM
(September 4, 2016)

For no reason whatsoever, *NBC* put on a show on the U.S.S. Intrepid — a decommissioned aircraft carrier-turned-military museum. The Intrepid survived five Kamikaze attacks and a torpedo in WWII. It was also a NASA recovery ship, and served in Vietnam. Yet it took a direct hit by a major television network to inflict any real damage to its dignity. The show was entitled "The Commander-in-Chief Forum" and the audience was filled with active duty service members, as well as generals, security experts, and *MSNBC* analysts.

It was moderated by Matt Lauer, because if you want to inform the public about a presidential candidate's foreign policy positions, who better to host it than the affable, non-threatening host of *The Today Show*? They might as well have called it "Commanders-in-Chief Share Their Favorite Chili Recipes" and put the candidates in aprons and big, goofy chef hats. We might have been treated to insights like "I think NATO countries should shoulder the financial burden of keeping Europe safe from Russian aggression and terrorist attacks. Plus, a touch of chopped Italian parsley can add color and pizzazz to your leftovers."

That would have had as much gravity as the actual proceedings, which began with a coin flip to see which candidate would be first to stand up to Lauer's intense grilling. A coin flip. Really. Why not rock, paper, scissors? Once, twice, three — shoot? Or, given the show's military theme, maybe thumb-wrestling.

Trump was up first, and when grilled by Lauer over his super secret plan to defeat ISIS, Trump replied "When I do come up with a plan that I like, and that perhaps agrees with mine or maybe doesn't. I may love what the generals come back with... I have a plan, but I wanna be... I don't want it ... Look, I have a very substantial chance of winning...Make

America great again. We're gonna make America great again. I have a substantial chance of winning. If I win, I don't want to broadcast to the enemy exactly what my plan is… and let me tell you, if I like maybe a combination of my plan and the generals' plan, or the generals' plan… If I like their plan, Matt, I'm not going to call you up and say 'we have a great plan'."

If only we'd had a military strategist like this as Commander-in-Chief during Vietnam, imagine the lives that could have been saved. I mean, really, how incoherent does a presidential candidate have to be before a moderator just looks him in the face and says, "You really have no idea what the fuck you're talking about, do you? You're just rambling, repeating the word 'plan' over and over so it sounds like you're actually saying something. Don't you realize the military people in the audience are looking at you like you're some kind of imbecile?"

Then it was Hillary's turn, and Lauer spent half the time grilling her about her emails. In the end, Hillary was judged for being too tough and confrontational, an odd critique for someone auditioning for the role of Commander-in-Chief. Maybe they should've just called it Nuclear Celebrity Apprentice.

JIMMY FALLON
(September 15, 2016)

Politicians go on talk shows to create the illusion that they're human by adopting an "I'm just a regular person" persona, while parasitically feeding off the likeability of the host. And Fallon is likeable. So freaking likeable. He sweats likeability, especially to women, who must find his boyish, grinning manner attractive. I'll confess: I like him. He loves music. And he's got an ear for clever song parody and mimicry.

But Fallon instantly donated that likeability to Trump by playing host to the Republican nominee, asking probing, hard-hitting questions like "Do you think your business background helps you with campaigning?" And "What has changed since you first started running?" If Hitler were a guest, Fallon would've asked, "If you'd been accepted at the Academy of Fine Arts in Vienna, do you still think you would have gone into politics?" This was legitimacy by association, a moment that occurred in that netherworld between politics and show business. Though it's hardly the first time. When Bill Clinton played his sax on the Arsenio Hall Show in 1992 it was a pivotal moment in his campaign.

Trump was in all his glory, grinning like he'd just evicted a poor family from one of his apartments. Then Fallon took a beat as if a tough question was coming — an in-your-face drone attack of a question that would force the candidate to give a straight-ahead, no-bullshit answer.

Then Fallon asked if he could touch Trump's hair. Really? The hair? After all this time, after all that's happened, he does a hair bit? Trump smiled, boyishly. You could see in his eyes that he knew he'd been set up with a giant softball. He also must have known that whatever shellac he sprayed on that piss-colored whip on his head would stand up to Fallon's gentle mussing.

Trump then leaned forward, and Fallon mussed him. And it worked. The bit made him seem so nauseatingly likeable I retched up a meal I ate in 2003. In one lame moment he turned Trump from a vicious, power-mad, political animal into an adorable, self-effacing scamp. It took a ton of stink off him, and I'm sure left many undecided voters thinking he's not so bad.

The following night, to preserve the image of fairness, Fallon had Hillary on as a guest. The underlying message seemed like a way of taking the stink off the flack he took over the Trump hair bit. As a joke, Fallon put on a surgical mask, a teasing reference to her recent health issues. She laughed it off, but in doing so, missed an opportunity.

Life doesn't often hand you the perfect straight line—a moment that arises as if it were a set-up on a TV comedy. And in those moments you need to have a mind that's agile enough to pounce on it. But she didn't pounce. What she should have said was, in reference to Trump's previous guest appearance, "you should have worn the mask last night." It would have gotten a laugh and shown her as quick-witted and likeable. She could have taken a backhand slap at Trump at a time when he wasn't there to hit back. All he could have done was tweeted, and that would have made him look even more petty than usual. The second her moment passed I flashed back eight years to Tina Fey's portrayal of Sarah Palin.

Throughout the 42-year history of *SNL*, many of the highlights have been impressions of candidates and politicians. Some have been lighthearted impersonations that played off a politician's demeanor and quirky inflections, like Dan Aykroyd's Jimmy Carter. Others were absurdist depictions, like Chevy Chase's Gerald Ford. And one—Dan Aykroyd's Nixon—hit a level of macabre, diabolical characterization that captured the dark core of the subject's being.

Ranging across the spectrum were Dana Carvey's wacky Bush I, Jon Lovitz's incredulous Dukakis, Phil Hartman's hungry, horny Clinton and jerky Reagan, Norm Macdonald's robotic Bob Dole and Will Ferrell's cocky, clueless, Bush Jr.

But not until Tina Fey's Sarah Palin did a characterization have political impact. It wasn't just that she benefitted from a physical similarity. Or the fact that she nailed Palin's erratic rhetoric with the wild, Annie Oakley spin she put on it. She turned the dial past impression and impersonation to caricature. She took Palin's popularity, filtered it through the Katie Couric interview, along with a few other gaffes, then re-presented the candidate as a sexy, clueless gunslinger who was completely out of her depth. The moment they passed each other on stage was simultaneously real and surreal. Fey took Palin's soul and with it, much of her power. And they both knew it. It was one of the most brilliant moments of televised political theater I'd ever seen. And it made a difference in the real world.

As I said, I like Jimmy Fallon. But I hope next time Tina Fey sees him she punches him in the mouth.

TRUMP'S BIRTHER
PRESS CONFERENCE

A MASTER CLASS
IN THE FINE ART
OF
TURD JUGGLING
(September 16, 2016)

Trump International Hotel, Washington, D.C. Spitting distance from the White House.

Sometimes you just have to give it up to someone who can keep that many shit balloons in the air at once, like one of those comedy jugglers who can flip a hammer, watermelon and chainsaw without missing a beat or losing a finger.

Let's put this in proper historical context. Trump made his name peddling birtherism, cynically trading on the race hate he knew was simmering in the country. He did it for five years. Five years! Even if you accept the claim that the idea for using it as a campaign tactic was originally raised by the Clintons, and that the picture of a young Barack Obama in Indonesia was released by them, they didn't pursue it, Trump did. For five years! He did it in TV interviews, at press conferences, and on Twitter. Whether he believed it or not, he ran with it, blowing his racist dog whistle because he knew it had power as a way of galvanizing anti-Obama sentiment. It was his calling card to angry, white America. But it's not like he was shouting into the wind. *Fox, NBC, ABC* and *CNN* all gave him airtime to flog his birther lies.

In an interview with *NBC* Trump stated, "I have people that have been studying it, and they cannot believe what they're finding!" He added that it could be "one of the greatest cons in the history of politics and beyond." Put aside whatever the fuck "beyond" means, it didn't matter. The more he said it without being effectively challenged, the more power it had.

Even after the president condescended to the noise and

released his birth certificate, Trump kept the accusation alive by trying to deny its authenticity. "How do we know it's not a forgery?" That was the real tip-off that he was full of shit and just wanted to keep it going because he felt it was playing for him. That it was always about the music, not the words. This alone should have tipped the country off to the fact that this guy was just an opportunist and pathological liar. You know, what Ted Cruz called him, before he eventually rolled over and became Trump's prison bitch.

But it served him well. It gave him a platform. An excuse to get on TV. A song to sing. But now he had a problem: the debates were coming up. This put Trump at a crossroads. He rode the talking point "I don't talk about that anymore" for a few months, but now it was in danger of sounding evasive and, even worse, becoming inoperative. He knew the birther thing was going to come up. He would either have to continue the lie, which would make him look ridiculous, or deny it in a forum he couldn't control. He'd painted himself into a corner. But you have to give the son-of-a-bitch credit, he never just paints his way out of a corner; he punches his way out.

Trump put out the word that a "major statement" was coming. Like a fanfare announcing the arrival of the king, he let the word go forth that there would be news. Then, as they'd been trained to do, the media flocked to the hotel, instantly launching into "team coverage," which once again made it news. Or more precisely, "breaking news."

Reporters vamped on camera, tossing out probing questions like: "Why is Trump doing this now?" And "what does he get out of it?" An *MSNBC* host asked Senator Harry Reid "Do you believe it?"

I didn't. I couldn't believe she actually asked that question. Why wasn't it obvious, particularly to news reporters that the man was using the event to shed his birther skin, the way he dispensed with trophy wives when they aged a year, gained a pound, or sprouted a zit.

How could they not get this? Or did they get it and not

have the balls to say it? Were they afraid it would have made them look biased or confrontational?

The stage was set, with a backdrop of tough old military types, including 14 Medal of Honor recipients. This was a nauseating sight—veterans donating their honor to someone so dishonorable. Like the guy in Virginia who offered his Purple Heart to Trump, which Trump accepted, commenting on the relative ease of being gifted a medal without having to go through the inconvenience of getting shot.

It made me think of the famous line used by General MacArthur in his farewell address: "Old soldiers never die. They just fade away." Yes, but sometimes, before their final fade, they make a momentary comeback and get used as political props by a lying scumbag.

Then the moment we'd been told would happen ... didn't happen. Instead, the live TV audience was treated to a hotel infomercial. Hey, this is some hotel. Fabulous hotel. Greatest hotel in the world. That went on for 20 minutes. Several news channels—*MSNBC, CNN*, and *Fox*—cut away, realizing they'd been played, though not before airing the assembled veterans' statements praising their host.

Finally, we were treated to the moment we'd all been manipulated into waiting for as Trump stated: "Hillary Clinton and her campaign of 2008 started the birther controversy. I finished it. I finished it. You know what I mean. President Barack Obama was born in the United States, period." Five sentences crafted to whitewash five years of racism. Racism as personal attack and political tactic. A tool to demean, and delegitimize the first African-American president. And no one in the media questioned the meaning of "I finished it." Finished what? There was no "it" to finish. There was only the "it" he created in the first place that he was now, with media complicity, successfully weaseling out of.

But the stunt worked. He ditched his junked car on the side of the road, tossed in a lit match, blew it up, and just walked away. But it wasn't just a simple ditching. It was a ditch and switch. As cynically as he polluted the national conversation he not only removed the stink, but blamed Hillary for fouling it, then took credit for cleaning it up. Then the backdrop collapsed. Like the hotel itself was saying it was all just an illusion.

Even if some in the media had been skeptical, even cynical, about the event they still showed up to cover it. And they talked about it; in effect, donating air time for Trump to pivot with a brand new talking point. Which was all he wanted. This was a master class in political shape-shifting.

Trump was right. It was one of the greatest cons in the history of politics. And beyond.

THE
MASTER
DEBATES

We don't have debates in this country. Not in the sense of a dialogue in which the participants exchange ideas in order to arrive at the truth. Not even in the debate-team sense of people making opposing cases on an issue to see who can make the stronger argument. Instead, we have contests. Head-to-head matchups. Mano-a-mano slugfests. And given our love for sports metaphors, they're discussed in the only terms we understand: winners and losers. Who scored what points? Who landed a knockout punch? Who slipped? Who stumbled? We have rules, timers, buzzers and referees.

We judge the contest with little regard for the content. We celebrate gotcha moments. Reagan's "There you go again" attack on Jimmy Carter. Lloyd Bentsen's "You're no Jack Kennedy" takedown of Dan Quayle. We dwell on the screw-ups: Obama's lackluster first debate performance; Romney's "binders full of women" comment at a later debate; Christie's takedown of Rubio's robotic catchphrases; Trump's takedown of, well, everyone in sight.

As we headed for the first debate, the media was in full pre-game mastication, analyzing the choice of moderators, the debate prep, the potential questions. Is Trump hunkered down with advisors, studying the issues, and preparing his strategy, or is he just winging it? Or is that a cover story? Who's playing Hillary? Who's playing Trump? What are they eating while they prepare? Who are they wearing? Will they start slow and throw a few opening jabs, or come out swinging?

They were dissecting an event that hadn't even happened yet. At some point they might as well just stage it as a boxing match. Have the nominees strut down a long carpet wearing robes with their nicknames embroidered in gold, along with the logos of their corporate sponsors so we're clear whose interests are really being served.

They could get some ring girls. And ring guys. Don't want to get caught up in gender stereotypes. Then a mic could drop down, and the ref could call the candidates to center ring, and state the rules. They'd do the steely-eyed stare, touch gloves, go back to their corners, and at the sound of the bell, they'd come out arguing. There'd be no need for fact-checking. Just hook up each candidate with electrodes, with the controllers in the hands of *Politifact*. Every time they lie — zap 'em! The crowd would love it. Then the public could vote on who won, like it's *Dancing With the Stars*.

In the end, the candidates are judged on their performance. Style replaces substance, half-truths become truth, and appearance becomes reality. Meanwhile no one is informed but we can live-stream it and go on real-time rages, screaming into our individual echo chambers. Then the spinners spin, in an effort to convince us that we didn't see what we saw, or heard what we heard, and that their person obviously won.

We've long since abandoned any Platonic search for truth. We've even gone beyond sophistry and the skill of making a compelling argument. We've entered a post-fact world where any lie can get floated into the public consciousness and go forward as truth until it can be successfully debunked. A world in which catchphrases, slogans, insults and tag lines masquerade as legitimate argument. First we dragged news down to the level of entertainment. Now we've dragged politics there as well.

THE FIRST DEBATE

THE INTERRUPTING CLOWN
(September 26, 2016)

Hofstra University. Hempstead, Long Island. NBC's Lester Holt moderating.

Not that there wasn't a lot riding on that first debate, but an estimated 84 million people tuned in, making it the second most watched event of the year, after the Super Bowl. The *FiveThirtyEight* election forecast had tightened to 54-45, down from a high point of 89-10, where it had been in mid-August. This was the closest it had been since the end of the Democratic convention. This wasn't just tightening. There was a palpable shift in momentum, and liberals were freaking out. The election could actually turn on this one single event.

The Trump media narrative was that if he could just refrain from drooling, farting, or lighting himself on fire, his performance would be judged a success. He just had to act "presidential." Toss in a few facts. Put on a serious face. Take a pause or two so it looked like he was actually thinking. Just act smart. Like when he claimed to be articulate by saying "I have the best words," even though articulate people don't say "I have the best words." That is an inarticulate thing to say. They also don't say, "I have, like, this amazing vocabulary" then moments later use the word "schlonged."

I'd written that the debates would be Trump's Waterloo. That he had no knowledge of domestic or foreign policy, and would finally be in a forum where facts would come into play, and insults wouldn't cut it. I thought it would lead to him getting exposed to the American public as a dope and a fake.

But it didn't. At least not right away. The first segment was about jobs, and when it was Trump's turn he didn't shit the bed. He launched right into his China and Mexico job-stealing NAFTA rap. He name-dropped Ohio and Michigan, Carrier Air Conditioning, and lied about Ford's small car division shutting down and moving to Mexico. He was on script, and on message. He may not have looked presidential but at least he looked presidential-esque, and was creating the impression to some that he knew what he was talking about.

But then something happened. He started sniffing. Once. Then again. What the fuck was this? He's on live, national television being watched by millions and he's snorting like a meth head. Then came the interrupting. "Wrong! Wrong!" This was crazy. It's a presidential debate and he's acting like a roided-out frat boy who just sucked down an Extreme Power Shake, then chased it with Adderall.

This guy was making a complete imbecile out of himself. Or he was revealing his inner imbecile. I thought Kellyanne Conway's head was going to explode as she tried to spin it. This was, in Trump-speak, a total disaster! He blamed the microphone. He blamed the moderators. He slut-shamed a former Miss Universe on Twitter at 3 am. He even tweeted that he won. It didn't matter what excuses he made or where he cast blame. He crapped his pants and lit himself on fire. On live TV.

His campaign was imploding. Hillary's poll numbers immediately started climbing. It couldn't possibly have gotten worse for him. Then it did.

PUSSYGATE
(October 7, 2016)

Two days from the second debate and Trump's campaign was sputtering out of control, like a balloon that was inflated until it was ready to explode, and then released, causing it to blast off in a wild, flatulent burst, finally dropping to the ground — shriveled, spent, and useless.

If the bar hadn't been set low enough for the first debate, this was like someone called in the Army Corps of Engineers to excavate the toxic waste dump where they'd buried the first bar, dig down another mile, then bury this one even deeper. At this point as long as he didn't expose himself he'd be declared the winner. Then he exposed himself.

It was a casual Friday night. Nothing much to do but settle in, turn on the TV and catch up on the news. And there it was: the Access Hollywood tape. Or as the scandal it generated came to be known — Pussygate. It's one thing to shoot your mouth off. It's quite another when your mouth crawls out of the past and shoots *you*.

It was on every channel, practically playing on a loop. Another social dividend of the Trump candidacy was that everyone was allowed to say "pussy" on TV. Saying pussy was all the rage. We're all saying it. Out loud. Although some bleeped out the word. Others played with the graphic, using the less offensive "p***y," as sort of a verbal merkin. Others just went for it, including Ana Navarro on *CNN*, sticking it to Trumpbot Scottie Nell Hughes, who was offended by Navarro's repeated use of the word. Not Trump's use of it. Or alleged grabbing of it. That was fine. As an interesting sidebar, political pundit Bob Beckel declared on the show that the election was effectively over.

Suddenly Republicans were scrambling for a way through the moral dilemma of pussy vs. party. Paul Ryan checked his conscience and decided that Jesus wanted him to disinvite Trump to a rally in his home state of Wisconsin. Others felt safe to whip up the obligatory Republican outrage, summed up by Mitch McConnell's heartfelt "As the father of three daughters, I strongly believe that Trump needs to apologize to women and girls everywhere, and take full responsibility for the utter lack of respect for women shown in his comments on that tape." You have to love it when these dusty, hypocritical old Republicans suddenly go full-cornpone Southern gentleman, declaring they've been deeply offended by some scalawag's insulting remark then demanding satisfaction on the field of honor.

Trump's defense, meanwhile, was pure Trumpian offense, hinging on the carefully constructed excuse that it was "locker room talk." A private conversation that took place years ago. He even added "Bill Clinton has said far worse to me on the golf course, not even close. I apologize if anyone was offended." Note his use of the conditional "if."

This was the opposite of the Karl Rove tactic of turning your enemy's strength into a weakness. This was taking your own weakness and trying to deflect attention by saying your enemy's even worse. First of all, he didn't even get the inflection right. It's not "locker…room…talk," with equal emphasis on each word. It's locker-room talk. Talk that takes place in a locker room. And given that this guy is 230 pounds of Trump steaks in a suit, I'd bet it's been decades since he's even seen a locker room.

This was classic Trump. Never surrender the moment. Turn, and attack, and use whatever language is necessary. Trump's words have always been weapons in a battle. The battle is the moment. And Trump can never lose the moment. To lose the moment is to appear weak, so he says whatever he thinks will win the moment, because he knows that if he wins the moment, there will be another moment right around the corner and no one will remember the previous one. They'll just remember that he didn't lose it. It doesn't matter if his comments are based in fact or are in response to the question he was asked. It's about getting the last word, because getting the last word means you won.

But he was far from getting in the last word. Pussygate

wasn't going away. This was a shit-storm he couldn't quickly ride out. And no one was letting up. His campaign was flailing and his odds started plummeting to an all-time low.

THE SECOND DEBATE

THE PRESS CONFERENCE
(October 9, 2016)

Washington University. St. Louis. Moderators: *CNN's* Anderson Cooper and *ABC's* Martha Raddatz.

If there was ever any doubt about how low this guy would go, how dangerous he is when backed into a corner, there was no need to look further. Trump set up a pre-debate press conference starring Bill Clinton's former accusers and a woman whose rapist was defended by Hillary Clinton when she was a court-appointed lawyer. This was some serious, rapey misdirection.

Trump wasn't about to accept that his candidacy was marooned on Pussy Island. If he was going down, he was going down in flames. He was James Cagney in *White Heat*, standing on top of a blazing inferno, screaming "Top of the world, ma!" Or DeNiro's Johnny Boy in Scorsese's *Mean Streets* trying to shoot out the lights of the Empire State Building while defiantly flipping off the world.

Then there was the actual debate, in which he went full-tilt loony. Stalking her around the stage. Humping his chair. Threatening to investigate her and put her in jail. This guy was so tweaky he couldn't sit still. On top of his disastrous first debate performance he was now in full metal meltdown—interrupting, snorting, sputtering. This was beyond comical. It was becoming theater of the absurd.

But one thing that kept nagging at me: she didn't close. She just stood back as if it would be obvious to the 66 million people watching that this lunatic was unfit for the presidency.

This was basic WWE. When the bad guy's on the matt, you don't turn and smile to the crowd, because the guy will always get up, grab a chair and smash you over the head. She should have grabbed him by that hair whip and flung him out of the ring. But she didn't. She let him up to fight another day. This was not only a missed moment. This was fatal.

THE THIRD DEBATE

TRUMP'S ACCUSERS
(October 19, 2016)

Vegas. Home of sleaze, drunken marriages, and boxing, where no matter how crazy the night, the next morning the Strip reeks of beer, sperm, and regret. Was there a more appropriate place on Earth to bring this hot mess of an election to a climax?

Just when you thought he might skate through with the "locker room talk" line, it went from bad to worse. Like the iconic scene in Hitchcock's *The Birds*, where he intercuts between a person on a bench and the playground as more and more birds ominously appear. So it was with Trump's accusers.

A *People* magazine reporter hit on by Trump in his house, with his pregnant wife in the other room. Allegedly. Another groped on a plane. Allegedly. And they were all speaking out, guided through the process by Gloria Allred, a woman who is no stranger to scandal.

In the world of measuring small amounts of time, there's the nanosecond and the colloquial New York minute, each connoting how quickly one event follows another. For the scientifically inclined there's Planck Time, defined as "…the time it would take a photon travelling at the speed of light to cross a distance equal to the Planck length. This is the "quantum of time," equal to 10^{-43} seconds.

No smaller division of time has any meaning. Except for one. Even quicker than Planck Time is the "Allreddy" which describes the near instantaneous amount of time it seems to take from the moment a celebrity scandal breaks to the moment Gloria Allred is attached to it. (Not a criticism, just an observation.)

From Heather Mills to Amber Frey to Robert Blake's ex, the alleged offense has barely been played out before the attorney is clinging to the victim's side like a barnacle in a pantsuit, strenuously defending the rights of the victim and declaring that there will be justice. And maybe book deals.

But she is a tough advocate and knows the drill. And frankly, I was happy to see her with another Trump accuser in tow, accusing him of doing the very thing he was busted on tape bragging about. But he still wasn't stopped. Trump was in full-tilt denial. They're all lying! It was a clear case of he said/she said, she said, she said, she said, she said, she said, she said, she said, she said, she said, she said and she said. You know — baseless allegations.

But here's the thing. Imagine you were in his position. You don't even have to be running for president. You could just be an average guy going about your business when suddenly, out of nowhere, twelve women accuse you of sexual harassment. And you knew you were innocent. Wouldn't you be shocked? Mortified? Humiliated? Screaming from the rooftops that that you didn't do it? Wouldn't the look on your face be one of horror, because you knew that, these days, people are guilty by accusation, and tried in the court of public opinion? The whole thing would feel Kafka-esque. You'd be shaking your head, softly muttering, "I didn't do it." But he didn't do any of that. There wasn't one moment of sadness or contrition. Trump was combative. Defiant. Insisting they were lying and that he'd sue them all.

The whole affair was becoming cringe-worthy. I didn't think I could make it through another debate. I needed a pressure release, so I joined in a live comment stream — an alternative to yelling at the TV, where I'm pretty sure no one hears me. I also expected, naively as it turned out, that the tape and the accusations would have built to a watershed moment, in which the final Bernie holdouts would shake off the last vestiges of heartbreak and embrace Hillary, just out of sheer revulsion at the alternative.

I naively expected the comments to reflect the choice between an experienced, albeit flawed candidate and an imbecilic, life-sucking sexual abuser and megalomaniac who only knows he wants to win this election like a shark knows it wants to eat. But it turned out to be less of a stream and more of a raging river. The tone ranged from broken-hearted despair to drunken bar fight fury, with a sidebar of a two-year-old's shrieking tantrum.

The Hillary haters were raging. "They're both full of shit!" "Hillary for prison!" "Hillary's a fascist!" "NeverHillary!" "Democrats put up a shitty nominee and they should get what they deserve!" It was like one loud, angry voice screaming "Aaaaaaagh!" "I'm gonna hold my breath 'til the country turns blue!" "Bernie!!!!!!!!"

This reminded me of an article I'd read back in May by Robert Reich, former Clinton Labor Secretary, in which he urged Bernie supporters to get behind Hillary. The article was smart, and pragmatic. And there were 14 thousand comments, many from Bernie people. And they were pissed. The same vitriol. "Traitor!" "Turncoat!" "Sellout!" "Hypocrite!"

What hit me both times was that these people were furious. And they were in no mood to compromise, let alone engage in a civilized conversation. All I could think was, ok, I get it. You're hurt. Disappointed. Break-ups are a bitch. You need to process the heartbreak and heal. But does that mean you jump on the back of some bad boy's Harley and fuck the pain away? Apparently it did.

(Or, that's how it struck me at the time, though it now seems possible that these were bots that had successfully blasted their way into the opinion stream. Now I realize their power, because I completely bought it. Even if the Russians didn't literally steal the election, they virtually stole it by feeding into the Hillary-hate.)

Finally, mercifully, the debates were over. And maybe the election. I wasn't sure how much more pounding the electorate could take.

FiveThirtyEight had the odds at 87.4% to 12.6%, the most lopsided they'd been since August. He was done. Like David Blaine trapped in a plexiglas cube suspended from a crane, it seemed that no one could get out of this. This was definitely over. Except it wasn't.

PUTIN
TAKES A
WIKILEAK

Despite Trump's protestations that we didn't know if it was Russia or China or some fat guy in a basement—it was Russia. A little Valentine from Vladimir to the Moscovian Candidate.

The actual revelations had little substance. Was it really surprising that people involved in a political campaign didn't always agree, and occasionally said mean things about each another? Primary fights are tough. Yes, the DNC wanted Hillary more than Bernie. And who cares if Donna Brazile slipped Hillary some debate questions? Did it really take a genius to figure out what might be asked during the debates? What's your favorite color? How much do you love puppies?

The power of the hack was in reinforcing the existing Clinton narrative in the minds of undecided voters by playing into the "crooked" meme. It sowed disunity in the party when they needed to pull together. It fed the Bernie outrage. Split the focus. Planted seeds of chaos. And lead to the resignation of the head of the DNC. Death by a thousand cuts. The slow drip of accusations worked on a segment of the electorate that wasn't aware it was being manipulated. And it all deflected the media from Trump's transgressions.

The real story should have been Trump's baffling pro-Russia statements, which were bizarre, right from the start. Historically, Russia-bashing is high on the Republican top 40 hit list, right up there with abortion, Social Security, and boys kissing. Trump's entire campaign was one love letter to Putin after another.

The lies ranged from "I never met him" to "We appeared on *60 Minutes* together." In reality, they were on the same episode but the segments were shot independently. They weren't splitting vodka and blinis in the green room. When it fed his story to say they met, he said it. When it suited him to say they'd never met, he said that. But no president or candidate for president has ever kissed up to a Russian dictator like this. What the hell was going on?

(On December 9th, *The Washington Post* reported that the government had evidence of the Russians meddling in the election in Trump's favor. And despite Trump's constant and belligerent denials of any involvement by his kleptocratic brother from another mother, in early January, after an intelligence briefing, Trump finally acquiesced, admitting they might have been involved. Though he added that unless they compromised the actual voting machines, it didn't matter. Whether it mattered is still under investigation.)

THE FINAL DAYS

THE COMEY LETTER
(October 26, 2016)

Less than two weeks from Election Day and Trump was still toast. *FiveThirtyEight* had the odds at 81.5% to 18.5%. Even though the polls were expected to tighten. And they did. I mean this shit was tight. Still, the pundits insisted it was in the bag. Trump was in damage control mode. Sexual accusers were lining up like someone was handing out 6-figure settlement checks. He stated he might not even accept the results. He was keeping America in suspense. Everyone was hypothesizing about his post-election plans. Maybe he'd partner with Steve Bannon in an alt-right media empire — Trump TV. "We Incite — You Decide."

Yet, there was Rudy Giuliani on *Fox News*, sporting the cocky sneer of an ambassador's son who used diplomatic immunity to beat a DUI, bragging, "I'm sorry, I don't believe in polls. Every election I ever won, I outperformed the polls...I think he, meaning Trump, has got a surprise or two that you're going to hear about in the next few days. I mean I'm talking about some pretty big surprises... We're not going to go down and certainly won't stop fighting. We've got a couple things up our sleeve that should turn this around."What was this? Arrogance? Denial? A Hail Mary? Or someone bragging about something he knew was coming?

Then it hit. Eleven days before the election. The Comey Letter. Three mind-blowing words that will one day take their place in what's left of American history, alongside "The Black Sox Scandal" and "The Kennedy Assassination." Bombshell! Breaking News! Clinton email investigation re-opened! Essentially, "we interrupt your regularly scheduled election with this important-sounding non-information."

For all the media sound and fury, this is what was in the actual letter sent to the eight Congressional committee chairmen: "... In connection with an unrelated case, the FBI has learned of the existence of emails that appear to be pertinent to the investigation. I am writing to inform you that the investigative team briefed me on this yesterday, and I agreed that the FBI should take appropriate investigative steps designed to allow investigators to review these emails to determine whether they contain classified information, as well as to assess their importance to our investigation. Although the FBI cannot yet assess whether or not this material may be significant, and I cannot predict how long it will take us to complete this additional work, I believe it is important to update your committees about our efforts in light of my previous testimony."

Appear to be? Whether they contain classified information? *Cannot yet assess whether or not this material may be significant?* Not exactly a smoking gun. Actually no gun at all. No bullets. No smoke. No nothing. Basically a heads-up about the remote possibility that there might be something gun-related. Eleven days before the most important election in modern history, with the fate of the world hanging in the balance, the FBI Director decides that sending this letter was his only legitimate choice.

Some said that Comey was forced to err on the side of impartiality, particularly after Bill Clinton's June 27 tarmac assignation with Attorney General Loretta Lynch while the email investigation was going on. Right. One non-event serves as justification for another. Despite the optics of that meeting, which sucked, if former President Clinton wanted to send a message to the Attorney General, do people really think he had no other means at his disposal? If you're trying to hold a clandestine meeting, why have your rendezvous in an airplane hangar? Granted, Clinton has a history of injudicious behavior, but he's hardly a political neophyte and had to be aware of the optics and potential blowback.

Even if the purpose of the letter was to pre-empt a leak from other members of the FBI, who cared? Whatever happened to the pro forma, "It is not the policy of the FBI to comment on ongoing investigations?" That line has deflected more tough questions than "I swear, honey, she's just a friend." If there was ever a time to trot it out, this was it.

Now, I'm no conspiracy theorist. Though there was definitely a plot to kill JFK. Maybe it was Sam Giancana getting payback for Bobby Kennedy's prosecution of the mob, particularly after they virtually delivered the Chicago election results to Jack. Or it was the CIA or members of the military who were nervous about a pullout in Vietnam. Or it was Fidel Castro in retaliation for the Bay of Pigs and the exploding cigars. I doubt Ted Cruz's daddy was involved, but who am I to question the journalistic integrity of the *National Enquirer?*

I mean, c'mon. I've never heard a credible theory explaining how Lee Harvey Oswald could first try to renounce his American citizenship and defect to the Soviet Union, then return to the U.S. with a Russian bride, and totally escape the scrutiny of law enforcement. And during the Cold War. And how did Oswald just happen to get a job at the Book Depository before the presidential motorcade route was announced? And why didn't he wipe the rifle clean and just meld into the crowd in the ensuing chaos?

And Jack Ruby? Give me a fucking break. A patriotic, mob-affiliated strip club owner who had access to the basement of the Dallas Police Department on the day they were transferring the most dangerous assassin in modern history? A man who was so outraged over the assassination that he took his .38 caliber revolver, waltzed through the apparently lax security, and strode right up to Oswald close enough to shoot him in the gut?

Either truth is stranger than fiction, or these were just cover stories fed to the public via the Warren Commission. We've been lied to for 54 years about the most seminal, life-changing, innocence-shattering event in modern history. I just hope that one day the records become public so that those of us who lived through it can finally get closure. It not only matters as history. It matters so that people know what their government is capable of. And how successfully we can be lied to.

Ok, so except for JFK, I'm no conspiracy nut. I know the moon landing was real. So was 9/11. I knew two people on the first plane to hit the tower, so unless they've been playing a very long game of hide and seek, they're gone. There are no aliens in Area 51 or any other area. There are no aliens, other than in our popular fiction. It's an amusing fantasy to play "we are not alone." But we are alone—just a tiny, insignificant speck in a vast universe. And given the mess we've made of the planet, if any creatures, however humanoid, mastered the art of space travel, why the fuck would they stop here unless it was to go to the can?

So… given Giuliani's coquettish "I know something you don't know" taunt on *Fox News*, along with the subsequent release of information about rogue elements in the New York FBI office who were infuriated that Clinton wasn't prosecuted, the reason for sending that letter still seems highly suspect.

Comey already conducted his investigation. He testified before Congress. He slammed Hillary as much as he could, given the fact that there was no evidence to move forward with an investigation. Some say he went over the line. Still, there was absolutely no rational reason to release this. How could the Director of the FBI be so disingenuous about the repercussions from the letter, and the timing?

Then, as if the initial letter wasn't damning enough, on November 6—two days before the election—we had The Comey Retraction. Sorry. Did we say "related to the email investigation?" We meant it was just more Weiner dicks, and totally unrelated to the investigation. Never mind.

Who cares if he took it back? Did I say you were a child molester? Sorry, I meant you're not a child molester. Have I said the word child molester enough? It just kept the story in the air, and played right into the "untrustworthy" narrative. It gave Trump more chances to scream that she was crooked and, according to some experts, sent college-educated white Republicans scurrying back home. Releasing that letter was a game-changer. Not just for the election, but for the world.

(December 20, 2016. Per an article on *Huffington Post*, legal experts agreed that the warrant that lead to the FBI search of Huma Abedin's laptop should never have been granted. So even the reason behind the original letter was bullshit. Oops. So sorry. Never mind.)

(January 2017. Comey's decisions in the investigation and release of information are being investigated by the Department of Justice. Maybe that could be followed up by an investigation by the Department of We Already Elected the Asshole So It's Way Too Fucking Late For an Investigation.)

(April 2017. A *New York Times* article provides a detailed timeline of events at the FBI, as well as insights into Comey's decision-making process. It all makes perfect sense. And we still got fucked.)

(May 2017. Comey testifies before the Senate Judiciary Committee and sticks by his story, adding that the decision made him "mildly nauseous." Given that his decision may lead to the gutting of the ACA, it's going to make millions of people mildly dead.

The decision to send that letter is even more baffling given that the FBI was simultaneously investigating ties between Russia and the Trump campaign—a probe that, unlike Clinton's emails, had a direct effect on the election. Since neither had reached a conclusion, Comey had the choice to reveal one, both, or none. Even if he had been called before a congressional committee after a Clinton victory to explain his rationale in not releasing any information about the investigation, he would have been justified in saying just that. Frankly, the more he explains his reasoning, the murkier it becomes, particularly after claiming that not releasing the information would have amounted to "concealment." Using that word, itself, felt like concealment.

Sending that letter changed history. And despite the motivation behind it, or the outcome of the Russia investigation, the one tragic irony is that the decision of the guy with integrity ending up giving us the president without any.

SHIT,
WE GOTTA GO
TO DETROIT!
(November 4, 2016)

No one wakes up in the morning, takes that first sip of coffee, then suddenly smacks their head and thinks, "Shit, I gotta go to Detroit!" No offense to the people of the Motor City, but I've been there. I stayed in a nice hotel that had an armed guard in the lobby. And while I love the music of Motown, it wasn't high on my list of places to get back to. If you're in a hurry to get to Detroit it can only mean you just spent a year in combat, your discharge came through, and you're rushing home to see your family — in Detroit. Or it means something in your life has just gone horribly wrong and you're panicking. Despite every cover story put out by the campaign, this felt like panic.

Even though no less an expert than David Plouffe, Obama's 2008 campaign manager and senior advisor, assured me during an appearance on the *Keepin' It 1600* podcast that the bedwetters could relax, I couldn't relax. I'd gone from bedwetting to full-on incontinence. Then the campaign bolted for Michigan like they were afraid they'd left the gas on and thought the house might explode. And they were right.

CHAPTER THREE

HOW THE FUCK
DID THIS HAPPEN?

CABLE NEWS
DR. FRANKENTRUMP

"Give my creature life!"

Young Frankenstein

Trump is our 21st century political Frankenstein monster. A creation built out of spare parts — rich guy's spoiled brat, real estate dealer, tabloid celebrity, shameless self-promoter, branded product salesman, reality show personality, and alleged swindler — then stitched together in a dank, dusty lab somewhere in a frozen Russian wasteland. But it was the media that shot lightning into his neck bolts and gave him life.

Just to be clear, in one sense there's no such animal as "the media." There's cable news, network news, radio, print, websites, podcasts, blogs, journalists, pundits, Russian hackers, Twitter and Facebook trolls, and assholes punking the world with fake news. However, if we make an analytic distinction, and designate cable TV news as "the media," then the media fucked up. They fucked up bad, and on many levels.

They created Trump via $2-3 billion in free advertising by airing his rallies in their entirety, turning them into virtual infomercials. No cutaways. No commentary. And the fact that they were covered with so much import afforded a de facto legitimacy to the candidate. You could almost feel TV executives quivering from the thrill of multiple Trump-gasms. And if he said something crude, stupid or, cross your fingers, racist, they got a sound-bite they could play for days, and righteous indignation they could mine for weeks.

In a post-election appearance at the Harvard University Kennedy School of Politics' Campaign Managers Conference, *CNN* President Jeff Zucker took flack over his network's airing of Trump rallies. While defending their coverage, Zucker admitted they probably shouldn't have done it as much. No. They shouldn't have done it at all. Of course some were more culpable than others. Obviously *Fox* was his champion, despite George Will's protestations and the Megyn Kelly flap; however, during the early stages of the campaign, *MSNBC* was equally guilty.

But it wasn't just a matter of allowing him to hijack the news. Trump became the news. He was the story. Day after day of nothing but Trump breaking news! Trump team coverage. He was the political O.J. trial.

His rallies were wild, spontaneous events — equal parts political theater, game show, and rock concert. And this made them great TV. And the candidate knew he could direct media attention by playing right into it, particularly by exhorting people to violence. "Get him outta here!" "I'd like to punch him in the mouth!" You have to give him credit. Trump knows how to play to the cameras. He seems to possess an almost out-of-body awareness of the event, and how he appears in it.

Finally they'd cut back to the studio commentators who desperately strained to analyze his statements under the assumption that they represented his policies, and that there was some sense in his nonsense. There wasn't. They were just tag lines crafted to work up the crowd. Trump was a child who ran into a room and scrawled on the wall with his own poop, then the media critiqued the paintings.

They never realized that Trump wasn't addressing an electorate; he was entertaining an audience. He was a clown, pulling streams of colored handkerchiefs out of his sleeve at a children's party. Personal insults, histrionic language, call-and-response audience participation. "Who's going to pay for the wall?!" "Mexico!" His supporters weren't listening to the words; they were banging their heads to the music.

The next level of media fuck-up was inviting Trump's flying monkeys on their shows to create a reality distortion field by insisting that no one heard what they heard, or saw what they saw. He was going to ban Muslim immigration, but he really wasn't. He was going to deport 11 million immigrants, but he really wasn't. Their lies were treated as simply conflicting, though equally valid, interpretations of reality. This was an informational Trojan Horse — bullshit smuggled in to create the illusion of legitimate political conversation.

And they all used the tools of Trump-Speak. State your premise, reject any facts that counter your premise, talk over anyone who tries to reject your premise then, when in doubt, blame Hillary. And never take a punch. Even if everyone saw you take a punch, never admit you took it because it's not the punch that makes you vulnerable, it's admitting you got hit. Never show weakness. Never apologize. And never back down.

The hosts never seemed to learn the tricks. His flacks would echo their boss' ludicrous statements but were never really forced to back them up. They were never challenged on how Trump would make urban crime magically disappear, or about his "secret plan" to defeat ISIS. Or why a presidential candidate would think he could get away with saying, "I have a secret plan," like a child who swears he did his homework.

Allowing themselves to be tagged as "the liberal media" forced them into a position of bending over backwards not to appear partisan. And by letting his people spread misinformation they became unwitting campaign surrogates. It was the journalistic equivalent of being in a boxing match where your opponent is hitting you with both fists and you hit back with one while punching yourself with the other.

Even if the conversation became contentious, it would end in a civilized "let's just agree to disagree and thank you for coming on the show." And that was their victory. Because their counter-narrative got through, which was always the intention. It was just about filibustering the conversation, and creating informational white noise — the political equivalent of the Monty Python Dead Parrot sketch.

And no one ever pointed out that they all referred to the candidate as "Mister Trump." Same exact inflection. "MIS-TER Trump." Like they had to pass an elocution test before graduating from Trump Spokesfuck University.

The nuttiest of them all was Katrina Pierson, who insisted that "MIS-TER Trump wasn't changing what he thought, he was just using different words." But the queen was Kellyanne Conway, his Florence Nightingale. A woman who looked like she'd had all the water, life, and decency sucked out of her. Assuming there was ever any there to begin with.

Although previously, as a spokesperson for the Cruz campaign, she stated on *CNN* that "Trump made his money on the backs of working people" and that he should "definitely show his taxes" this was a new day, with a new boss, and a new reality.

Conway came along when Trump was doing terribly with women. Then she plastered on that shit-eating grin and began covering up the stink of her boss like a fresh coat of paint slapped over black mold in the bathroom. The strategy was brilliant. Her frozen smile and confident manner carried a subliminal message. It was "Look, I'm smiling. And I work for Donald Trump. So he must be non-threatening, and a good guy, because I'm a woman and I'm smiling." It was literal lipstick on a pig. All part of the ad campaign for the re-launch of their product—New And Improved Trump! Now, 20% less sexist!

The third level media fuck-up was in adopting the Trump campaign narratives. When it seemed that his language and behavior were about to negate him as a serious candidate, they were handed new words and concepts, implying that he could "soften his tone" and "pivot" to being "presidential." They not only bought the concepts but adopted the lingo and looked for evidence and confirmation. Trump baked a shit cake and the media discussed what flavor frosting to put on it.

After Trump's Mexico trip, they spent days discussing how he "pivoted" during the awkward joint press conference. They analyzed his demeanor, even the color of his tie. They allowed Trump to stand behind a podium, slap on his mock serious face, read from a teleprompter and not say anything racist for five minutes, then declared it a rhetorical triumph.

They gnawed on the dog bone of who told whom in public or private that they would or wouldn't pay for a wall. Then, after they were done with the wall narrative, they pivoted to the "outreach" narrative. They followed Trump to a black church and covered him taking pictures with black people. This wasn't news. It was a staged event, the purpose of which was to send a message to white people who were nervous about Trump's racism.

There was no outreach. In some polls, Trump's support among African-American voters was 0%. 0%! Even if the stunt sent his numbers up tenfold, he still would have had 0%! Yet the video of this lumbering stiff in a black church, awkwardly swaying to gospel music was all over the news. He couldn't even clap on the fucking downbeat. (It's on the 2 and the 4. It seemed to matter at the time. Now it doesn't.)

And if they got access to the candidate himself, they just got played. They didn't press him on why being an "outsider" was a good thing when applying for the most important job in the world. This is a man with all the sincerity of one of his gold-plated hotel bathrooms, and none of the qualifications we traditionally look for in a president. Honesty, intelligence, experience, humility, honor, class, a respect for American democracy, a sense of history, an awareness of the state of the world and America's role in it. Granted, past leaders have had these qualifications in varying degrees. Others seemed to possess them, only to eventually disappoint. But no one person elected to the presidency has been utterly bereft of all of them. It was a stunning act of political alchemy to take a history of greed, larceny, lies, and scandal and reconstitute them into a political resume.

The other failure was in treating him like a conventional candidate, someone who had coherent positions on domestic and foreign policy. They thought he could be held accountable by the standard benchmarks of truth and ideological consistency.

They assumed calling him inconsistent in his position was a damning attack. They parsed his statements, not realizing that the shit that flowed from his mouth was simply crafted to rile up the crowd, demean his opponents, or negate his critics. They never questioned the possible motives behind Trump's wet kisses to Putin, his shots at NATO, nor the simplicity of the statements themselves. "Wouldn't it be great if we could be friends with Russia." Friends? Are we schoolchildren? These were not the sober observations of a foreign policy visionary trying to transcend Cold War thinking and guide the country through the geo-political realities of 21st century. (Their real intent is only now becoming clear in the context of the Russian hacking investigations.)

Meanwhile, they parroted the Hillary "untrustworthy" meme, citing polls detailing what percentage of which voters in which states believed she was less than honorable. But reporting what people think is not the same as probing whether a thing is true, or digging into the history of the meme and how it was successfully planted in the public mind. (Check out judicialwatch.org for a decades-long history of Clinton bashing.) By flogging endless "email" stories they turned the allegations of mishandling classified information from a political attack to a guilty verdict. This set the table for Trump to rant about the "33,000 emails."

This was always the goal of the Benghazi hearings. Ultimately, it didn't matter that two Congressional show trials ended up in the same place, i.e. nowhere. The story wasn't that she withstood eleven hours of partisan interrogation without cracking. What mattered was the picture of Hillary Clinton sitting at a witness table for eleven hours while Republicans puffed themselves up with righteous indignation and lambasted her for being personally responsible for "four dead Americans."

They put her on the defensive, and anyone put in that position looks guilty. The hearings were pre-emptive character shots, so that during the election, every Republican candidate could stand onstage and scream "Benghazi!"

Yes, they reported on the Trump scandals, but they never seemed to make the distinction between Hillary's mistakes and Trump's crimes. Like allegedly bribing the Florida Attorney General to drop a lawsuit against Trump University. Or for that matter, Trump University itself, and the character of a man who would cook up a scheme that resulted in settling several lawsuits for $25 million. The high price of innocence.

Every single thing Trump said over the last two years, let alone the last five years, should have instantly disqualified him from being seriously considered for the presidency. Of course, many journalists fact-checked him, and pressed his people on their ridiculous arguments, but only Laurence O'Donnell consistently called out the nominee as an "imbecile," and "pathological liar." Someone unworthy of the presidency.

Trump didn't just play the media, he conducted them like a maestro leading an orchestra. He used their own ratings lust and dedication to fairness against them. He called into shows when it suited his needs. He raged against Megyn Kelly then agreed to participate in a softball "apology" show because he knew *Fox* would air it. And why not, it was great TV. And it let him fix a problem with women by changing the narrative. But if you look back at it, he never actually said the words "I'm sorry." It was "Did I offend you?" Oh. Well, then excuse me." Even in a special that was touted as a kiss-and-make-up session, he refused to apologize because an apology would have meant he'd done something wrong, and that would make him look weak, and weakness would make him vulnerable.

Trump fed the sources that nourished him while inoculating himself against voices he considered unfriendly. Unfortunately it took too long for many in the media to figure it out. Seasoned political commentators mocked his clunky language, the contradictions, the malapropos—the naïve if not childish understanding of policy and history. And none of it mattered. The charge of ideological inconsistency is only effective against someone who's playing in the real world. He wasn't. Instead, he dragged the game into his world and made everyone play by his rules. He told a simple story using simple language, slogans, and props. Hats, signs, and T-shirts are the usual detritus of political campaigns, but they're supposed to function as visual representations of the candidate's message. In Trump's case, they were the message.

Of course, the media didn't pack those halls with thousands of enthusiastic, if not angry, supporters. There was a legitimate phenomenon going on. Whether that phenomenon was created by Trump, or the news shows, or some unholy combination of the two, it was still the responsibility of journalists to frame the events by adding context and a level of healthy skepticism.

Of course there was outstanding reporting, most notably by *The New York Times, New York Magazine,* and *The Washington Post.* The *Times* ran a late October, two-page spread detailing Trump's history of Twitter insults and accusations, but it didn't matter because the people who should have read it didn't read *The Times.* David Fahrenthold's relentless coverage of the Trump Foundation was extraordinary journalism. The sad fact was that while it mattered in reality, in Trump World, it didn't.

Trump's campaign wasn't made for print. It was made for TV. And it was great TV. To borrow and bend a phrase from one of the most brilliant movies ever made — *Network,* written by the great Paddy Chayefsky — Trump was reality television incarnate. A crude, low-rent form of programming that cynically played to the worst in us.

Even though the media was compliant, and to some degree complicit, in Trump's rise to legitimacy and ultimate victory, it's an oversimplification to lay it all at their feet. Trump shape-shifted from a rich, preening, egomaniacal, self-aggrandizing, amoral, solipsistic, vindictive, status-hungry, ego-starved, political arriviste, alleged sexual abuser, and gold-plated douchebag, to a working class hero. That required more than media exposure. That took a master mind-fucker.

CHAPTER FOUR

WHAT THE FUCK DID HE DO?

TACTICS

TRUMP-SPEAK
PSYOPS
BRANDING
TWEETSTORMS

"If you know the enemy and know yourself,
you need not fear the result of a hundred battles.
If you know yourself but not the enemy,
for every victory gained you will also suffer a defeat.
If you know neither the enemy nor yourself,
you will succumb in every battle."

Sun Tzu
"The Art of War"

TRUMP-SPEAK

Philosophy of Language explores the nature of meaning, and the relationship between language and reality. Not exactly topics that come up in everyday conversation. Yet if you initiated a dialogue on the subject, most people would accept that words are what we use to describe our experience of life and communicate that experience to others. They're a bridge that takes us out of our solitude. They're also the building blocks for thoughts and ideas, grounded in a belief in truth, whether as some Platonic ideal, or just as a standard to strive for.

Language is a social contract, based on the premise that words have meaning. That's why some Democrats, journalists, and political pundits would reach near orgasm when they thought they'd busted Trump in a lie or contradiction. It was a triumphant gotcha moment, in which the fatal charge of "liar" or "hypocrite" was thrown down like an atomic mic drop, instantly vaporizing his bullshit into intellectual rubble. And in ordinary reality it would have worked that way. The problem was, in Trump World, it didn't.

Trump World was and still is an alternative, parallel universe where words don't have meaning; words have power. In Trump-speak, words are not social conventions used for communication, they're weapons in a rhetorical war, utilized to evoke emotion, create illusion, or deflect blame.

Trump weaponized language, creating a world in which truth didn't exist. Where false statements lurked behind a reality distortion field protecting them from being debunked by facts. Phrases like "believe me," "trust me," or "this is inarguable" were sales tricks. You know how a con man says "fuck you?" "Trust me."

He'd make a claim then add "and everyone knows it." This conveyed the illusion that it was objectively true. His "people are saying" line carried the same connotation while protecting him against a lawsuit for slander. After all, he was simply repeating something he'd heard.

The generic "just look at what's going on out there" phrasing was employed to convey the impression that there were real events in the world that backed up his claims, while simultaneously masking his basic ignorance. Another Trumpian word game involved distorting an allegation made against him then vehemently denying the distortion, allowing him to play the role of the victim who'd been falsely accused.

He even taught his kids the game, as well as his surrogates. Unfortunately no one in the media seemed to pick up on it. Instead they would try to break down his statements in order to arrive at some core truth or belief. There was none. Trump created reality on an ad hoc basis and it didn't matter if there was any consistency from one day to the next.

These rhetorical devices fueled his campaign and he used them as needed. Like with the issue over his taxes. He knew during the primaries that releasing his tax returns could only hurt him. He also knew that if he lost the election, no one would care, and if he won he'd have the power to avoid the problem indefinitely. So he settled on the "audit" lie and stuck with it even though it had no basis in reality.

When the subject of his taxes came up during a post-election press conference, he repeated the lie, saying he couldn't release them because "as you know, I'm under audit." The "as you know" line framed the lie as an accepted fact. When the reporter tried to follow up, citing the tradition of presidents releasing their tax returns, Trump did a sudden but interesting pivot. He said, "You know, the only ones who care about my tax returns are the reporters." He then went on to state that he won the election, and that the American people didn't care about his taxes. This revealed the fact that he never intended to release them. In April, he declared just that.

(This one example is indicative of Trump's behavior in any controversy. He never admits guilt. He always attacks. He denies everything. Then he throws out a series of wild counter-factual statements, like verbal smoke bombs, while he continues to outrun the truth and play for time.

Even as he battles back against Russia-gate and mounting cries for impeachment, he acts as if he's untouchable. If he eventually beats that rap, the non-denial denials will fade away and "I didn't do it" will change to "Yeah, I did it, and I'll do it again.")

Another Trump word game involved using generic language that sounded meaningful, like with his Muslim ban, which called for "a complete and total shutdown… until our elected officials can figure out what the heck is going on." What does "what the heck is going on" mean? Like in national security terms. Or in English. And where? In a specific country? In the Middle East? In the minds of radicalized young men all over the world? Besides, he knew what the heck was going on. His boyfriend Rudy said it in his convention speech. Terrorists were coming to kill us.

The line that surfaced during the campaign about taking him seriously versus literally was an interesting distinction. But it didn't get to the heart of the matter. Trump's words should rarely be taken literally. They should always be taken seriously. But most importantly, they should be taken tactically.

Think back to the flap over his crack about John McCain and the "I like people who weren't captured" remark. There was outrage at the statement but no awareness of the intention behind it. Forget the fact that denying the heroism of a POW was completely anathema to Republican orthodoxy. The statement itself was loopy. As if it was McCain's fault that his plane was shot down over North Vietnam and he was taken prisoner. Trump wasn't knocking McCain's service. He was neutralizing an attack by lashing out at his attacker.

I'm surprised he didn't go for "He was tortured for five years by the enemy. How do we know he didn't give up any secrets? All we have is his word." Yes, it demeaned any POW who endured his captivity and made it out alive. But that wasn't the point. The point was deflecting criticism in the moment.

Trump never defends himself. That would imply guilt

or remorse. Instead, he attacks. That's why he claimed all the women who accused him of sexual improprieties were lying, that all the lawsuits against him were baseless, all the critical news stories were fake, and that the intelligence community was wrong about Saddam having weapons of mass destruction and therefore had no credibility when it came to Russia meddling in the election.

When he wasn't deflecting accusations, he was fending off contradictions in policy statements. In one instance, Trump reversed himself once on climate change, and twice on guns in schools, in the same sentence. He was challenged on his alleged $1 million contribution to veterans, and his flip-flopping on self-funding. The accusations were dead on, backed up by facts and research, and delivered with an air of finality like a final checkmate move in which one's opponent has no choice but to topple his king and admit defeat. And that would have been true, had this been a chess game. But it wasn't. It was a street fight. And only Trump knew that, which is why he couldn't be hurt by conventional political weapons, like facts. Contradictions bounced off him like bricks off Superman because he was playing a game in a parallel universe. The media was in Metropolis. Trump was, and still is, in Bizarro World.

Go on *YouTube* and check out the *60 Minutes* interview he and Mike Pence did with Leslie Stahl, soon after Pence was selected as his running mate. No need to suffer through whole piece. If it had been any more of a ventriloquist act, Pence would've been sitting on Trump's knee with a finger up his ass. When the subject of his anti-Iraq War stance came up, Trump stuck with the talking point that he was against it, while Hillary was for it. Even though there was video evidence that negated his claim, he never backed down.

When Stahl pointed out that his running mate voted for the war, Trump replied, "I don't care." Perplexed, Stahl pressed the point, saying, "What do you mean you don't care that he voted for it? ... You used that vote of Hillary's that was the same as Mr. Pence as an example of her bad judgment."

Trump gave Pence a jocular shoulder nudge, quipping that everyone's allowed to make a mistake every once in a while." Stahl continued "But she's not." Trump: "No, she's not." This was pure contradiction. And it didn't stick.

Another revelatory moment that just slipped by was when Hillary chose her running mate. Trump immediately attacked Tim Kaine for "doing a terrible job in New Jersey." This was his warning shot. But he shot the wrong guy. A confused Trump was referring to Tom Kean, former governor of New Jersey. Hillary's choice was Tim Kaine, Senator from Virginia. (How's that going to work out when, as Commander-in-Chief, he bombs Athens instead of Aleppo? Oops. Sorry.)

Even Mike Pence took Trump-speak out for a spin when he said, in defense of Trump's man crush on Putin: "It's inarguable that Vladimir Putin has been a stronger leader in his country than Barack Obama has been in this country." No, it was not "inarguable," at all, in actual reality. Comparing a dictator to the president of a democracy is absurd. But it didn't matter. Saying it was "inarguable" made it sound real. Just like I could say it's inarguable that Mike Pence is a spineless, pandering, vertical loaf of Wonder Bread with a balloon on top, who sold his soul to the devil in exchange for power. He's not here to argue with me, so that statement becomes inarguable.

The media constantly took Trump's words as if they had conventional meaning instead of deconstructing his language to uncover his intent. Any war of words wasn't about the words; it was about the war.

Accuse him of lying and he'd strike back on Twitter. And you can't beat him on Twitter. There's no judge on Twitter. No ref. No fact-checkers. And he's not visible which means he's not vulnerable. Or he'd call in to some morning show to offer a one-sided rebuttal. And he'd rarely be challenged because the friendly shows supported him, and the others were afraid of losing access.

At his rallies, Trump's language was crafted to rile up

the crowd. And it worked, because they didn't know what he was saying, they just loved the way he said it. No wonder he gloated about loving the poorly educated. They're so easy to manipulate. And Trump knew how to play them. They'd cheer or boo on command. He even threatened reporters, branding them as "dishonest" to the point that some required security. He could have manipulated that crowd into anything. If he'd told them to throw pencils at the press, symbolically attacking them with their own weapons, they would have thrown pencils. Conversely, he could have held forth on the vital role of the Fourth Estate in our democracy, stating that journalists should be showered in roses, and they would have thrown roses.

The love his people had for him wasn't intellectual. It was emotional. On his post-election victory tour he announced to a crowd in Cincinnati that he was going to appoint "Mad Dog" … And that's as far as he got. The crowd burst into applause at the sound of "Mad Dog." They didn't know it meant that General Mike Mattis was his pick for Secretary of Defense. They just knew that "Mad Dog" sounded tough.

When he wasn't fighting off attacks or whipping up the crowd, he was spewing out words in order to mask his ignorance. That was behind his "I'm very smart" rap. You know who goes around saying "I'm smart?" Stupid people who don't want to get found out. Intelligent people don't brag about their "intelligent brains." They just have intelligent thoughts and communicate them intelligently.

He bragged about having an amazing vocabulary yet spoke in simple, declarative sentences. "My bank account is huge!" "My rallies are fantastic!" "Our leaders are stupid." "Our country's a disaster!" Articulate people don't say, "I have the best words." It's a stupid person's idea of being articulate. But none of this mattered. No one was pining for the next William F. Buckley. Not everyone was thrilled with the first one.

This was also behind his use of the word "disaster."

"Obamacare's a disaster!" "Our military's a disaster!" By using the catch-all "disaster" he could convey the impression that he had a thorough knowledge of the subject and was just speaking short-hand.

Trump even managed to turn the notion of "political correctness" on its head, perverting it from an attempt to have language reflect an ideal of fairness, to the notion that people were being forced to be empathetic. It was even in his phrasing. The deliberate way he said "African…American." Like he'd just learned the word, so he took a big pause in the middle to make sure the wrong word didn't accidentally slip out. Because growing up in Queens I'll bet that's not the phrase that was usually en route from his brain to his mouth. That's where he should build a fucking wall.

Sometimes, words would come out because he'd been put in a position where he was expected to speak. Take his comments to members of the press in late December while outside his Palm Beach home with Don King. First of all, if you were trying to convey the impression that you were taking the responsibilities of being president seriously, would you really trot out Don King? And not even Don King in a suit. Don King sporting a shit-eating denture grin and dressed like some old lady waiting to board a bus to Atlantic City to play the slots and gum some buffet food.

When the subject of Russian hacking came up, Trump responded with "I think the computers have complicated lives very greatly. The whole age of computer (sic) has made it where nobody knows exactly what's going on."

The press aired the clip. They mocked the fact that it was gibberish. An older guy trying to pretend he's plugged in by talking about how it's fantastic what the kids are doing these days with the computers. (Even if what he thought he meant was that while computers have put a world of knowledge at our fingertips, the downside is that they have simultaneously made us vulnerable.)

When he wasn't using language as a weapon, or vomiting up word salads, he was just plain lying. But Trump's not simply a pathological liar. Nor is he a clever, debate team-type liar like Ted Cruz, who carefully hides his lies inside language. Trump is a George Costanza-type liar in the sense that "it's not a lie if you believe it." He's the guy who gets caught in bed with another woman by his wife and denies it with "Who you gonna believe, me or your lyin' eyes?"

Protestors in Jersey City after 9/11? Absolutely. Planes unloading pallets of cash for Iran? He saw it. And if busted, he just doubled down on the lie. In the context of the Russian hacking scandal, you can understand Trump's comments by using the above scenario. Just substitute "Russia" for "the other woman," and the "American people" for "his wife."

For Trump, words are weapons in a battle. That's why, in Trump World, he was never losing the election. He was always winning because he said he was winning. And saying he was winning meant some perceived him as winning, which meant they could vote for him, confident they were voting for a winner.

Whether his mendacity is calculated or habitual is academic. Now that he's president he's using the same rhetorical tricks he used during the campaign. He rarely means what he says. But he always says what he means, and what he thinks he has to say in any given moment. His agenda is buried in the words. And because he plays so loose with facts he's going to be challenged constantly which means he has to come up with more counter-attacks by dismissing the attacks as lies and the attackers as liars.

There's an adage in advertising about pitching clients a campaign. "Tell them what they're about to see, show them, then tell them what they saw." Create your reality then tell them how they're going to live in it.

In Trump World, lies become truth. Everyone is played but no one is informed. Even worse, we get the illusion of being informed, which renders us ill-informed, and, ultimately, misinformed. Because sometimes reality is what I can convince you it is. For Trump, language is about framing reality to suit his ends then denying the existence of any other reality, thus dragging everyone else into his.

But once you figure out the game, it becomes easy to deconstruct his statements. Just consider what he wants you to believe then ask yourself why he wants you to believe it. What are his motives? His words have meaning only insofar as they have purpose. And power. It's not language. It's Trump-speak.

PSYOPS

Psyops. Psychological operations. A tactic employed by military and intelligence networks to take advantage of an enemy's vulnerabilities in order to achieve a specific objective. In the case of this election it was, in simple English, mindfucking the electorate. Floating lies into the culture, or trading on memes that already existed, repeatedly pounding them into the public consciousness to the point that lies became truth.

"Crooked Hillary." She's crooked, because everyone knows she's crooked, and we had the 33,000 deleted emails from her private server, so obviously she was hiding something because, as we all know, she's crooked. Most people couldn't tell you what a server is, what it does, and why having a private one is bad. But because she had one, she was crooked. And "33,000" emails was a big number, which made it sound worse.

On the day of the third and final presidential debate, a reporter on *MSNBC* was interviewing some local voters about their impressions of the candidates. Their opinions were across the board, but one woman said she couldn't trust Hillary because of "the emails and, of course, Benghazi." Propaganda works.

Then there was the lie about Hillary's health. Trump literally pulled it out of his ass but it worked because he knew the press would report it even if it was completely unsubstantiated. You just make an allegation then the media reports that an allegation has been made. Then the person against whom it was made has to deny it. Then the absence of a denial itself becomes news, whether or not it ever had any basis in fact. When she vanished from the 9/11 Memorial, then collapsed on the sidewalk, it was the perfect confluence of bullshit and reality.

The Clinton "dishonest" meme goes back decades. During the election there were Judicial Watch "bombshells" on "HILLARY CLINTON'S SECRET EMAIL SCANDAL" and the "BENGHAZI COVER UP." They've been dogging the Clintons for decades, since the days of the "vast, right wing conspiracy." It was always a political hit job. Maybe because Bill Clinton was the personification of a Republican nightmare: a good-looking, intelligent Southern Democrat with small town roots and an affinity for connecting with regular folks. Clinton not only talked the talk but walked the walk, even if it involved an occasional walk on the wild side. This seriously screwed with the folksy Republican narrative, and the traditional demographic map. Clinton won the presidency with 370 electoral votes in 1992, and 379 in 1996. His presidency was successful until reality played into the narrative with an actual scandal. By the time this election rolled around, the Clinton-hate was baked in. And since Bill was heavily involved in the campaign, it was easily transferable.

The second part of the psyop war was the Karl Rove strategy of taking your enemy's strength and turning it into a weakness. That gave us John Kerry's 2004 "swiftboating." But Trump ratcheted up this tactic to a level of mind-fucking previously unseen in politics by accusing his enemy of doing exactly what he was doing. It was a form of psychological projection, not as a defense mechanism, but as a tactic.

By blaming his enemy he created a brilliant smokescreen for his own activities. It worked because no one ever imagines that the person doing the lying is actually guilty of the crime, especially not someone in a position of power. We just don't think on that many levels.

It reminded me of a 1970 Italian movie—*Investigation of a Citizen Above Suspicion*—about a police inspector who murders his mistress, then becomes part of the investigation to catch the killer, so he plants clues at the crime scene to deflect blame.

We like to say "all politicians lie" because it gives us the illusion that we're sufficiently skeptical. But just think about all the things he said to deflect attention from his own character and behavior.

The dumb guy accused his enemies of being stupid.

The guy with the erratic temperament accused his opponent of being unstable.

The guy who was lying accused his enemies of being liars.

The guy who couldn't fake his way through a single Bible verse accused his opponent of being immoral.

The guy who was crooked enough to be sued over 3000 times accused his enemies of being crooks.

The guy who attacked a judge in one of those cases for being potentially biased based on his ethnic heritage accused his opponent of being racist.

The rich guy who (allegedly) stiffed contractors and screwed his workers accused his opponent of being out of touch with working people.

The guy who was snorting so badly during a debate he looked like he was tweaking accused his opponent of being on drugs. (What drugs could she have possibly been on? Lipitor? Frankly, a little coke bump during one of the debates might have given her the energy to go for his throat.)

The guy who complained about rigged elections was allegedly colluding with a foreign power to influence the election.

The guy who complained about voter fraud was in the party that had been actively engaged in voter suppression.

The most corrupt person ever to seek the presidency accused her of being the most corrupt person ever to seek the presidency.

The guy who complained about violence against his supporters urged his supporters to violence.

He even called out his people to go to Pennsylvania to "help me stop crooked Hillary from rigging this election." He urged his supporters to go to "those neighborhoods — and we all know who we're talking about — and be on the lookout for people who come in and vote five times."

Did people signing up on the website think they were going to race to Philly and stand outside polling stations with digital cameras and laptops equipped with facial recognition software? Did they really think someone was going to vote, then put on a disguise and return to cast another ballot under a different name? Did anyone in the media question the lunacy of the allegation or whether it was simply an attempt at voter intimidation?

It didn't matter whether there was any truth to any of his comments. What mattered is that he was able to say them and get away with it. Kellyanne Conway even copped to the strategy on *Fox*, in response to Bret Baier's comment about a likely indictment over the Clinton Foundation "scandal." Even when the host walked back his comment as "inartful," Conway said it didn't matter, noting, "the damage was done."

Or, as Goebbels put it: "That propaganda is good that leads to success, and that is bad which fails to achieve the desired result."

BRANDING

People like to call Trump a marketing genius. I don't like using the word "genius" in this context because it demeans the concept. Why take a word used to describe people like Albert Einstein, Pablo Picasso, Jimi Hendrix, or Steve Jobs, and sully it by assigning it to anyone who exhibits a particular ability or skill? Would you call a clever balloon-folder a balloon-folding genius? We have other words in the lexicon to describe someone who can take long pieces of colored rubber, inflate them with helium then quickly configure them into the shape of a sword or dachshund.

The word should have some component of the quality of the result. So let's keep "genius" reserved for those whose creative breakthroughs have added a unique understanding or artful quality to life. Let's not call Trump a branding genius. Let's just say he's very, very good at it. The guy can brand the shit out of anyone, if they let him. And most people aren't prepared to fight off the attack, particularly when it's the last thing they expect in a presidential election.

The method is simple: Toss out a stock phrase then say it over and over, like an advertising slogan. It doesn't matter if it's debunked. Once it's out there, it's out there. You can't un-drop a bomb. Seventeen candidates slugged it out in the Republican primary like it was a political rugby scrum. And one by one, Trump stuck each one in a box they weren't clever enough to punch their way out of.

He always started with his toughest challenger. Jeb had the name, the money, and the party behind him, so he took the first hit, getting branded as "Low Energy Jeb." Trump hammered this poor guy mercilessly, on national TV. I couldn't believe Jeb let him get away with it. Of course, if he didn't have the balls to fight off being taunted, then he didn't have the balls to be president. But watching it still made me sad.

Make no mistake, I completely disagreed with Jeb Bush's brown paper bag Republican dogma, and I did not want this guy to be president. Bush 41 was innocuous enough, but after Bush 43, no one was dying for the three-peat. But watching Jeb take a national beat-down while offering up little more than a hapless pathetic shrug was just too painful. Trump might as well have pantsed the poor bastard on Christmas morning in front of his kids, while groping his wife. My heart went out to him. It was like the end of *Rocky*. I sat in front of my TV yelling, "Get up, Jeb! Get up!" But he couldn't get up. He literally didn't know what hit him. I even screamed out his lines for him.

Imaginary Jeb: "Low-energy? What's the matter with you, you idiot. This is the presidency of the United States. It's not about energy; it's about experience. Of which you have none. Zero. I've been the governor of the fourth most populous state in the country. You went bust peddling steaks and phony universities. Just go back to your con games and your golf courses and leave governing to the people who know how to do it…"

I could've riffed that speech all day long. But Jeb couldn't fight back. He just took it. By the time he did that pathetic New Hampshire town hall where he had to beg people to clap, I wanted to send the poor bastard a therapy dog. Jeb had no balls. Even one ball would've been fine. But Trump picked his pocket clean and soon Jeb was gone.

Then it was on to "Li'l Marco." Trump mocked his size, along with his infamous dry mouth and awkward water grab during his 2013 GOP response to President Obama's State of the Union address. Trump really worked it, flinging around a water bottle like some hacky prop comic doing a midnight slot at the Komedy Korner.

But it landed. And you could see Marco was not going to get tagged like Jeb, so he eventually hit back, in kind. The "tiny hands" crack stuck. It got traction. People were laughing. Everyone did their "tiny hands" joke. And it took us to the lowest point in the history of American politics, in which a man running for president of the United States stood on a stage and bragged about the size of his dick.

Marco tried to defend himself but it ultimately failed, because it was fake. It was a comic doing someone else's material. Rubio may be many things. Spineless. Opportunistic. Ambitious. But the one thing he's not is authentic. And voters want authentic. They don't seem to care if the person is a scumbag. They just want an authentic scumbag. He wasn't, as Chris Matthews put it, "comfortable in his own skin." My feeling was that Rubio was shopping around for a skin that seemed to fit, but Trump wouldn't sell it to him.

In the meantime, Trump took shots at Carly Fiorina's face. Then sort of apologized when he thought it might have hurt him with women. He mocked Rand Paul's looks. The orange, fat-faced, yellow-haired clown mocked someone else's looks. He did fat jokes and bridge jokes on Christie, and dumb jokes on Rick Perry (now his Secretary of Energy). He knocked Ben Carson (now his Secretary of Housing and Urban Development, though his only qualification is that he's "urban"). He lampooned Carson's "knife in the belt buckle" story, calling him "pathological." He just floated it out there as a stand-alone insult. He didn't even finish it. Pathological what? Pathological liar? Pathological masturbator? He didn't say. Just pathological, which had no meaning, but it sounded bad. He even gave out Lindsey Graham's cell number. Graham tried to fight it with a TV spot in which he destroyed his phone in amusing ways, but it didn't land. It was also fake.

Trump blew away the field. Despite all his vulnerabilities — the lawsuits, the hair, the steaks, the bogus university — no one could land a punch. No one could do Trump but Trump. And once he closed the deal, he bragged how hard he was going to hit Hillary. Her campaign should have assumed the worst and come up with a counter-strategy, but they didn't. And he came out blasting.

The Iraq War vote. Super-predators. Goldman Sachs. Monica. "Crooked Hillary." "Founders of ISIS." "Emails!" He hit the Clinton Foundation as a "pay for play deal." He called her evil. The devil. A criminal who should be locked up. Or shot.

And the events in her life played right into it. As I heard it put on the *Keepin' it 1600"* podcast, she was "a guilty verdict in search of evidence." Did her behavior and evasive language over decades of public service occasionally open a door for her political enemies? Shit, yes. But you tend to tread carefully when you're walking through a minefield. Is she ambitious? Probably. Anyone who wakes up in the morning, looks in the mirror, and thinks "I could be president" should immediately be taken away for a psych eval.

It seemed obvious she was running for president the moment she moved to New York to run for Pat Moynihan's open Senate seat. Did that make her a carpetbagger? You could say that. People said that about Bobby Kennedy when he ran for a New York Senate seat in 1964. She lost the primary eight years ago, yet she dusted herself off, sucked it up, and served in the administration of the guy who beat her. You could say that showed class, and a dedication to shared ideals. Or you could say it revealed her political opportunism and a desire to build her resume so she could run again.

She even said in her speeches that she needed to have a public and private position. The context didn't matter. It played into her negatives. Was Hillary pure? Hell, no. You want ideological purity? Go live in a monastery.

There's a difference between people who want power for power's sake and people who understand the responsibility that goes with power. Government is about getting shit done. LBJ didn't exactly have a history of high-minded idealism. But he got shit done, like the Civil Rights Act and the Voting Rights Act. He knew how to wield power.

Trump neutralized his primary opponents, then he demonized Hillary. He completely outplayed everyone. He was the consummate flim-flam man. He even copped to it in a post-election rally, telling his people that he was unsure whether the "swamp" line would stick. Imagine the arrogance of a con artist who looks his marks in the face and brags that he wasn't sure if they were stupid enough to believe him. He even told them he didn't need their votes anymore. And they still applauded.

He's still using the same tactics because he thinks no one can figure out what he's up to. And, as much as it induces severe mouth-vomit to write this: in many cases, he's right. We're just too gullible. Bullshit works on us.

Nicotine isn't addictive. Seat belts don't save lives. Climate change is a hoax. We can bomb ISIS out of existence. We can keep terrorists from entering the country through "extreme vetting" because "extreme" vetting sounds tougher than regular vetting.

Lies become truths unless they're successfully debunked. Traditionally, big lies required big venues. But our methods of communication have changed. Big lies now also come in small packages.

TWEETSTORMS

Throughout our history, presidents have used various methods to address the American people. Whether a soaring, provocative oratory to thousands in a stadium, the folksy give-and-take of a town hall, a one-on-one interview, or an intimate statement to camera from the Oval Office, it's always been about the medium as well as the message.

Lincoln's Gettysburg address. FDR's fireside chats or Pearl Harbor address to Congress. JFK's "ask not" inaugural. LBJ's "I will not seek, nor will I accept…" withdrawal from running for a second term. Nixon's "I am not a crook" press conference. Obama's 2008 speech on race in America. Even W's bullhorn speech on the smoldering wreckage of the World Trade Center had power. Of course, given the emotions of the moment, a chimp in a Yankee jacket could've brought the crowd to tears, but I'll give him credit, he rose to the occasion.

And now we have the presidential tweet. Trump was built for Twitter, the use of which he tries to fob off as just a modern form of communication. It's what all the kids are doing. And, of course, his personal Cruella de Vil spun it as Trump's way of reaching out directly to the American people. Right, because the president of the United States has no other means at his disposal.

(According to a *Vanity Fair* article from August 2016, sources differ on the real number of his Twitter followers, noting that many are bots, dead bots, or people not actively engaged. Though given the fact that he's president, I'm guessing those numbers will rise. And if they don't, he'll say they did. On Twitter.)

Whether or not Twitter makes it into the future, and I hope it does because I own some stock, it will remain Trump's favorite mode of communication. And misdirection. Why? Because he has limited intelligence, a short attention span, no ability to engage in meaningful dialogue, and no patience for looking vulnerable or being contradicted. Just imagine if there's another 9/11-style attack and the president tries to calm the fears of a nation with a tweet.

Trump didn't just use Twitter; he weaponized it. News shows now begin with the line "The president tweeted." Then the panel rings in on Trump's tweets. Then the Trump-talkers invade the chat shows, explaining the true meaning of the tweet. He throws up the news candy of a provocative new mind-spurt, knowing the media will chew on it, thus avoiding the story he doesn't want discussed, or creating the story he does.

Think back to his post-victory tour, when he swooped into Indianapolis to announce the Carrier Air Conditioning deal that allegedly saved 1100 jobs. When Chuck Jones, President of United Steel 1999, criticized the deal, Trump instantly denounced him on Twitter. Though Trump was criticized for being petty and punching down, the media didn't seem to get that he was simply reacting to criticism. Jones was throwing shade on his stunt so Trump had to strike back.

Trump's tweets all mean the same thing: don't fuck with my optics. Or stop investigating me because I'm guilty as shit and you're getting too close. It doesn't matter if the recipient is Rosie O'Donnell, Alec Baldwin, Hillary Clinton, James Comey, or any of the 289 people he lambasted on Twitter, per *The New York Times*. It's not about the insult; it's about self-preservation.

Lies, psyops, branding, Twitter — all weapons in his arsenal, aimed at creating illusion, or whipping up emotion. It takes a strong mind to guard against an avalanche of propaganda and disinformation, particularly when we don't know we're being hit with it. In many cases, it seems a simple lie goes down easier than a complex truth. Although, it raises the next question: who are we, and why did these tactics work on us?

CHAPTER FIVE

WHY DID IT WORK ON US?

WELCOME TO DUMBFUCKISTAN

"The root of the Wallace magic was a cynical, showbiz instinct for knowing exactly which issues would whip a hall full of beer-drinking factory workers into a frenzy — and then doing exactly that, by howling down from the podium that he had an instant, overnight cure for all their worst afflictions… Wallace assured his supporters that the solution was actually real simple, and that the only reason they had any hassle with the government at all was because those greedy bloodsuckers in Washington didn't want the problems solved, so they wouldn't be put out of work."

Hunter S. Thompson
Fear and Loathing on the Campaign Trail – '72

AMERICA'S
SOCIAL AND POLITICAL
SCHIZOPHRENIA

"One nation under God." Words we've mindlessly, and robotically chanted since we were schoolkids, while gazing up at the flag. Though no one ever questioned why we had to start the day by reciting a national loyalty oath. And we readily accepted the God part, even though it was added during the Eisenhower administration. So, technically, America didn't receive divine sanction until 1954.

We're not a nation of thinkers. We're a nation of believers. And our strongest belief is in our own mythology. Unfortunately after the last eight years, and particularly after this last election, the "one nation, indivisible" part rings particularly hollow. We're one nation, divisible. Red, blue, left, right, liberal, conservative, rich, poor, atheist, believer, small town, big city. The 21st century U.S.A. — United Schizophrenics of America. No wonder we can't get anything done. Given the voices raging inside us, it's not surprising it takes a war to focus national attention.

You could look at our political differences in Freudian terms, as the outward manifestation of our inner psychological impulses. Our politics is essentially a war with ourselves. The id gives us Republicans, who extol individual rights and resist any impediment to a person pursuing their self-interest. (Unless of course it involves sex, in which case the government must step in and the guilty must be slut-shamed.) Our superego gives us Democrats, who value the role of government and our responsibility to one another. And, like a functional person with a healthy ego, we need both aspects of who we are to live life to the fullest. That's why we have a Defense Department, and Medicare.

Historically we've drifted left and right, but usually rejected the extremes. We flirted with fringe candidates, whether it was Barry Goldwater playing the tough-guy card or George Wallace playing the race card, but ultimately our need for stability won out. Not this time. Throughout the campaign, Trump spewed a stream of ignorant bile that would have been considered over the line from a drunk at the end of a bar. He not only degraded the electoral process—a process one would think couldn't be degraded any further—he demeaned the presidency, itself.

So, why was it that for 63 million Americans this behavior wasn't just acceptable, it was desirable, even empowering? Why were 63 million Americans not only open to dating Trump, but to running off to Vegas and marrying him? Why were people at his rallies raising their fists, grunting their approval at the prospect of building a wall, punching out protesters, or hurling insults at the press? It's in our nature to look for saviors, but what was going on in the American mind that made people think they could be saved by fat, dumb, rich orange Jesus?

TRUMP
FEAR

Elections are snapshots in time. They become flash points for whatever's pushing our buttons; reflections of the zeitgeist, thermometers up the ass of the nation. And while most presidential campaign themes are centered on hope, change, and a bright, shiny American future, the theme of this election became fear of an ugly, dangerous present.

Trump campaigned on fear, and unfortunately, the times backed up his play. Since JFK's assassination in Dallas, the names of American cities have morphed from places to live or visit to synonyms for mass murder: Austin, Oklahoma City, Littleton, Aurora, Tucson, Newtown, Phoenix, Boston, Charleston, San Bernardino, Orlando, Baton Rouge, St. Paul, then Dallas all over again. And it wasn't just American carnage. There was Paris, Nice, Istanbul, Madrid, Manchester and, most recently, London.

To paraphrase Joseph Heller, just because you're paranoid doesn't mean people aren't trying to kill you. When fear is in the air, people look for protection, and someone to blame. And who better than foreigners?

Even though the only thing that ties most Americans together is that we're either immigrants or the children of immigrants, we seem to conveniently forget that fact when the next group moves into the neighborhood. Once upon a time, people railed against the Irish, Italians, and Jews. Now it's Mexicans and Muslims. You know, those strange people with the weird customs who are coming to kill us.

No one sold fear better than Trump. Bad things are happening! Mexico's sending rapists and murderers! Terrorists are sneaking into the country! ISIS is coming to kill us! Hillary's going to take your guns! The military's weak! We need a wall to keep out illegals! A ban on Muslim immigrants!

Despite the fact that Syrian refugees are subjected to an 18-24 month vetting process, he whipped up hysteria by claiming they're pouring over the border and we don't know who they are. He used the Orlando attack to back up his claims, even though the shooter was raised in New York. Post-9/11 feelings of vulnerability along with a series of attacks all over the world played right into his narrative.

We focused on the fight against ISIS because it was the brand name we were given, even though there are terrorist groups all over the world. But there hadn't been an attack on American soil to rival 9/11. While we've had demonstrations against police shootings that have bought social tensions to a boiling point, it's not like the late '60s when cities were going up in flames. The only American carnage has been the daily body count of gun deaths, to which we've sadly grown numb.

Fear was just another branded product. Trump University, Trump Institute, Trump steaks, Trump wine, then Trump Fear, peddled by a demagogue who scared the shit out of people who just wanted their jobs, their guns, their God, and their football. The code words of Nixon's "law and order" message were gone, replaced by the actual words. There was no dog whistle language. The dog was barking out loud: "Our country has become a bleak, desolate hellscape and I alone can save you."

ECONOMIC
FEAR

There was no rational argument for Make America Great Again in 2016. Reagan used the same slogan in the 1980 campaign at a time when we were suffering from inflation, gas shortages, the Iran hostage crisis, and perhaps a little too much Jimmy Carter introspection. We were vulnerable. Insecure. It was the perfect time for a handsome actor to come along and tell us that no matter what anybody said, we were beautiful. The patriotic equivalent of (now Senator) Al Franken's *SNL* Stuart Smalley character: "You're good enough, you're smart enough and doggone it, people like you."

Ok, so maybe some people were pissed because factories closed and jobs moved overseas. And maybe it's true that Democrats didn't speak to their concerns. Hillary didn't make her case to the people who needed to hear it. I couldn't tell you Hillary's economic plan, though I have a feeling it wouldn't have departed too far from the Obama administration policies that led to 15 million new private sector jobs over the course of his two terms. Perhaps it would have included incentives for companies involved in clean energy, which would have created jobs while addressing climate change. I'm just guessing because she didn't make her case.

There may have been an economic dis-ease running through the country but things were not bleak enough to back up Trump's rhetoric. America was not a dust bowl wasteland. The landscape wasn't littered with the corpses of rotting factories. No riots in the streets. No bread lines. No families in rickety old trucks roaming the plains, looking for work and roasting potatoes over open fires. We did have a level of economic inequality that was at its worst since the 1970s, but the irony was that people looked to Trump as the one who would solve the problem instead of realizing that he was part of the cause.

There was no American carnage. But there was something going on at those rallies. They had all the sobriety of a UFC cage match. People were pissed off and ready for violence. In some cases, they were actually violent. Though maybe some just wanted to be part of the show. To dress up in their T-shirts and MAGA hats, and do the call-and-response. "Who's going to pay for the wall?!" "Mexico!" Only Trump could drag politics down to the level of Wheel of Fortune.

But were these really America's downtrodden? According to a *FiveThirtyEight* exit poll taken during the GOP primaries, the mean annual income of Trump voters was around $72,000. That doesn't exactly back up the case that his support was rooted in desperation. Those rallies weren't exactly the blue collar equivalent of the Davos forum. I didn't see one person holding up a sign reading, "I'm extremely upset that economic growth has stalled out at less than 2% of GDP!" How do you make the case for economic anxiety when it breaks down along party lines?

As noted, the argument might have had some validity if you reversed the records of the previous two administrations. If President Bush rescued the country from a near depression, saved the auto industry, created 15 million new jobs, got unemployment under 5%, and appropriately responded to the devastation caused by a hurricane, but then President Obama tanked the economy, lost 750,000 jobs a month, risked a second Great Depression, let New Orleans drown, allowed 9/11 to occur, and lied us into a divisive war that further destabilized an already unstable region, I would have understood the anger and the cries for change.

Hell, if a Republican administration presided over eight years of economic growth and relative safety and a Democrat came in and wrecked it all, I might have been tempted to vote Republican. I wouldn't have, but I would have been tempted. But the truth was exactly the opposite. Trump's promise to return America to some mythical Reaganesque utopia was empty. But people ate it up. And even if there was real economic fear, you can still acknowledge the existence of the disease without buying snake oil as the cure. Something else was going on. Something irrational. Something that made people put aside their values and elect someone, despite his obvious moral failings.

During the McCarthy hearings, the plea from attorney Joseph Welch to the junior Senator from Wisconsin was "have you left no sense of decency?" It was a sobering, poignant reminder that we still had a sense of morality. This election seems to have buried that notion forever. Along with the dumbing-down of our national dialogue has come a lowering of the bar for acceptable behavior. It's one thing when it's an actor or an athlete, but we've now extended it to those seeking public office.

So why were so many people willing to give him a pass? How was it that language and behavior that would have instantly disqualified someone from teaching kindergarten suddenly became acceptable in a presidential candidate?

WE FORGAVE
HIS SINS AND
FAST-TRACKED
HIS REDEMPTION

Even with our differences on economics, social issues, taxes, and the proper role of the federal government, the one place we can usually come to some agreement is on the value of basic human decency. If pressed, most Americans would probably say they believe in some standard of absolute morality. Most wouldn't identify themselves as moral relativists. Most people couldn't define moral relativism, let alone have an intelligent discussion on the subject. But they might hold fast to their religious beliefs, perhaps expressed in the Ten Commandments, the Sermon on the Mount, or the Golden Rule.

Self-professed atheists might reach for Kant's Categorical Imperative: "Act only according to that maxim whereby you can, at the same time, will that it should become a universal law." Even existentialists, who might disagree philosophically with the existence of objective morality, would probably accept that there are standards of behavior that contribute to the betterment of society.

These may be our beliefs, but it's not what we practice. Culturally, we've not only defined deviancy down, an observation from the late New York Senator Patrick Moynihan. We've gone a step further and defined decency down, then fast-tracked redemption.

When a celebrity has a misstep, they instantly embark on the Mea Culpa Tour. Get a DUI? Get busted sending a dick pic, or having actual, old-fashioned sex with someone who's not your wife? Call a cop "sugar tits" and make hateful remarks about Jews or African-Americans? Engage in a little extracurricular dog-fighting? No problem. Set up a press conference. Face the cameras, make a sad, pouty face, throw some cash at a charity and poof! You're redeemed and reinvented. Instant Karmic cleanser. We no longer care about actual atonement, just the appearance of it.

Still, at one time, it didn't hold true for politicians. George Allen's "macaca" insult took him right out of an election. As did Gary Hart's affair. As did John Edwards' affair. Larry "wide stance" Craig is gone. Elliot Spitzer's gone. Mark Foley. Anthony Weiner. Not that he went quietly. Yes, David Vitter got another shot. As did Mark Sanford. But why did we lower the bar on acceptable behavior this time?

Traditionally, candidates have used optimistic, uplifting language when announcing their run for higher office. Expressions like "hope and change" or "American dream" are the expected clichés. Yet no one seemed to think it was anything more than an odd rhetorical choice when Trump used the word "rapists."

None of his supporters stopped for a moment of reflection when he encouraged violence at his rallies or when a guy got punched, and then threatened by his attacker, who said, "If he comes back we may have to shoot him."

No one squirmed when he mocked a reporter with a disability.

Guys who took pride in being tough voted for someone whose main mode of attack was banging out petty revenge tweets.

He bragged during the campaign that he could stand in the middle of Fifth Avenue and shoot somebody, and wouldn't lose voters. No problem.

He implied that Hillary could be shot if she appointed judges in favor of stricter gun control. Then he threatened to imprison her. Still not over the line.

No one slammed the brakes over Pussygate.

No one thought that even if one woman accusing him of sexual assault might be looking to cash in, twelve such accusations might have indicated a pattern of behavior. When this came out, there were still undecided women. Undecided college-educated women. What in the world could make college-educated women waver in their choice between a female candidate who spent a lifetime working for women, and a male candidate who allegedly spent a lifetime abusing them?

Perhaps it's no accident that Trump arrived by way of reality television, a medium in which we not only lower the standards of acceptable behavior, we celebrate them. We live for those extreme moments—the anger, the insults, the fights.

We not only lowered the bar on his behavior, we fast-tracked his road to redemption. TV pundits smacked their heads at the horrible remarks, yet the sin became less important than whether it could be politically transcended. They framed it like he was MacGyver trapped in a windowless basement with just a shoelace and a paper clip. It was "how the hell does he get out of this one?" Then they allowed his spokespeople on the air to make their ridiculous counter-arguments and in doing so, became complicit in excusing his behavior.

Take the Megyn Kelly episode. Imagine the level of misogyny it takes to imply that the only reason a female reporter asked a tough question was that she was having her period. Then imagine the balls it takes to claim that you didn't really say what you said, then continue to insult the reporter on Twitter. Then imagine the level of cynicism it takes to stonewall the blowback, then use it as an excuse for a TV special.

It was so sickeningly fake when he flashed that stupid, cutesy grin, cooing, "Did I call you a bimbo? Excuse me." He should've just given her a red heart made out of construction paper with "Donald loves Megyn" scribbled in crayon. It all played so cloying and fake. But it worked. He was able to power through the crisis and move on.

Once he transcended that disaster, it was open season on anyone. Carly Fiorina's face? Insult and apology. Crisis averted. Fat-shaming and slut-shaming a former Miss Universe? No problem.

But the acid test was Pussygate. This was heralded as "game over." Un-survivable. First Trump issued a belligerent, sneering damage control statement—the "I'm really not sorry" non-apology video. Then there was the half-assed "locker room talk" excuse followed by "These words don't reflect who I am." No they didn't reflect it. They defined it. Or they would have if we had retained any traditional standards of behavior. Even his idiot son tried to explain it away as "alpha male" behavior.

A dozen allegations of sexual misconduct were fought off with one blanket denial. They're all liars. Of course, the sheer number of allegations made that necessary. Then he tossed in the counter-factual "no one respects women more than Donald Trump," which was a remarkable, bold-faced lie but it became true because he said it. And enough people bought it. Even though there was the obligatory Republican outrage, it was all ultimately hollow. It was party over morality, as the people who brought you Christian values gave a pass to the pussy-grabber.

Even the allegation that there was video of Trump getting peed on by Russian hookers didn't derail him. It was still deny and attack. Accuse the accusers. Ride out the storm, and live to fight another day.

During the 2012 election, Mitt Romney advisor Eric Fehrnstrom suggested that the candidate was going to Etch A Sketch his personality and tone in order to pivot to the general election. During Trump's "presidential" metamorphosis, his then-campaign manager Paul Manafort tried to reassure GOP leaders by saying that Trump had just been playing a part, implying that the candidate would soon act in a way befitting the office.

Per Manafort, "You can't change somebody's character, but you can change the way a person presents himself." (So said the man who people say did public relations for a murderers' row of, well, murderers, and has since become one of the main players in Russia-gate.)

When it became disturbingly clear that Trump would be the Republican nominee, he went on stage and bragged "I'm going to be so presidential." It was as if the "presidential" was a suit he could buy from the Trump catalogue that came with an extra pair of pants, a shirt, and some dignity. When did the benchmark for national office become whether you could successfully fake decency? Presidential? Why not presidential-ish? Presidential-esque? It seemed that no matter how ugly the offense, he was able to do a spin-move away from it, engage in some political shape-shifting, and voters were still eager to go along for the ride.

There were other factors in play that allowed Trump to extricate himself from his sins: the classic American values of reinvention, as well as religious notions of sin and redemption. Both are hard wired into our national psyche. We're a nation based on second chances. We're all sinners. And all sin is forgivable, as it's the essence of the human condition. We atone, do penance, and move on. Hate the sin, not the sinner. Trump's "I never claimed to be perfect" was just a more belligerent version of "Let he without sin cast the first stone."

All his missteps, comments, and misdeeds were branded as one-offs, as opposed to evidence of a pattern of behavior. He used the language of atonement to weasel out of any genuine remorse. Not that there was any. He was just pissed off at having been busted.

In the age of moral relativism, it's not a matter of where the line is. It's that there is no more line. We've lowered the standards of decency, trivialized immorality, and fast-tracked redemption. If this were 1945, we'd dispense with the Nuremberg Trials and just demand the Nazis issue formal apologies, do highway cleanup all over Europe, and write "I will not commit genocide" a million times on the blackboard.

Trump's victory turned out to be a test of our nation's fundamental decency. And we failed. We elected an immoral, perhaps amoral man to a job we like to think should be held by someone who at least values morality. His supporters forgave his moral transgressions, misogyny, multiple accusations of sexual assault, shady business deals, and even his alleged collusion with an enemy to influence the election. The question is, why.

I think it's because the candidate was scratching a more powerful itch, one that wasn't rooted in fear of terrorism, economic desperation, or the promise that he'd fulfill their American dreams. Something deeper was also going on in a segment of the American population. Something he played on with his birther campaign, and rode all the way to the White House.

THE
LAST GASP
OF
ANGRY
WHITE
AMERICA

For many, the election of the country's first African-American president was an important milestone and a sign of hope. But for others, it was the cause of an existential freak out. After eight years of President Obama, Trump promised redemption and re-empowerment. This was angry, white America's last stand. It wasn't the totality of the Trump phenomenon, but to suggest that it wasn't a major factor is to ignore the obvious.

Once upon a time, when it was morning in America, even the poorest poor bastard could step out of his trailer, crack open a beer, and take that first deep breath of air that smelled like dog piss and gasoline, and still feel that life was ok, and that the world was in its proper place. Because what got his ass down to the filling station to clean toilets eight hours a day was the feeling that, as bad as life was, at least he was better off because he was white. But when a black guy got elected president that rationale was gone. And that was unsettling, because it caused people to lose their social bearings and accept that the world was changing. Obama didn't fuck up "the" world. He fucked up "their" world. They were pissed off. They were scared. And they wanted things to go back to the way they were.

Trump's birther campaign was grounded in Obama blowback. It was a shout-out to uneducated, socially castrated white guys who yearned to be re-empowered because they couldn't get over the fact that we elected a black president, then re-elected the black president, then failed to impeach the black president for the high crime of bring president while black. It was never about the words. It was about the music. And the emotions.

But it's not like he was shouting "birth certificate" in the forest, with no one around to hear it. Trump was on every network and cable outlet. Even if the hosts tried to challenge the claims, they never got him to recant, which allowed him to keep the notion in the air. Trump could say he had people on the ground, studying it, and that they couldn't believe what they were finding. Even though it was an obvious lie—made even more obvious now because he never released any of the "unbelievable" findings—no one successfully challenged him in the moment. But it wasn't just a matter of failing to debunk his claims. The original sin was in allowing him on TV in the first place. So even before some news outlets aired his rallies as infomercials, they already had blood on their hands. They were complicit in giving the birther lie a foothold in the American mind.

But Trump knew the minds of the people he was reaching out to, and why they would respond. He rode a wave of racist backlash that began the day Obama won the election, and manifested itself with the rise of The Tea Party, and an onslaught of insults, and accusations. "Obama's a tyrant! A king! A dictator! He's trampling on the Constitution!" Yes, the guy who taught Constitutional Law was trampling on the Constitution.

There are only two possible explanations for why Trump ran around the country for five years slinging this shit. Either he was dumb enough to believe it. Or he was dark, cynical, and cunning enough to use it by stoking the lingering cells of racism still alive in the body politic.

I think it's the latter, because even when it crossed the line of absurdity and Trump was in danger of looking like a clown, he still wouldn't let go. Even after successfully forcing the president to release his birth certificate, he shifted to questioning its authenticity, tweeting, "An 'extremely credible source' has called my office and told me that Obama's birth certificate is a fraud."

Then he pivoted to casting doubt on Obama's college records. No sentient human being could be stupid enough to insist there was any truth to it. And not just in private, but in public. And if this guy is about anything, it's about his public image.

He may have kicked off his campaign by taking a shot at Mexicans, then segued over to Muslims before spraying fire at the press corps, but his basic platform was racism. After eight years of President Obama, Trump was white folks' revenge.

A week after the election, while still reeling from the aftershocks, I was taking a morning walk and listening to Ezra Klein's *Vox* podcast. The guest was *Atlantic* writer, Ron Brownstein, and they were doing the post-game analysis. Despite the many factors in the mix, one word kept wafting out of the conversation: "whites." Non-college educated white men. Non-college educated white women. College-educated white men. College-educated white women. Nothing but whites. Like a laundry soap commercial. The word itself began to sound like a strangely anachronistic holdover from our ugly past. An era Trump promised to bring back.

Even if you chalked up those 77,759 rust belt votes to a combination of some Obama voters switching to Trump, other Obama voters not showing up, and more white voters coming out for Trump, economic anxiety didn't explain 63 million votes. These people weren't acting based on a rational fear of losing their lives. Many were afraid of losing their way of life. It wasn't just the change Obama symbolized; it was the totality of social change. Gay marriage. Pot legalization. LGBTQ rights. The Kardashians' daddy becoming a chick and wanting to pee in God knows which bathroom.

Trump's railing against political correctness was a shout-out to those who didn't want to let go of their prejudices and accept a changing world, with new rules. He reached out to those who were not happy in this new, multi-cultural America. People who wanted their old world back and their old *words* back. It takes too long to say "African American." Five syllables are too many.

These people just wanted to go back to a simpler time,

when a guy could go down to the local bar, knock back a few, rant about how this used to be a great country, then get in his truck and drive home without being pulled over at some bullshit sobriety checkpoint. But electing a Black president meant that world was fading away, so they reached out to someone who promised to bring it back. Trump was selling re-empowerment to guys who just wanted their Caucasian balls back. He was a human boner pill.

People can play the Black Lives Matter/All Lives Matter game all day long, but Black Lives Matter is just the modern iteration of the NAACP, or the Black Panthers. Different words, same music, same meaning: racism still exists. We've obviously made some progress as a society but we're still not over it. This shit's still happening. And Trump is the proof.

In a climate where protests erupted over police shootings, and cops are, in turn, getting shot, it was no accident that Trump grabbed on to Nixon's "law and order" line. But what does it say about us that it worked? What does it say about us that after eight years of relative economic growth, safety and security we still responded to the racist dog whistle?

Racism is just the manifestation of an even broader phenomenon: the reason social progress in this country takes so long. Metathesiophobia—fear of change. Real change in this country has occurred over time. It took a century to get from the Civil War to the Civil Rights Act, and standing in the way was the same ignorance and fear of change that exists today. There has always been blowback from people who just couldn't deal with it. Trump wasn't promising to take people into the future. He was about going full speed ahead to the past. Make America Great Again? No. Make America White Again.

Some have discounted race as a major factor in favor of level of education. Maybe so. Or maybe it was just a perfect storm. Economic insecurity, racism, sexism, fewer Obama voters turning out for Hillary, more non-college educated white people coming out for Trump, debilitating primary battles, a vote-sucking third-party candidate, and Russian meddling. At this point, the various factors are just individual strands of a rope that's been tied into a noose and is hanging around our necks.

Reflecting on the mistakes of the past won't change the outcome, though it can lead to lessons for the future. It's in that spirit that I can't help but wonder about things that might have been. Were there missed opportunities? Errors in judgment? Extenuating circumstances that affected the outcome of this election? 20/20 hindsight — it's a beautiful thing.

CHAPTER SIX

WHAT IF...

WHAT COULD HAVE GONE DIFFERENTLY WHY IT DOESN'T MATTER AND WHY IT DOES

*"Those who cannot remember the past
are condemned to repeat it."*

George Santayana

After experiencing tragedy, it's human nature to look back through the tears and wonder, "what if." What if I'd given the relationship another shot? What if I hadn't panicked and sold that stock? What if we hadn't elected a mentally unstable, temperamental, man-baby to the presidency, maybe we wouldn't all be living in underground bunkers fighting over the last potato chip while trying to Google the half-life of plutonium.

I'll put aside whether Hillary was the right candidate at the right time. Whether she ran a flawed campaign too focused on metrics while failing to deliver a broader, more inspirational message. Yes, she won the popular vote by three million. However, considering everything Trump said and did, she should have destroyed him. Flayed him open like a sushi chef slicing a tuna. She had the chance. But she didn't do it. And in that respect, she blew it.

Everything that went down in the campaign was, essentially, trash talk before a heavyweight fight. Yes, there were some highlights and momentary game-changers. Hillary's 9/11 memorial disappearance and subsequent street collapse. And Pussygate. And they all played out in the media while the candidates did damage control via speeches and surrogates as the polls narrowed and tightened. But it was all essentially political shadow boxing until the debates.

These were heavyweight fights. No pundits. No surrogates. No signs. No hats. No excuses. No packed houses or partisan cheering crowds. No tweets. Just two candidates trading punches with millions watching live.

For the first time, they were in an arena where she had the clear advantage: intellect, and actual government experience. All she had to do was expose his ignorance. Pull his pants down in front of the world and expose him as an ignorant fraud, con man, and pretender to the throne.

Twenty minutes into the first debate she had her first shot as Trump began imploding. He was virtually punching himself out. Snarling. Growling. Interrupting. Practically foaming at the mouth. The more he name-called, the more juvenile and un-presidential he looked. This was her moment. She had him on the ropes, but she didn't knock him out. She didn't close.

ABC. Always Be Closing. The famous line from *Glengarry Glen Ross*, delivered by Alec Baldwin's slick, snarky real estate middleman in a scathing takedown of a group of sad bastards in a pathetic, hole-in-the-wall Manhattan office. The despair in the room was so thick it practically stuck to the walls. And Baldwin was so powerful you momentarily forgot that Al Pacino, Jack Lemmon, Alan Arkin, Kevin Spacey, and Ed Harris were also in the room. He didn't just take stage; he owned it, to the point that the tag line has worked its way into the vernacular: ABC — Always Be Closing. From the second you get your foot in the door you're always working toward making the sale.

Yes, the campaign was ready to get under his skin, knowing he'd react. But it wasn't enough to let him crumble and just lay back as if his mania would be self-evident. As an attorney she should have known that you're always setting up your closing argument. She had to humiliate him in front of the entire country, especially those "undecided voters" who needed to be smacked out of their baffling indecision.

She should have known what was at the root of his support. Why his people were behind him. Trump was their big daddy, the guy who'd fix everything. They thought he was smart. Because he told them he was smart. But his obvious lack of intelligence, experience, and grasp of the issues was his Achilles heel. He knew that. She should have known that. She should have jabbed in the early rounds, attacking his statements as "ignorant," "uninformed" and "unintelligent." All subtle synonyms for "stupid." It would have worked on his insecurities. Being criticized, even humiliated, by a woman, on TV, with millions of people watching, would have been his worst nightmare.

Once his knees buckled, she should have knocked him down, then stood over his body, like Ali defiantly staring down at Sonny Liston. Then she should've turned to camera, branded Trump as a dangerous idiot, and then made the case for herself. Instead, she stepped off and smiled, assuming that any intelligent voter would see his obvious flaws. She was trying to win on rounds instead of knocking him out.

Whether she didn't have the rhetorical ability or the taste for the jugular, I don't know. My sense was that it was an extension of her "high-road" campaign stance. She may have been showing class, but she needed to show strength. By letting him up, she let his people hang on to their image of Trump as their hero.

I watched the debates, shouting lines back at the screen, but apparently she never heard me. So this is my imaginary Hillary. The Hillary I wished showed up when he was flailing like an imbecile. She should have beaten him senseless with his own idiotic branding lines. Like when he referred to her and the president as "The Founders of ISIS." (Note: The profanity is just for flavor.)

"FOUNDERS OF ISIS?"

Nice try, Donald, but you don't know what the fuck you're talking about. ISIS—the Islamic State of Iraq and Syria—started as Al-Qaeda in Iraq, the result of an incompetent, unprepared occupation force that had no clue how to maintain order after getting rid of Saddam Hussein.

Instead of using Saddam's army to keep the peace, we disbanded it and sent those men away—armed, trained, and angry. As for withdrawing our troops, the 2011 date was negotiated by President Bush. President Obama lived up to it. Neither of them could get a status of forces agreement because the democratically elected Iraqi leader refused. He also refused to form a coalition government, which fomented even more anger.

Colin Powell said it: "If you break it, you own it." And he was right. That's why presidents need to know history. They have to know that a dictator who rules over a divided people may keep their hatred in check through violence, intimidation and even murder, but displacing a dictator leaves a power vacuum that can lead to a bloody civil war. And we created a power vacuum. Sometimes there's no perfect decision, just a list of imperfect choices. It's called history, you fucking moron. Knowledge is power. And stupidity is dangerous. But in a president, it can be lethal.

YOU'RE GOING TO PUT AMERICA BACK TO WORK?

You? The guy who's famous for saying "You're fired!" is going to put America back to work? It's because of people like you that they're out of work, or out of business because you screwed your suppliers, then claimed it was because their work was unsatisfactory. Really? All of them? If that's the case, how can you be such a great businessman if you keep hiring incompetent people?

Plus, you went broke in the casino business, a business where companies have made billions. A business where people literally walk in the door and give you their money. A business where you have math on your side. How dumb do you have to be to pull that off?

"I ALONE CAN FIX IT"

First of all, that's insane. No president acts alone. If you knew anything about the job, or American history, you'd at least know that. We have a system of government based on checks and balances, a way of preventing the rise of dictators. Do you even know the three branches of government? I'll give you a minute to answer. Beat... beat... That's ok; you can Google it later.

You're not going to fix the problems in this country and in the world by the force of your personality. At the end of the day, it's not about personality; it's about policy. And your policies and those of your party don't work. They led to one depression in the '30s and nearly another one eight years ago.

No one wants a third. We tried trickle-down economics. Several times. It ends in, and I'm quoting you here — a disaster.

Yes, some manufacturing jobs have gone overseas. You should know; you sent them there. But they've also been lost to automation. I know people are hurting. But we can't go backwards to a 20th century economy. We retooled during WWII to fight the Nazis and we need to re-tool again to fight climate change in the context of a 21st century energy policy. This isn't anti-business. It's a business opportunity. It's called "the future," Donald. Plug into it. You can't drive a car forward by looking in the rearview mirror.

And by the way, climate change is not a Chinese hoax. That's not just dumb, it's dangerous. Unless you think you breathe different air than the rest of us. I know sometimes it seems like you're living on another planet but the fact is we all live on this one. Deal with it.

YOU'RE WORRIED ABOUT MY MENTAL HEALTH?

Me? You're the one who's delusional. Protestors in Jersey City cheering after 9/11? Sorry, but it didn't happen anywhere but in your disturbed little mind. I don't know where you get your facts but it's not from the same reality the rest of us live in. And that's the reality presidents need to live in.

If someone insults you, you go on a Twitter rampage. Lyndon Johnson fought the war on poverty. Nixon fought the war on drugs. You fought the war on Rosie O'Donnell.

You need to toughen up, Cupcake. You want to be in public service? Get used to being insulted. I've been taking hits for 40 years. Sometimes that makes me a bit guarded. Who wouldn't be? I fight back when I have to, and sometimes I let things go. But I'm still standing. That's called stamina, asshole.

Yes, I've made mistakes. I own up to them. That's what

adults do. You learn from your mistakes and you move on. And if you want to take cheap shots at my marriage, go for it. Everyone goes through hard times. Marriage can be tough. You should know—you've had three of them.

YOU'RE UPSET ABOUT POLITICAL CORRECTNESS?

Bullshit. That's just an excuse to legitimize hate-speech and racism. You can use extremes like university "safe zones" to lampoon and delegitimize a change in social consciousness, but the point of this country is to move away from prejudice and discrimination to assimilation and inclusion.

I'M THE CROOK?

Why? Because of an email server? Show me one real-world, national security consequence of my using a private email server. Or I'll ask you an easier question: what's an email server?

It's not like I outed a CIA agent for political retribution. My husband and I operate a foundation that does humanitarian work all over the world. You shuffle other people's money through your so-called foundation and use it for paybacks, and bribes to a state Attorney General to avoid legal prosecution for your bullshit university. Allegedly.

You're being sued thousands of times. Phony universities. Phony charities. Now you're trying to con the American people with your phony candidacy, a job for which you have zero experience. I've spent my life in public service. You've spent your life in private service.

I grew up in tough times and had to work my way up. You grew up with a silver foot in your mouth. I've worked for decades to help people get ahead in life. It's not always easy. When you work in government you have to work with those who may not share your views, and find solutions together. You can't steamroll people because then nothing gets done.

Your party has been guilty of obstruction for the last eight years and the president still managed to right the economy and pass a landmark health care bill that may have flaws, but it sets us down a path toward full coverage. And I know twenty million people who agree with me.

You're a fake, Donald. A con artist. It's one thing to screw banks by reneging on loans. It's pathetic to con people who are struggling, and take advantage of their fears by tricking them into thinking you can wave a magic wand and make it all better…

Anyway, that's what I would have said. Though I wasn't the one on stage and under all that pressure, trying to debate an erratic, snorting lunatic. Of course, none of this matters now, but I had to get it out.

LEG TINGLE

Yes, Hillary was smart. And experienced. And tough. But, to quote Chris Matthews' reaction to a 2008 speech by Barack Obama, there was no "leg tingle." Matthews confessed that he felt a "thrill going up his leg." Political commentary, with a sidebar of eroticism.

Matthews has a Biden-esque, everyman way of making his point. Which was that Barack Obama had charisma. FDR had it. Kennedy had it. Reagan had it. Bill Clinton had it. Even Trump, in his own demented way, has it. Hillary didn't.

Before she chose her running mate, I'd written that I thought Senator Sherrod Brown of Ohio would have been a solid VP. Nothing against Tim Kaine. He's intelligent and experienced but unfortunately, no fireball. Brown was from Ohio, one of those states that swung for Trump. His voice, alone, screamed blue collar. He could roll up his shirtsleeves, grab the mic and talk to folks. He wouldn't have to pretend to be that guy. He was that guy. He could've laid out an economic plan and made the case in language that would have resonated with voters not just in geographical Ohio, but in psychological Ohio. Pennsylvania, Michigan, Wisconsin. Tim Kaine was a safe choice at a time when she needed a charisma transplant.

Or, if that wasn't a real option, they could have taken into account the Podesta emails, WikiLeaks dump, the flap over Debbie Wasserman Schultz, the anti-Bernie DNC conspiracy, and the existence of Jill Stein, and solved the entire mess with one simple move: Bernie.

BERNIE!!

Compared to the bad acid trip that was the RNC convention, the Democrats pulled off a professional, well-produced affair. There were passionate, eloquent speakers, both politicians, and regular folks with a story to tell. There were real celebrities and a shitload of righteousness. Woodstock on the moral high ground. But what was missing was some Trump magic. Drama. Showmanship. And while I'm sure there were a million reasons why this never would have happened, I wanted a moment; one that could have been created by Hillary and Bernie walking out hand-in-hand, as candidate and running mate.

The campaign could have kept the country in suspense about the VP pick. Put out false leads to raise expectations and keep the rumor mill churning. It would have created excitement. The media loves rumors. This could have built to a moment where they did more than talk about unity. Instead of negotiating with Bernie to include his policies in the platform, she needed the "leg tingle" of walking on stage with him. It would have galvanized the base and sent Jill Stein and her smug smile back to the irrelevance from which she came.

Of course, there could have been a downside. Politics has always been a game of move and counter-move, strategy and counter-strategy. If Senator Sanders became the VP pick, Trump would have unloaded on him, aiming his message at those same non-college educated white voters. "He's a Socialist! He and Hillary are going to raise your taxes a million percent!" "They're going to steal your hard-earned money and give it away to immigrants and terrorists!"

It wouldn't have mattered if anyone tried to make the distinction between a Socialist and an Independent who caucused with the Democrats. What would have mattered was that the word "socialist" would have been shooting out of every unholy orifice in Trump's body.

So, maybe choosing Bernie would have backfired. It needed to have legs beyond the initial moment. And maybe they calculated that. Still, it would have added some excitement to the ticket.

Of course, some still argue that Bernie should have been the nominee. I'd written that, while I agreed with his vision of life, and government, he never really made the case for how he would have gotten the necessary tax reforms through a Republican Congress. They spent eight years in a steel cage death match with a left-of-center Democrat. Why would they suddenly lose their appetite for obstruction when they were up against a self-proclaimed Socialist?

Still, she lost. And in a two-person race, second place sucks. There's no silver medal. So, he couldn't have done worse. Still, in that moment, it felt like you couldn't send a unicorn to kill a dragon.

She also could've chosen Elizabeth Warren but I doubt Warren wanted it. She seems to be gearing up for 2020. Besides, our innate sexism would've really kicked into high gear. Two women on the Democratic ticket? The optics would have worked against her. I wasn't sure the country was ready to elect one woman, let alone two.

I also wondered what might have happened if she picked a Republican, someone like John Kasich. While it would have freaked out the extreme wings of both parties, it would have siphoned off many Republican voters who were repulsed by Trump, and cut into his support.

They could have campaigned on a spirit of bi-partisan cooperation and ending Washington gridlock. It would have made her look reasonable and less ideological, someone who really wanted to find common sense solutions to our problems. It could have been a game changer. Out-of-the-box thinking. And being from Ohio, Kasich also had rust belt credibility. Of course, we're still not grown up enough to embrace that kind of cooperation when it's so much fun to just fling your shit at your opponent.

CITIZENS UNITED

Citizens United allowed dark money into politics so that candidates could pound their opponent to death with negative ads. The Willie Horton attack ads Bush used on Dukakis. The swiftboating of John Kerry. Going negative has become accepted political wisdom. And in this election it didn't mean shit.

Jeb outspent Trump by millions and yet he crashed and burned. He could have literally gone door to door with a bag of money, offering people cash to pull the lever for him and he still wouldn't have been able to buy a vote. Hillary may not have had any leg tingle, but Jeb had no legs.

Hillary out-raised and out-spent Trump, two to one. $1 billion to $500 million. She ran 187 spots on broadcast TV. Trump ran 40. Her ads were professional, slick, and emotional, and played to our highest ideals. His were cheesy, infomercial, no-money-down real estate type spots, with shitty graphics and the frantic, rapid-fire voice-over at the end. Low-rent commercials for a low-rent candidate. And he still won.

But the money story of the campaign was not about paid advertising. It wasn't about 30-second or 60-second spots. It was about billions in free advertising in the form of rallies transmitted without interruption. I lost my voice, and my mind, screaming at my TV. Cut away! Say something! Make a comment! This is a fucking infomercial! It was like watching *MSNBCSPAN*.

The cable news media has to own this one. They got played by their own ratings lust. Trump rallies became wild, spontaneous events in which no one knew what would happen. Would he say something outrageous? Would there be violence? Trump obviously knew all this. He knew he could bait them with the promise of a moment, and a story.

Citizens United still perverts the electoral process, but given the present make-up of the Court, it's not going anywhere. We can bitch about SuperPacs, and assume they operate independently from and don't have contact with the respective campaigns, which no sane person believes. We can scream our heads off about dark money, as we should. Money and attack ads will still be a major factor in upcoming elections. But in this presidential campaign, it wasn't the story.

There's an adage in advertising about selling the sizzle and not the steak. She was all steak. He was all sizzle. He sold it. The media help sell it. And 63 million people bought it.

JEB SHOULD HAVE
RUN THIRD PARTY

Republicans pick the strangest times to get honorable. Usually, it's about self-preservation. From the moment President Obama was inaugurated, they lined up and marched in unified opposition, reciting their anti-Obama talking points on command. Except for the few flashes of morality and social conscience, like when Republican senators crossed the aisle to vote for the ACA, they were steadfastly united in their obstruction.

But when they saw that their party was in danger of being hijacked by a madman, they launched the mealy-mouthed "Never Trump" movement, which was never good. It was basically political chat show appearances by consultants, and weak-ass attack ads. What they needed was a giant, meaningful "fuck you." That's why Jeb should have run.

Forget Reince Priebus' dumbass pledge. It wasn't a legal document. It looked like the "certificate of authenticity" on one of those infomercials hawking specially minted silver dollars for fifty bucks.

Just having the balls to announce a third-party run would have given him a much-needed charisma transplant and political B-12 shot. Not that he would have won. He would've split the vote and handed the election to Hillary, which would have been fine, given the alternative. But, more importantly, it would have been political payback—a smack in the face to the guy who humiliated him on national TV. This would have been my pitch:

Jeb. You don't know me. I'm a Democrat. I dislike your policies. They hurt the country and bring misery to the lives of regular Americans. I do, however, feel your pain. Because Democrats are compassionate. Not from of any religious dictate, but from basic human decency.

It must be killing you to have to sit back and watch that bloviating parade float, Donald Trump become your nominee.

America's Berlusconi—a guy who's turning your precious GOP into the Bunga Bunga party. It must be torture to turn on the TV and listen to his moronic statements on serious issues without cringing. Or weeping.

I know how humiliated you must feel. He mocked you. Taunted you. Called you "low energy." Insulted your wife. And all you could do was stand there and take it, because you were incapable of slamming him back. Not that you didn't try. But it just wasn't you. The man gutted you on national TV. And all you wanted was to give America another Bush presidency. Not that we wanted it. The last one was quite sufficient, thank you very much. And I know you think there's nothing you can do but sit back and watch Trump cut a swath of destruction through the country, like a tornado ripping through a trailer park. But you're not powerless. There is something you can do, something that would really hurt him. Run. Run third party.

Yes, I know there's talk of Ben Sasse getting in. But, c'mon, there's no irony in Ben Sasse. No one's ever heard of Ben Sasse. Yes, he's bright, articulate, and telegenic. But Ben Sasse has 2020 or 2024 written all over him. This is now. This is your time. Just do it! That's actually not a bad slogan. Better than "Jeb!" Maybe you could wrangle a Nike endorsement.

All through the primaries Trump taunted the party by refusing to sign "the pledge." Then he signed it. Then he flirted with backing out. He thought he was the one with the third-party power. But now you've got it. Do the very thing he taunted you with. Stick it to him. Cut him with his own sword. You must still have a few bucks in the coffers. Go Green Party. Libertarian. Bull Moose. Or, given the intellectual level of the debates, the Know-Nothing Party. You'd siphon off enough old-school Republicans to make sure he'd go down in flames. C'mon, you're the one who could hurt him. You know you want to.

Though I get it if you're just too wounded to get back on the campaign trail. It might be too hard to summon up the facial muscles needed to force out that sad clown smile. Then, do the rest of us a favor — pass this on to the other losers in the Sweet 16. I know they're already plotting their political futures but maybe for once they could put country ahead of party.

Carly. He mocked your face. Christie. You endorsed the bastard then he dragged you around like a pug on a leash. And if he didn't call you fat, he was thinking it. Yet you stood on stage behind him with a look on your face like he had your kids trapped in his basement. And Marco. Li'l, sweaty Marco. I know you're saving your reputation for 2020, but get out there now and talk some shit. Hit him with the small hands thing again. Lindsey. You're a fun guy. Have a bourbon and let that acid tongue loose. Kasich. For a brief, shining moment, you were the least ugly guy in the bar at last call. Get back out there and stuff your face with ethnic food. And Ted. Lyin' Ted. Instead of venting your anger by forearm smashing your wife, take that evil that swirls around you like Fukushima fallout and channel it into some good, old-fashioned revenge.

Or, if none of you wants to go it alone, you should all run. I know that sounds way too socialist, but you could unite to defeat a common enemy. Imagine the look on Trump's face when you all declared your candidacies. Marco and Jeb could sting him in Florida. Cruz could bushwhack him in Texas. Kasich could handle the rust belt. Pataki and Christie would gut him in the northeast. Carly would handle California. Someone there must like her. Jindal and Lindsey could take the south. It would be like the ending in Agatha Christie's *Murder on the Orient Express*. The suspects' hatred for the victim ran so deep they all killed him.

If you can't do it for country or party, do it for the most Republican reason of all: political payback. Hook yourselves together like rodents pulling a ratfuck Santa sleigh. Now Kasich! Now Walker! Now Graham! Now Carly! On Ted! On Bobby! On Marco! On Christie! It would truly be Christmas when that cocky smirk is wiped off that asshole's fat face, replaced by a befuddled what the fuck just happened?!

It would be a perfectly insane ending to an insane year.

Unite. Go rogue. Gut the arrogant son of a bitch. Because you know damn well he would have done it to you.

JILL STEIN-NADER

What's left to say but "Thanks, Jill. Thanks a whole fucking lot." The votes you pulled from Hillary in Michigan, Pennsylvania, and Wisconsin swung the election for Trump. I hope at least he sent you a carton of Trump steaks, or a voucher for 10% off a 2-night stay at one of his fantastic Trump International Hotels. They're the finest hotels in the world, you know.

So, now that the rest of us will be suffering for at least the next four years, what did you get out of it? Name recognition? Maybe. I'd never heard of you but I swear I'll never forget your name. What was the upside? You think we'll end up with a four-year teachable moment, where we'll see the wisdom in your platform then all come together and usher in the Age of Aquarius? Shit. We'll be lucky if the planet's still here in four years.

You knew what happened in Florida in 2000. You saw where this was going. You could've pulled out at the last minute like nutty Gary Johnson. He knew he was done. His running mate knew they were done. He couldn't stop rolling his eyes when his candidate screwed up on live TV. You could see all he wanted was to get off the crazy train and hit the bar.

Oh, and fuck your recount. If you really wanted to do something positive after the election, you should have taken the money you raised, bought a time machine, travelled back six months, and gotten out of the race.

And fuck your self-righteousness. I hope your smugness keeps you warm in these dark days. You're the reason people hate liberals. I'm a liberal and I hate you. I don't hate you personally, because I don't know you and that would be judgmental. You may be a very nice, good-hearted, well-intentioned person with friends, pets, high ideals, and compassion for all humanity. I just hate you politically. You weren't the sole reason Trump won, but you didn't fucking help.

Frankly, if I were a conspiracy freak I'd ask what you

were doing in Russia in 2015 at a banquet table with Michael Flynn and Putin, celebrating the 10th anniversary of RT. Some people could draw the conclusion that your candidacy was just a Russian gambit to suck off votes from Hillary. I'm not saying that. But some people could.

So take your smile and your stink of liberal superiority and go live on a commune, record dulcimer music and put it on SoundCloud, teach a course in political commitment at some backwater junior college, or maybe self-publish a book of vegan brownie recipes. Just get the fuck out of politics.

THE ELECTION IS HISTORY
AND MAYBE SO ARE WE

The Russian-orchestrated WikiLeaks email dumps may have sent a powerful disinformation shit-wave that played into an existing Hillary narrative, scrambling the brains of undecided white voters, but unless the Russians hacked the voting machines in Michigan, Wisconsin and Pennsylvania and jiggered the vote tallies just enough to tip the results in Trump's favor by a small enough margin to appear consistent with the laws of probability, then this election wasn't stolen. 63 million Americans voted for this guy. Or you could just say that 77,759 voters in three swing states rat-fucked the rest of us. Ultimately we weren't screwed. We, the people, screwed ourselves.

There were direct causes, indirect causes, things that might have been, things that shouldn't have been, media failures, an angry, dumbed-down electorate, racism, sexism, economic desperation and third-party spoilers. Or you could say that some people just liked Trump better. I can't fathom it but it's obviously true.

And you have to acknowledge that, from a purely political standpoint, he played the election brilliantly. Stonewalling on his tax returns with the phony "audit" excuse. Well-played. If he lost, no one would care about his taxes. If he won, which he did, he could continue to stall before just coming out and saying that everyone can just suck it—he wasn't releasing them. Which he did.

The surrogates. Nice job. Like Scientologists, they never gave an inch. From the smiling, desiccated Conway, to Boris and Steve, wacky Katrina, Jeffrey Lord and stone-faced Michael Cohen. They even had Palin in there for a while before they realized that even she was too stupid.

Pussygate. No politician could have survived that. Not even Bill Clinton.

Not even Republicans thought he would win. In fact, anticipating a loss, they were already trumpeting their anti-

Hillary strategy and it didn't involve a honeymoon. It didn't even involve a wedding night. More like a gang bang in a dark alley. In the spirit of coming together as Americans and solving our problems, squirrel-faced Chairman of the House Oversight and Government Reform Committee, Jason Chaffetz, had already stored up two years' worth of Clinton investigations, like nuts for the winter. (Now that he doesn't get to investigate her, it seems he's taking his nuts and going home.)

It would have been a continuation of the Obama obstruction, with more Email-ghazi show trials, while they played for time, hoping a more attractive nominee would emerge in 2020, forever bleaching the Trumpstain from the party. I imagine Paul Ryan was already working on his announcement speech, while Ted Cruz stared in the mirror, screwing his face into a smile that wouldn't frighten small children. Each would have positioned himself as a leader in the new holy war against Clintonism.

You also have to give it up to Republicans on their Supreme Court gambit. There was absolutely no political reason to give Merrick Garland a hearing before the election. There was a patriotic reason, but no one gave a shit about that. So they hid behind the ad hoc fabrication that President Obama was in his last term and therefore had no right to make an appointment. It didn't matter if it was true. It wasn't. But it didn't stop them from saying it.

There was no downside to stalling. If Hillary won, they probably would have confirmed Garland out of fear that she'd appoint someone more radical. I always thought the supreme "fuck you" to Mitch McConnell would have been to appoint Barack Obama to the Court and watch Republicans freak out in the confirmation hearings. But she didn't win, so they were free to basically dig up Scalia and reconstitute him in a younger, more photogenic package. And even if something went crazy wrong during the hearings, they had a deep bench of originalists.

What a Clinton presidency would have been will be

relegated to the scrap heap of alternative history. We'll never know whether she would have moved on a more progressive agenda, taken a more centrist approach, or if her presidency would have been hijacked by the chaos of world events.

The 2016 election was like an episode of *Survivor*. Democrats got outwitted, outplayed, and outlasted. But unlike the TV show, we don't get to leave the island. We're stuck here.

But we are where we are. So, strap in as we race toward an uncertain future by going forward to the past—back to the good old days of a paranoid president, enemies' lists and political retribution. There's a wave out on the ocean and it's bringing in a shit-ton of evil, while washing poor people and the middle class back out to sea.

So, how do we survive the Trumpocalypse?

CHAPTER SEVEN

SURVIVING
THE
TRUMPOCALYPSE

*"He's out there operating without any
decent restraint, totally beyond the pale
of any acceptable human conduct."*

Apocalypse Now

COMMENTS FROM THE
TRUMPOCALYPSE

*"Oh, my God, put Emperor Trump's face
back on the screensaver!
You want to get us all killed?!"*

*"I don't know what your third arm is for!
Figure it out for yourself!"*

*"Nobody knows what's on the other side
of the big, beautiful wall.
According to legend, it's Jews."*

*"I've told you 100 times: they used to grow food
in the dirt on a place called a farm.
Now, shut up and eat your brother."*

*"It's not about love. It's about propagating
the species. Now, stop asking questions
and go fuck your cousin."*

*"Ok, one more bedtime story
but then you have to go to sleep.
Once upon a time, there was a magical
kingdom under the sea called Miami…"*

*"Nobody knows what a private
email server is. We just know it's evil."*

*"There's no more Christmas. Santa ate
his reindeer because he was starving,
then he died of radiation poisoning."*

*"No, you can't change your name! It's the law!
All girls must be named Ivanka."*

President Trump. Hitler, without the artistic ambitions; Nixon, without the warmth and charm; Eric Cartman, without the emotional maturity. After the election, some people said that Trump would eventually realize the awesome responsibility of the job and work to uphold its highest traditions. Unfortunately, it's just not shaping up that way. I have no illusions that the office will ever shape the man. If his performance to date is any indication, I think the man is going to rape the office.

Look back at his inaugural address. Put yourself in his head, if you can stand it. Imagine if you defied the pundits, the critics, and the popular wisdom, and pulled off one of the greatest political upsets in American history. How would you handle it? After the initial shock, and the ego rush and sense of vindication, would you begin to ponder the awesome responsibility that had just been placed on your shoulders? Not just to your 325 million fellow Americans, but to the 7 billion people on the planet. Would you look at the speech you were about to deliver as an opportunity to express a positive vision for the country? Would you enlist the help of the sharpest minds and most talented writers, asking for their help in drafting an address that would demonstrate your desire to lead with strength and, yes, even compassion? Would you look back at famous presidential speeches in history? Lincoln, FDR, JFK. Would you dig deep into your soul and look for just the right words to encourage your supporters, and mollify, even embrace your critics by promising to work together to fulfill the ideals of those who shed their blood 240 years ago to create this great nation, and guide the American dream into the 21st century? You might, if you were a normal human being. But he didn't, because he's neither normal, nor human.

He kicked off his campaign with "rapists and murderers," and ushered in his administration with "American carnage." With a worldwide audience not nearly as huge as the one in his head, Trump was bellicose, belligerent, and defiant. He fought his way to the top of this shining city on a hill, then whipped out his dick and pissed all over it.

Then he began ranting about his popular vote loss, insisting 3-5 million people voted illegally or were dead. Amazing how 100% of dead voters went for Hillary. What is it about the dead that makes them vote Democratic? It certainly can't be the health care, or the minimum wage. They don't have to work anymore, which is one of the perks of being dead.

He then visited the CIA and rambled about the crowd size at the inauguration and how many times he was on the cover of *Time*. Standing right in front of a wall of stars, symbolizing CIA agents who gave their lives for their country. He's still locked in a battle with the intelligence community, though it may be more accurate to say he's locked in a battle with intelligence.

He instantly shape-shifted on the campaign promise to build his pet wall by claiming he would hit Mexico with a 20% tax on imports. "Who's going to pay for the wall?! Mexico! ... Eventually! ... We'll invoice them!" I wonder if they'll pay in dollars, pesos, or cocaine.

Then he went after the press. Or, as he called them, "the enemy of the American people." The days of the traditional press conference may soon be over. Trump can't hold an intelligent conversation on his feet. He's borderline illiterate when he's reading from a prompter. He doesn't like questions. And he hates follow-up questions for the simple reason that he expects his initial line of doublespeak to be accepted, regardless of whether it makes any sense, or is in any way related to the question he was asked.

Instead of the traditional game of question and evasion, we may eventually have some version of carefully constructed news events with handpicked media, all stage-managed to present the illusion of information while transmitting the party line. Live from Mar-a-Lago, it's "Believe Me! The Best, Most Fantastic Five O'clock Follies and Propaganda Info Dump from Our Dear Leader!"

Whether or not he eventually moves the press out of the west wing, he'll make every effort to stack the deck with *Breitbart, Fox,* and other friendlies. He'll refuse to answer any question he doesn't like by firing off the accusatory "fake news," his new favorite phrase, with which he tagged *CNN* and *Buzzfeed* for the crime of having the audacity to report the Russian pee-tape story. Trump may actually hate the media, but in this case the "fake news" gambit was just a tactic, a way of inoculating himself against the Russia investigation by pre-emptively discrediting the major sources most likely to uncover it while putting out false counter-narratives for everyone to chase down various rabbit holes.

It doesn't matter whether he does the job himself, or if he sends in hapless Sean Spicer, or pathologically mendacious Kellyanne Conway. Within the first several weeks of the new administration, Conway not only coined the term "alternative facts," but invented a massacre to justify the initial not-a-Muslim ban. Quite an accomplishment, considering she's also busy with her side business of selling poison apples on ebay.

It's frightening to think that every crazy ass thing that's going on in our country has sprung from the dark, twisted mind of one man. We've handed power to a thin-skinned, hot-tempered, insecure, ignorant, volatile, vindictive, solipsistic, narcissistic megalomaniac. And while the selfish man/boy in him feels entitled to it, deep down in that secret compartment where most people keep their soul, he knows he's not up to the job.

He knows that because the daddy in his head keeps telling him that. And now, a man with all these demons in his head has the nuclear launch codes in his pocket, and like a coiled viper, could instantly strike back against anyone who might piss him off.

This could turn into the perfect nuclear shit-storm. Trump has repeatedly expressed his quasi-phallic affection for nuclear weapons. "Why make them if we're not going to use them?" As he said, he refuses to take any of his options off the table, such as destroying the world in order to save it. Sure, for the moment, his tiny fingers are just raging on Twitter, but why assume there'll be any governor on his fury now that he can stage a nuclear tantrum.

But until he decides whether to end life on Earth, he's going to make sure life in America reflect the darkness inside him.

DEATH
TO
AMERICA!

LEGISLATIVE
EDITION

The Republican faux outrage at Trump's campaign behavior is gone. Paul Ryan orgasmed the second Wisconsin tipped the election for Trump, as he realized he might achieve his Ayn Randian wet dream of obliterating health care, lowering taxes on the rich and slashing entitlements. Mitch McConnell finally got his Obama payback, a belated Christmas gift for eight years of obstruction. And like many on the religious right, Mike Pence put aside his deeply held Christian beliefs to join forces with an accused sex offender so he could do God's will and get rid of abortion. They all think they can ride the bull to achieve their political goals, no matter the cost. As if lower taxes on the rich will save us from nuclear radiation.

Then there's Steve Bannon, a guy whose only goal in life is to bleach the planet, so that life becomes one unending Happy Hour at a restricted country club, as God meant it to be. If Bannon is the endgame of western civilization, then western civilization needs a serious re-think.

Trump, Ryan, McConnell, Pence and Bannon—Satan's law firm. Though, despite their individual styles and rhetoric, when you break it down, it's just old swine in new bottles. They're already doing everything they can to slam the breaks on social and political progress and turn the 20th Century New Deal into the 21st Century No Deal.

Hanging in the balance are *Citizens United*, *Roe v. Wade*, Planned Parenthood, gay marriage, religious freedom laws, voting rights, civil rights, health care, climate change, clean energy, Dodd-Frank, the Consumer Financial Protection Bureau, Medicare, Medicaid, Social Security, immigration reform, public education, student loans, marijuana legalization, prison reform, gun control, infrastructure spending, the First Amendment, tax policy, and the Middle East. Oh, and all of our lives.

And then there's the sixth Beatle: Vladimir Putin. Whether he and Trump made a sweetheart deal to plunder the world or if Putin's got a pen drive with videos of the orange menace getting whizzed on by Russia's finest hookers, it no longer matters. Unless he's impeached Trump's going to live up to his campaign promise to give the Russian leader free rein in Crimea and Europe while turning NATO into a protection racket. "You've got a nice little country there, Denmark. Be a shame if anything happened to it."

And never forget the Koch Brothers. While they seemed to hedge their bets during the election, with Trump at the plate and Mike Pence on deck, I imagine they're now looking at a future that belongs to them. It'll be like a re-make of *It's a Wonderful Life*, but one that ends with Jimmy Stewart successfully committing suicide, Donna Reed avoiding a life of poverty by marring Lionel Barrymore, and Bedford Falls descending into a bleak, Pottersville dystopian nightmare.

To get a sense of their vision of the good life, look no further than the platform of the 1980 Libertarian Party ticket, when David Koch ran for Vice President. He lost. But it resulted in him taking a more behind-the-scenes role in politics. At the time, this was his American dream:

Repeal all federal campaign finance laws.

Abolish Medicare and Medicaid.

Opposition to any plan to provide health services.

Deregulate the medical insurance industry.

Repeal Social Security.

Abolish the Postal Service.

Repeal all taxation, personal and corporate.

Repeal any and all minimum wage laws.

*End all government ownership, operation,
regulation and subsidy of schools and colleges.*

End all compulsory education laws.

Abolish the EPA.

Abolish the Department of Energy.

Abolish the Department of Transportation.

Abolish the FAA, FDA, and OSHA.

Abolish the Consumer Product Safety Commission.

*Opposition to laws requiring individuals
to buy or use safety belts, air bags or crash helmets.*

*Opposition to all government programs,
or relief projects that aid the poor.*

You know—what Jesus would do... if he were a selfish prick.

Meanwhile, the Democrats' power seems limited to the 60-vote threshold in the Senate, along with their rhetorical abilities to battle the administration in the media while investigating Russia-gate and galvanizing public outrage, along with plotting a course toward 2018 and 2020.

Whether Trump escapes this investigation remains to be seen. We may be heading for a Constitutional crisis and another stress test for American democracy. Many people are saying there's a raging fire behind all that smoke. As clever as he thinks he is trying to hide behind misdirection and fake denials, while declaring the investigations a "witch hunt," his behavior is actually transparent. The closer Congress and the media get to the truth, the more he screams. The more the Trumpsplainers insist there's nothing to look at, the more obvious it is that there's something to look at. We'll just have to see where the investigations lead. Constitutional showdown? Impeachment? Resignation? With the Comey firing and the hiring of Robert Mueller as special counsel, along with Trump's daily self-incriminating logorrhea, the only guarantee is that it will be great TV.

Still, although it's been a constant distraction for the president, it hasn't deterred him from living up to his campaign promises, or down to his campaign threats. He's not backing off his agenda. And even if he's impeached we'll still have to live with President Pence or, depending on the evidence and the repercussions, President Ryan; different personalities, same legislative goals.

As infamous tax cutter and government-hater Grover Norquist stated in a 2011 speech to the American Conservative Union: "We don't need a president to tell us what direction to go. We know what direction we want to go. We want the Paul Ryan budget which cuts spending six trillion dollars... We just need a president to sign this stuff. We don't need someone to think it up or design it... Just pick a Republican with enough working digits to handle a pen to become President of the United States."

Well, I guess if you work hard and stay pure in spirit, your wish will come true. Because we now have a president who has demonstrated that he has the working digits to handle a pen and scribble his signature, which looks like the brain scan of a serial killer. Norquist should also be happy that he's realized another dream: he finally got a government worthy of being drowned in a bathtub.

While still in its 100-days infancy, we had the aborted Muslim bans, hijinks in a Congressional investigation, the Flynn firing, Sessions' recusal, and a flurry of insane tweetstorms, including accusations of wiretapping against the former president. Still it's hard to know whether to be more afraid of the things he's done, or the things he hasn't done.

As the saying goes: "Power corrupts. And absolute power corrupts absolutely." But what happens when you hand power to someone who's already absolutely corrupt? Who the fuck knows what he's capable of? We already know his intentions coming out of the gate, but let's break it down, based on the same Rumsfeldian paradigm of known knowns, known unknowns, and unknown unknowns.

THE
KNOWN KNOWNS

Trump's big ass hadn't hit the chair before he issued an Executive Order for a Muslim ban that wasn't really a Muslim ban except when he felt like insisting it was a Muslim ban. But it still resulted in a storm of public protests, and an acting Attorney General being fired for standing up to him. Then it was repeatedly shot down in the courts.

As is their habit, many in the media dwelled on whether it was, or wasn't, a Muslim ban. You have to give them credit for finding a way to focus on a side dish and chew on it like it's the main course. Here's the deal: It was a Muslim ban in the sense that all the people being banned were Muslim. It wasn't a Muslim ban in the sense that not all Muslims were being banned.

Still, it's tough to make the case that selective discrimination isn't discrimination. That's sort of the definition of discrimination. But even if you momentarily put that aside, there was no strategy to it—no attachment to any direct intelligence or increased security risk based on country of origin. Neither Saudi Arabia nor Egypt was part of the ban and the 9/11 hijackers were from those countries. Saudi Arabia is not only considered the biggest state sponsor of terrorism, but the chief exporter of a radical, fundamentalist interpretation of Islam.

This wasn't intelligent policy designed to protect the homeland. It was pure optics, the illusion of quick, tough action. A way of showing he was delivering on the campaign promise of "extreme vetting." But what if he institutes "extreme vetting" and there's another attack? Does he then move to "extremely extreme vetting?" Maybe we need to go back to the Bush administration's color-coded threat thermometer. I'll always fondly remember Director of Homeland Security Tom Ridge standing next to the poster as he raised the threat level to "code orange." I'll also never forget how he did that just before the 2004 election. (In 2009,

Ridge admitted that he was forced to do it by the administration, for its political impact.)

After getting shot down in courts, in early March he issued his revised, "Ok-this-one's-really-not-a-Muslim ban," which was apparently tailored to avoid the legal problems with the first one. It was also blocked. He then threatened to cut off federal funds to sanctuary cities that refused to cooperate with his deportations, which resulted in the mayors of Boston, New York, and Seattle staging press conferences, and politely telling the president to go fuck himself. As did a federal judge, though not in those words.

In late April, a San Francisco judge ruled that the president couldn't withhold all federal grants, and that his January executive order violated several fundamental principles in the Constitution. In June, the Supreme Court allowed parts of the ban, and will rule on the case in the fall. So annoying when you have to adhere to the damn Constitution when all you're trying to do is keep the bad people out of the country. Sad.

It's also ironic that local Democratic mayors are the ones resisting Republican government overreach. Only several months in to his administration and he succeeded in turning our world upside-down. Call it "the new abnormal," or, maybe just the new Trump-normal.

It's also open season on the press. Steve Bannon has already told the media that their job is to shut up and listen. Which he got from reading the First Amendment. Look it up. It just says that Congress shall make no law…abridging the freedom of the press. It doesn't say that that the president's nanny can't tell the free press to shut the fuck up. Trump is still complaining about the way the media is treating him, while making noises about looking into our libel laws to make it easier to sue. Maybe a few lawsuits would deflect his attention, like a cat chasing a laser pointer up the wall.

Trump served up an initial budget with a monstrous $54 billion hike in military spending while cutting domestic spending and foreign aid. Despite his campaign claim to drain the swamp, he loaded his administration with the swampiest swamp dwellers in the bog.

He didn't have to eliminate the EPA, or the Departments of Education or Energy. Instead, he began a process of gutting those agencies by handpicking a group of domestic terrorists to lead them. Like injecting cancer cells directly into healthy organs to destroy them from the inside.

The Secretary of State is an oil CEO, who loves Russia and never spent a day in public service. The United States of America — a division of the Trump Organization — a wholly owned subsidiary of PutinCorp.

The head of the EPA is a climate change denier whose favorite pastime is suing the EPA. He's a former Attorney General of Oklahoma, a state that is experiencing a staggering increase in earthquakes — a phenomenon that has been traced to fracking. Trump was hellbent on cutting $6 billion from their budget, but couldn't pull it off when faced with the prospect of a government shutdown. But he'll be back. Might as well just drop the pretense and change it to the Environmental Destruction Agency.

The Education Secretary is a billionaire Jesus freak whose goal is to privatize education, weaken or eliminate federal standards, and put God back in the classroom. Something she calls, "giving people choice," a phrase Trump cleverly snuck into his February 28th address to Congress, when he called education the "civil rights issue of our time."

While many in the media were falling over themselves praising the orange chimp for reading words off the screen without having a meltdown, most didn't pick up on his intention to slash public school funding and give people the cash to go to Jesus Memorial High School. Go, Fighting Saviors! Maybe DeVos can work in mandatory school trips to the Creation Museum so the kids can post selfies riding the dinosaurs. You know, just like the cavemen.

Before withdrawing his nomination, Trump's first Labor Department appointee was a fast food mogul who hated working people, preferring machines because they didn't get sick or need vacations. He made his fortune serving up shitburgers (allegedly), so at least we knew what to expect.

It seems he grew tired of the confirmation hearings, as well as the accusations from a former spouse of wife-beating. Now he's free to replace all the workers in his restaurants with robots. Then when everyone moves away because there are no jobs, there will be no one left in town to buy his burgers. Just extend this to every town in America: if you get rid of workers, you simultaneously get rid of consumers who patronize other businesses, so that the people in those businesses lose their jobs, cutting down on the number of people who can patronize your business. Workers are consumers. Sorry if they ask for a living wage, and maybe an annual family trip to Disneyland.

The Secretary of the Treasury made millions off the housing crisis. Allegedly. In his Senate hearings he claimed he didn't want to foreclose on all those poor people, the government made him do it.

The Secretary of Health and Human Services is a bloodless, snaggle-toothed Southerner who looks neither healthy nor human, and allegedly traded health care stocks of companies he subsequently had influence on as a Congressman. He's on a lifelong mission to destroy Obamacare, while avoiding the political blowback they've seen at town hall meetings.

It's unfortunate that Price, a physician, doesn't seem to notice that people tend to get sick when they get older, which is also when they tend to stop working, which is when they need affordable health insurance. This is not a liberal plot to suck money from the government. It's the reality of human life. Disease doesn't play favorites based on party loyalty.

Still Republicans have been hell-bent on returning to the beauty of a free-market system, in which insurance companies get to cover people for everything except what happens to them, and where we all have the right to get sick, go broke, and die, just as God wanted.

From audio that leaked out of a private meeting of

Republicans in January, it became obvious that the main concern of moderates was the political ramifications of repealing the law, not how it might affect the lives of millions of Americans. This wasn't about actual life and death; it was political life and death.

In early March, House Republicans finally released their counter proposal, the long-awaited and hastily slapped together American Health Care Act — the high-fructose corn syrup of health care bills. They should have just called it WeReallyJustDon'tFuckingCare. Yet, the House Freedom Caucus — America's Christian Soldiers — cockblocked it because there was too much compassion in it. The extremists wanted to kill it. Centrists knew that snatching it away would be political suicide. Even the great white dealmaker in the White House couldn't navigate these waters. It was a stunning act of legislative incompetence. The Art of the Choke.

They were so close they could taste it, but they couldn't seem to squirm out of the Gordian Knot they'd tied themselves into. Repeal and replace? Repeal and revise? Retool and rethink? If only they could figure out how to hand it all back to the insurance companies and not take away the coverage people have come to depend on, while simultaneously taking credit for junking something that could've been fixed in the first place.

Still, they never gave up. It was like some old western movie where the bank robbers get run off by the armed townsfolk, then ride off into the hills to make camp and plan their next raid. Which they did. In early May House Republicans narrowly passed a version of their bill that had enough cruelty for the hard-core right while retaining the illusion of compassion.

What happens in the Senate remains to be seen or, more to the point, unseen, as Republicans operated with all the transparency of a meth lab. Then they released a bill that, according to the CBO report, would essentially rip coverage away from 22 million people.

As of this writing, they failed to get enough votes, so its

fate hangs in the balance. But if they do end up passing some form of the bill, the details won't matter to the president.

Trump said on *60 Minutes* that he'd like to keep the parts covering pre-existing conditions and letting people under 26 remain on their parents' plans. Many in the media assumed that meant he was committed to those principles. Sadly, they still don't seem to get that the president doesn't give a shit what he said. He was just saying what was politically expedient at the time. Congress could eventually pass a bill that mandates euthanizing people with pre-existing conditions and selling their organs on ebay, and he'd happily sign it. He just wants to stand behind a podium and say, "We have repealed and replaced Obamacare."

The Secretary of HUD's only qualification is that he's urban… ish, and has a personality the president once described as "pathological." So far it seems his primary responsibility is showing up when Omarosa put on a Black Stuff photo-op. Then he's allowed to go back to his office to nap.

The Ambassador to the U.N. has no diplomatic experience but she has Indian heritage, so as far as Trump's concerned, she looks international. And we've already had walrus-impersonator John Bolton in the job and he didn't blow up the world so how much worse could it get.

Haley was amenable to taking the Confederate Flag down from the South Carolina statehouse when she realized that some people took offense. Of course it took nine people getting murdered in church, but it seems even devout Christians need their come-to-Jesus moments. Still, Haley seems nice enough so it didn't seem like she'd come out pissing all over the U.N. Until she did. On her way to present her credentials to the Secretary General, she told the press that "for those who don't have our back, we're taking names, and we will make points to respond to that accordingly." Nothing like kicking off your diplomacy job by demonstrating that you possess all the diplomatic skills of a loan shark collector.

Trump's Supreme Court pick is an intelligent,

experienced appeals court judge, just to the right of the late Antonin Scalia. Neil Gorsuch describes himself as a Constitutional originalist, which is the excuse the right uses to justify their attempts to take the country back to the 18th century.

I just read the Constitution, which states that to run for president a person has to be born in the U.S.A. and be at least 35 years old. There is no mention of term limits, nor were the framers prescient enough to include a "no asshole" clause. Oh, and slaves were 3/5ths of a person, so you could own them and trade them like baseball cards, despite Ben Carson's theory that they were just tourists who overstayed their visas. And it took a war to change that, one we're still fighting in more subtle ways. It also seems that some of the original stuff was less than enlightened. Hence, Article V.

Article V
(Mode of Amendment)

The Congress, whenever two thirds of both Houses shall deem it necessary, shall propose Amendments to this Constitution, or, on the Application of the Legislatures of two thirds of the several States, shall call a Convention for proposing Amendments, which, in either Case, shall be valid to all Intents and Purposes, as Part of this Constitution, when ratified by the Legislatures of three fourths of the several States, or by Conventions in three fourths thereof, as the one or the other Mode of Ratification may be proposed by the Congress; Provided that no Amendment which may be made prior to the Year One thousand eight hundred and eight shall in any Manner affect the first and fourth Clauses in the Ninth Section of the first Article; and that no State, without its Consent, shall be deprived of its equal Suffrage in the Senate.

I'm not a constitutional scholar like our former president. You know, the one who trampled all over the Constitution. I've never even been to law school. But where I come from, the world "amend" means "to change." So why include the concept in the original document if the framers didn't think life was going to change, and that our laws might have to be adjusted accordingly.

Given that there have been 27 amendments, including those giving black people full 5/5ths personhood, women the right to vote, and all people regardless of race, creed, or color the right to drink alcohol, after removing it with a previous amendment, it does seem that the built-in fluidity has come in handy. And, while I know the real legal arguments are infinitely more subtle, maybe we should frame them in their proper context or dispense with the talking points. Politically speaking, a Constitutional originalist is a judge who rules in your favor. An activist is a judge who doesn't.

With Gorsuch's confirmation the ideological balance on the Court has shifted back toward its Scalia-era Conservative majority, which could alter the fabric of American life for generations. The fate of the world may rest on 84-year-old Ruth Bader Ginsberg's shoulders. If she gets a cough, I'm moving to one of those underground homes in the Australian outback.

Trump also put Iran "on notice." No one seemed to be able to define exactly what that meant, but it sounded like a cross between detention and double secret probation. Then he pissed off the Australian president on a phone call. And authorized a raid in Yemen that resulted in a Navy Seal being killed. So, he's already made his bones. Although he subsequently came out and blamed the generals for the screw-up, then trotted out the fallen soldier's distraught wife during his address to Congress for some gratuitous applause.

How dark do you have to be to use a military widow as a photo op, and then offer up the bizarre notion that the dead soldier would be looking down from heaven, pleased that the mention of his heroism generated a record for congressional applause time. Then he tweeted that the former president bugged Trump Tower. And, of course, there's the ongoing Russia-gate investigations.

So much for the honeymoon period. By the time this guy's done, he's going to need to build a wall to keep Americans from escaping into Mexico. Yet with all that, he remains undeterred, insisting to anyone who reads his tweets that he's doing an incredible job. As he told a *Time* interviewer: "I must be doing something right. Because I'm the president and you're not."

Those are just some of the highlights of the shit we know. The known knowns. What about the known unknowns?

THE
KNOWN UNKNOWNS

With Trump it's hard to have many known unknowns, as who knows what the fuck he'll do. I don't even think he knows what he'll do from moment to moment. Maybe they haven't fully explained the job to him yet, or maybe with his short attention span he can only keep so many evil plates in the air at one time. The fate of the world may be riding on what they say about him on cable news, or when his Adderall kicks in.

And of course, there's the great big beautiful wall. The media always seems to focus on the possibility of building it, as opposed to whether it was always just a stupid campaign stunt. An over-simplistic, nitwit solution to a complex problem that's not as dark as it's been made out to be, but infinitely more complex when you factor in visa overstays, along with the fact that we could increase border security using modern technology. You know, instead of cinderblocks and rebar.

He's still trying to strong-arm Congress into funding it. Maybe they should just throw him a few bucks so he can start building. He likes building things. It'll keep him occupied. Children need activities. He could do the stupid photo op with everyone in suits and hard hats holding the shovels and pretending to dig, while smiling for the cameras. Then they could cut the big ribbon with the giant scissors. The media would cover it, and everyone would assume he's living up to a campaign promise. Just dig a big hole then keep announcing construction delays. It took two thousand years to build The Great Wall. That would let him play for time and afford a measure of plausible deniability for why it's taking so long. In time, we'd all forget about it and the wall would exist in people's minds, which was always the intention. It was always a rhetorical wall, not an actual physical barrier.

Congress may be warming up with health care reform, but what they really have in their sights are so-called entitlements. Bush tried to privatize Social Security after he won in 2004, though it turned out to be yet one more thing seniors had a hard time digesting. But Ryan goes to sleep at night dreaming of the day he can turn the Social Security trust fund over to Wall Street, while handing old people Medicare vouchers and releasing them into the private sector. Like giving them $10 in chips before they board the casino bus. Only now they'd get to gamble with their lives.

During the campaign, Trump claimed he wouldn't screw with these programs. Which doesn't mean he won't go after them at some point. When the OMB Director refers to Social Security as a "Ponzi scheme" and wants to end Medicare as we know it, it doesn't exactly inspire confidence. Even raising the retirement age amounts to a virtual death panel, as they'd just be playing the actuarial odds so that more people would die before they got to file for benefits.

Action on gun control — none. Well, one actually. Republicans revoked the Obama law that made it tougher for the mentally ill to buy a gun. So, it's officially hunting season on the American public. With about one gun per person and roughly 30 thousands gun deaths a year, you'd think someone would make the connection that this is a public health issue.

If, or more likely when there's another mass shooting there won't be any expression of compassion from this president. No singing Amazing Grace. Just a call for more guns. And they're working on a law to expand open carry laws and cut restrictions on silencers. This way when someone sneaks up on you and blows your head off, you won't have to suffer through the loud, annoying bang.

The Consumer Fraud Protection Bureau. Fuhgetaboutit. We have a president who made a fortune in the consumer fraud business. Allegedly.

The Trump budget proposes adding billions to military spending while cutting taxes for the rich and slashing government programs that feed or educate people. It would also result in massive increases in the federal deficit, which the GOP will begin referring to as the "we never really gave a shit about the federal deficit."

Stop and frisk could become national law, though I suppose it's better than the old version of "stop and shoot."

Immigration. He's already kicking up the deportation optics by sending ICE agents on raids and deputizing local cops to enforce stricter laws. How long before it leads to a confrontation between the feds and local authorities? Instead of trying to find a rational balance between national security and the words on the Statue of Liberty, he may just kick everyone out then shut off the lights in the country and pretend no one's home.

Of course Republicans' real wet dream is getting rid of abortion. But the political blowback of overturning the law would be enormous. Though they might not have to get rid of *Roe v. Wade*. Instead they could gut it with tougher state restrictions, like the 2016 Texas law that was struck down by the Supreme Court. They might not have to abort the actual law. Instead, they could just keep throwing it down a flight of stairs.

That's just a taste of what could be coming or is already in the works. But what about the unknown unknowns? The shit we don't even know yet.

THE
UNKNOWN UNKNOWNS

As erratic as he is, Trump's capable of anything. He could wake up tomorrow morning, randomly throw a dart at a map then bomb whatever country it landed on. Sorry, Ecuador. Not your lucky day.

But given that we live in an unpredictable world, his particular mania will eventually run head first into reality. He can mind-fuck the public, screw with the press, create the optics of having important meetings, and even launch a few missiles when the situation calls for it. But he won't be able to control the uncontrollable. The world may have to bow down to him, but chaos theory may not respect his authority.

ECONOMIC CRISIS

In an interview with the *Hollywood Reporter* shortly after the election, Steve Bannon stated his intention for the economy, which was to bring back shipyards and iron works. "Just throw it all at the wall and see what sticks." Sounds like solid American thinking, if this were the 1930s and we were gearing up to fight the Nazis. Maybe we are, depending on which Nazis you're talking about.

Gutting Dodd-Frank might just be the first step in returning to the Bush-era economic policies that led to the 2008 crash. If banks are allowed to engage in speculation without being adequately capitalized to protect against a downside risk, how long before Wall Street comes up with the next credit default swap? And how would we know? Economic statistics come from the government. It's certainly not beneath this president to make sure that government economic data adheres to the same standards of truth as Soviet crop reports. It might take ATMs running out of money before people realized there was a problem.

In an interview with David Axelrod, former Secretary of the Treasury Lawrence Summers stated, "If you went back to the pre-Dodd-Frank world you would be taking immense and systemic risks of another financial crisis…It would be a catastrophic kind of error." Then again, "catastrophic kind of error" may be the slogan of this administration.

He summed up his concerns by saying, "I'm not just worried that we're going to do impudent things. I'm worried that we're going to do irreversible and imprudent things that will cripple us for a generation…"

CYBERTERRORISM

Also in an interview with David Axelrod, Mike Morell, former Acting Director of the CIA, stated, "Cyber crime now generates more revenue than the illicit drug trade." This could also become the new terrorism. Why blow up a building when you can shut down a power grid?

And who's going to protect us from it? The guy in the White House who just learned the word "cyber?" You can always tell when he learns a new word because he repeats it, getting the same thrill and sense of empowerment a child gets when he realizes that if he says "fuck" out loud, the adults will react. You can see the thrill in his eyes when he thinks he's found a way to make himself seem informed on a subject of which he is totally ignorant.

This was Donald Trump during the second debate: "We have to get very, very tough on cyber and cyber warfare. It's a huge problem. I have a son—he's 10 years old. He has computers. He is so good with these computers. It's unbelievable. The security aspect of cyber is very, very tough. And, maybe, it's hardly doable. But I will say we're not doing the job we should be doing. But that's true throughout our whole governmental society. We have so many things that we have to do better. And certainly cyber is one of them."

May 12, 2017. A massive ransomware attack hit 99 countries in what was called one of the most damaging cyberattacks in history. So rest easy. Trump's got this. Or maybe he'll put his kid on it.

TERRORISM

From the beginning of his campaign, Trump played the terror card to a country still cowering in fear from 9/11. The 2013 Boston Marathon bombing reminded us that we could never really feel safe. The attacks that have plagued Europe over the last several years have exacerbated the fear that we could get hit anytime, anywhere. Even though the Orlando and San Bernardino shooters were American citizens, the problem has still been reduced to one, idiotically Trumpian oversimplification: just keep out the bad people.

But fences won't stop dangerous ideas from getting into the minds of people who are already here. Despite what Trump thinks, the Internet doesn't have an on/off switch. His tough guy persona and bellicose public statements are an invitation to terrorists to strike back. Particularly home-grown terrorists. A recent study revealed that those in the U.S. who become radicalized do so after they're here. And we've certainly made it easier for them to get their hands on weapons of mass destruction, like AR-15s, if they decide to shoot up a mall or nightclub.

The immigration ban was just dangerous showboating. A hastily concocted, amateurishly rolled out Executive Order designed to create the illusion of decisive action. Just an arbitrary ban on a select group of people based on the false notion that anyone who wakes up in one of those countries and decides they feel like emigrating to the U.S. can walk right in. There were systems already in place, including an 18-24 month vetting process for Syrian refugees. And there's a difference between immigrants and refugees.

You can stand up in public and scream, "Islam hates us." You can enact a thousand Muslim bans. Expand the number of countries, and even make them permanent. Put in place the most super, extra special extreme vetting. Make everyone who wants to come into the country stop at customs, eat a hot dog and spit on the Koran. You can drive ISIS out of Iraq and Syria and bomb the shit out of every terrorist you can find, but that won't wipe out the mindset that gave rise to them.

That's the problem with the way we think, as well as the way the situation is presented to us. We've got a cult of personality approach. Once upon a time the bad guys were the PLO. Then al-Qaeda. Now ISIS, which formed as al-Qaeda in Iraq. According to the State Department website, per section 219 of the amended Immigration and Nationality Act, there are over 60 FTOS—Foreign Terrorist Organizations— worldwide.

The Trojan Horse argument is exactly the kind of dangerously idiotic oversimplification Trump is famous for, and that his supporters love. Bans won't block dangerous ideas from coming into the country. They also won't stop people who were raised here from becoming radicalized. As well, our nascent nationalist movement, along with others in Europe, could add a level of resentment and increase the likelihood of young men becoming radicalized, leading to more attacks. It's a virtual terrorist perpetual motion machine.

The terror threat didn't suddenly escalate the day Trump got into office. And given that we haven't been attacked on that scale since 9/11, it's obvious that the systems that have been in place have been working. That plots have been discovered, and foiled. However, it seems highly unlikely that there won't be another attack.

And with a madman in control, it could easily turn into a worldwide pissing contest. He's promised to "bomb the shit out of them," "kill their families," and "wipe ISIS off the face of the Earth." There's nothing like provoking an enemy that's already on a messianic quest. Would it be a shock if they decided to spit in this guy's face by attacking one of his hotels, either in this country or overseas? And if there were another attack, there would be no limit to his response. We're in just as much danger from extremists eager for another holy war whether they live in the Middle East or work in the White House.

And if the benchmark is "danger," as Giuliani bragged

about, then the more clear and present danger comes from easy access to guns — a far greater threat to public safety than terrorism. Especially after the new Republican Congress reversed a ruling, making it easier for those with mental illness to buy guns. Ultimately, it doesn't matter whether you're shot by a radical extremist or some unloved suburban teenager who wants to make the world pay for his misery. Dead is dead. And the chances of the latter happening on American soil are infinitely greater than the former.

Congressional Democrats may kick and scream, make passionate floor speeches, hit the talk shows, and register their outrage, but the balance of power has shifted in favor of a man who is not a fan of checks and balances. Calling him a dictator may be hyperbole, but it accurately describes his temperament.

He loves sitting behind the big desk, signing his name on shit, and handing out pens. And until the Russia investigations play out, he still gets to play pretend President and be the boss of America. But what if he starts figuring out how government works and how to cut deals with Congress? He could do some serious damage. Then it comes down to the ultimate unknown unknown: is Trump insane?

IS TRUMP
INSANE?

Given his behavior, many people have begun to question the mental health of this president. They're saying he has psychological problems, or may even be insane. I'm not saying that, but many people are. Many, many people. Like members of Congress, as well as some trained psychiatrists who met at Yale University in April and concluded that President Trump has a "dangerous mental illness," and was "paranoid and delusional."

He's seemingly on a quest to make American life fit his dystopian vision while eradicating President Obama's legislative record as payback for the public humiliation he suffered at the 2011 White House Correspondents' Association Dinner. A dark soul and a lust for revenge — qualities you look for in a world leader.

Obviously the guy has serious issues. Maybe he's still dealing with feelings of abandonment, having been shipped off to military school at a young age, along with the stress of having to prove himself to a demanding father. Just what we need: another Republican in the White House with daddy issues. That worked out so well the first time. He's also an egomaniac, yet with massive insecurities and a constant need for validation. And there's his obsession with money, and dominating women. And inauguration crowd sizes. Ultimately, there are five possible explanations for his behavior:

1) The president is psychologically damaged, probably the result of receiving no love as a child. This explains his constant need for validation and praise. His fragile ego rises and falls with public acknowledgement of his greatness. As *New York Times* writer Michael D'Antonio put it after conducting a long interview with Trump: the man is a "bottomless pit of need."

2) The president suffers from Histrionic Personality Disorder, characterized by wild and exaggerated behavior, a

need to be the center of attention, a hypersensitivity to criticism, and emotional volatility.

3) The president is master mind-fucker, sending out relentless waves of lies as misdirection. The "fake media" slams, along with shots at the intelligence community, were pre-emptive strikes against those who could uncover his crimes.

4) The president is a thug and a moron, an alchemist who turned his base talents into gold. He just wanted to win the election because he loves to win but now he clearly has no idea what he's doing.

5) The president is fucking crazy.

If it's the first, he needs to see a shrink and work out his shit so he can focus on the job he has; i.e. being President of the United States. If it's the second, he probably needs therapy, and meds. If it's the third, he needs to be called out in the press and stopped in the courts. If it's the fourth, he needs to take some night classes in government, just to get the basics. And if it's the fifth, he needs to be impeached and shipped off to his golf course in Scotland to hunt for lost balls in the woods, or walk along the shore and stare out to sea at the pretty wind turbines. Hopefully, their rhythmic motion will have a calming effect, like giant fidget spinners.

Of course, the most frightening prospect is that Trump may be some noxious cocktail of all of them: A true imbecile, or a genius doing an impression of an imbecile to throw everyone off the scent. It's obvious that winning the presidency was crucial to his ego, but having won it, he soon discovered he had to do a job he never realized was so hard. So far, he just doesn't seem to care for it. But his ego won't accept the slam of being a failure, especially a one-term failure.

Unless you're inside his head—and frankly, who wants to spend more time there than we have to—it's hard to know what's driving him. Whether his mania is at the service of his agenda, or his agenda is at the service of his mania. Still, how twisted do you have to be to ride hate to power? How cynical do you have to be to play off people's desperation? How narcissistic do you have to be to make it all about yourself? How much disdain do you have to have for people to lie right to their faces? How malevolent do you have to be to incite violence at your rallies? How morally bankrupt do you have to be to think it's just about winning at any cost? How dystopian is your worldview that you would inflict it on the entire world?

In a January 25th interview with *ABC News'* David Muir, Trump was asked if he thought his Muslim ban would provoke more anger around the world. He replied, "There's plenty of anger right now. The world is a mess. The world is as angry as it gets. What, do you think this is going to cause a little more anger? The world is an angry place." Was he talking about *the* world? Or was he talking about *his* world?

Or maybe there's another explanation entirely. One that escaped media scrutiny because entertaining the possibility is just too terrifying. His behavior, along with his many public statements over the years, may be rooted in an even more sinister desire. Apologies to Dana Carvey—but maybe Trump is... Satan!

IS
TRUMP
SATAN?

Or the son of Satan. Or the Antichrist. I don't really give a shit about the distinctions. The question is: is he the personification of evil on Earth? Many people are saying he is. Yes it seems crazy, but is it? Who else is so unrepentantly bad? Many have been whispering for some time that Trump's real goal isn't money — it's power, and corrupting mankind.

Yes, reasonable people say it's ludicrous. That there is no "devil." That it's just a metaphor for the evil in the human heart. Or is that itself a meme that has been floated into the public consciousness to distract us from the activities of someone with an agenda of world domination? Of course when allegations like this are made, rational people respond by asking: where is the proof? What possible evidence could there be for such an accusation? The proof, some say, is on his head. The mark of the Antichrist: 666.

It's a well-known fact that the mark of the devil — 666 — is imprinted on the head of his spawn. This is documented in the Book of Revelations, Verse 18: "Let him that hath understanding count the number of the beast: for it is the number of a man; and his number is Six hundred threescore and six." The Bible also says that the Antichrist will first accrue great wealth as a steppingstone to political power.

But where is the proof that it applies to Trump? The proof is in the man himself. The proof... is in the hair. It is a fact and inarguable that Trump is a vain, arrogant egomaniac. He takes great pride in his appearance. However, no man with even a modicum of self-respect would orchestrate that ridiculous front-to-back, side-whip comb-over cotton candy confection.

The only reason could be that he's hiding something — something that would out him as the personification of evil. Something... like the mark of the devil.

Trump obviously suffers from male-pattern baldness. And while baldness has been the bane of existence for men over the ages, recently the shaved-head look has established itself in the culture as a legitimate fashion choice. So, why hasn't he shaved his head? Some say it's because he can't risk anyone seeing what has been imprinted there. 666. The mark of the devil.

Some apologists counter that this is mere conjecture. Maybe so. But it's not the only evidence. Not by a long shot. There is something even more frightening: Trump's birthday. Donald John Trump was born June 14, 1946 in Queens, New York. New York. Home of many Jews. But there's more. Look at the date itself: June 14, 1946. 6/14/46. The first number: 6. The last number: 6. And the middle: 144. 1+4+4=9. And 9 upside-down... 6. 666.

Yes, it's shocking. Frightening. But now that he's the most powerful person on Earth, people need to know the truth. That is why President Trump must settle this question in the only way possible: by shaving his head on live, national television. This will put the controversy to rest, easing the minds of God-fearing Americans who need to know that the president of the United States is not the personification of evil.

Ok, I'm just fucking around, trying to freak people out. He's not the only one who can play mind games. There is no Satan. Or maybe there is. No, of course there isn't. Unless there is. See? Anyone can play.

But let's assume there isn't. Let's assume that there's no God and no Satan and they're just the outer manifestations of our conflicting psychological impulses. In the end, it doesn't matter whether he's the Prince of Darkness or just a deranged, unloved bastard who's hell-bent on making the world pay for his own miserable childhood.

He must be resisted. And if history has taught us anything, it's that autocrats may do everything they can to stay in power, but that public outcry and a sustained, passionate resistance movement can eventually bring them down.

Just like in *The Exorcist*, man can do battle with evil, and goodness will triumph, although it may take goodness throwing itself out the window of a D.C. townhouse in a Christ-like act of self-sacrifice. Or, maybe just marching in the street, holding up a sign.

CHAPTER EIGHT

RESISTANCE

THE
PEOPLE
ARE
REVOLTING

"The notion that a radical is one who hates his country is naïve and usually idiotic. He is, more likely, one who likes his country more than the rest of us and is much more disturbed than the rest of us when he sees it debauched..."

H.L. Mencken

This election was a thermometer up the ass of the nation. Despite Barack Obama's 2004 convention speech, in which he stated "there is not a liberal America and a conservative America — there is the United States of America," it turns out there isn't. There might have been if Obama's election had been treated as an important step forward in the evolution of American democracy instead of as a symptom of a dangerous trend that had to be reversed and permanently squashed.

Hence, eight years of monolithic Republican obstruction, leading to our current state of raging hyper-partisanship. Now we can't unite around anything other than a terrorist attack, or the Super Bowl. As expressed in the subtitle of my previous book, we have officially become the Dumbed-Down, Disinformed, Dysfunctional, Dis-united States of America.

As we slowly get accustomed to the new abnormal, over half the country is freaked out by the fact that we've succumbed to our worst instincts and put a madman in the White House — the darkest, most dangerous president since Nixon. Or Cheney.

But you can only scream at your TV, rant on social media, or bitch to your friends for so long. It may be cathartic, but ultimately it's just a temper tantrum that changes nothing. Easier to pop an Ativan, sip a coffee drink, or retreat to the safe space of some virtual reality. But we can't treat this as something that can be processed via denial, anger, bargaining, depression, and acceptance. This cannot end in acceptance. It must be met with resistance.

The emotions in the air are suddenly feeling eerily familiar to the anti-war protests of the '60s and '70s, in which I participated as part of my own political awakening. Outrage. Fear. Powerlessness. Feeling like a lone voice screaming into the wind, raging against a damaged, power-hungry president.

And whether it's called raising one's social consciousness, or getting woke, it's about being rocked out of your self-obsessed complacency. Though my own awakening was less a gradual loss of innocence than the result of culture shock — of growing up in simple times and being catapulted into a new, complex reality.

SELF-INDULGENT
BOOMER
REMINISCENCE

I grew up culturally isolated and historically oblivious in a Caucasian New York suburb. My ancestors were chased out of Russia by Cossacks, came through Ellis Island then settled in the melting pot of Manhattan's Lower East Side. They held fast to their cultural heritage while trying to assimilate into a society that didn't always welcome them. Their kids discovered subways and stickball, went to war, came home, attended college on the G.I. Bill, got jobs, got married, moved out to the burbs and started banging out baby boomers.

Growing up there were only select moments that broke through our blissful bucolic ignorance and forced us to realize there was an outside world. The first was when Kennedy defeated Nixon in the 1960 election. I remember thinking it was a good thing though I had no idea why. The second was during the Cuban Missile Crisis, when we had to leave the classroom to kneel down in the corridor, heads buried against the wall, in preparation for a nuclear attack. Another was when my teacher was called out of class then came back moments later to tell us that JFK had been shot. I watched the funeral procession on TV but somehow remained untouched by its larger significance.

Getting stoned in high school was as close as I got to any expanded consciousness. Civil rights demonstrators got assaulted with fire hoses and attack dogs. Freedom riders were murdered. Members of the Black Panthers were investigated by Hoover's FBI, and some even killed. Demonstrators at the Days of Rage in Chicago got their heads cracked by Mayor Daley's finest.

The nightly news brought "body count" stats from Vietnam reported with all the gravity of sports scores. If we killed more of their guys than they killed of our guys then we won. But nothing seemed to break through. It was like they took place in some fictional, alternate reality.

That slowly began to change my senior year with the shootings at Kent State, which was brought home more dramatically by the fact that one of the four dead students — Jeffrey Miller — was from my hometown. His mother was our Assistant Principal. Yet even when the news rumbled through the school and there were cries for a walkout I was still skeptical. Not that my teenage skepticism meant a damn thing but I was confused. I didn't know what walking out would accomplish, which was the question I put to one of my teachers and I still remember his pointed, simple answer. "When something like this happens, you have to do something." And he was right. The absence of a reaction would carry a message of acquiescence. So I walked out. At our graduation ceremony later that year many wore peace signs on their gowns. For what it was worth. It seemed more about style than political commitment.

College, however, brought instant culture shock. Self-styled radicals like Abbie Hoffman came to speak, dropping more F-bombs in a public arena than I'd ever heard in private. Jane Fonda showed up with her then-husband Tom Hayden, and we all went to Cornell to see them. Though most of the guys were there less for the politics than to check out Jane Fonda. She did not disappoint. Anti-Vietnam protests and talk of revolution were in the air. People ran around with signs calling for "Peace Now." I could never figure out if the slogan was a statement of defiance or the political expression of an indulged generation accustomed to instant gratification.

I wasn't exactly a campus radical, more of a suburban kid getting bombarded with the news that there was a world out there. And that people were getting killed in it. I went to demonstrations where the speakers railed against injustice, their fists raised in defiance.

Cries of "power to the people" and an ever-present cloud of dope smoke wafted over the crowds. It was resistance with a sidebar of dilettantism. People affected the look and language of revolution while being safely ensconced in a bucolic upstate New York college. Jeans ripped just so, open denim works shirts. The only callouses on their hands were from playing guitar.

Still, it seemed impossible to escape the times. Everywhere you went, some sign, poster, or person seemed to insist that if you weren't part of the solution you were part of the problem, like the guy who hung out every day in front of the student union. We called him "Leaflet Larry" because he'd stand there passing out flyers detailing stories of U.S. atrocities in countries I couldn't find on a map. I occasionally took a pamphlet and said I'd look into it. I never did. There was also a group of young, self-described Maoists who worked in a local factory and walked around brandishing Mao's Little Red Book. I think they were laboring under the delusion that they were organizing the workers and bringing about the revolution and inevitable dictatorship of the proletariat. I don't think they pulled it off.

Otherwise it was just the daily chatter, people hitting you with "Did you hear what Nixon said today." I would take it in, somehow feeling that Nixon didn't give a shit whether I heard what he said or whether I took any offense to it. Still, I went to anti-war marches and rallies, where speakers raged from podiums, and the crowd overdosed on defiance and righteous indignation. But no one's life was really on the line. We all had student deferments. And when our chances of being called up were subjected to a draft lottery, I pulled 365 — the best you could do. Unless World War III broke out, cats and dogs would get drafted before me. It was the only game of chance I've ever won.

But there were other, more personal and powerful moments that slowly broke through my innocence. Like the guy I met when I tried out for the soccer team. During practice, I noticed he wore a large silver medallion around his neck with one word: WAR. After nonchalantly trying not to stare I politely asked what it was about. He said he'd fought in Vietnam and that it was the medal his buddy was wearing when he was killed. I might have coughed up a pathetic "sorry" before we kept playing. I never found out if he wore it literally, sentimentally, or politically. I already felt stupid for asking the question.

Then there was the night several of us got high with a guy named Dan, another Vietnam vet. Amid the laughter, music, and haze of dope smoke he related a story about being next to his buddy in a firefight, then suddenly seeing his head get blown off. I can't quite remember what I said. It might have been "Oh, wow."

As we headed toward the '72 presidential election, people were feeling the Bern about George McGovern's candidacy, in that it was grounded in his pledge to end the war. While some took the position that change was possible within the system, the protests continued. After a speech by Chicago 7 defense attorney William Kunstler, a friend and I were inspired to hitchhike to D.C. to take part in a massive demonstration that was billed as a march to "shut down the war machine." The theory was that thousands of protesters would physically block traffic using trashcans, tree branches, human bodies and other implements of destruction, thereby preventing people from getting to work at the Pentagon and other government buildings.

Obviously, there was more romance than strategic planning involved but our presence added bodies in the streets. Though it wasn't quite peaceful. We got chased by riot police then tear-gassed in a dormitory when a cop car rolled up and tossed a grenade in the bushes. Tear gas is not fun. Your face burns, and snot drips out of every hole. We ran up the stairwell to escape the gas, holding wet rags to our faces. Taking the pain felt noble, but what it accomplished, politically, I had no idea. We got our sinuses drained for peace.

The next morning I woke up on the floor of a dorm at George Washington University and looked out the window at the war machine being shut down. Traffic was backed up. People were pissed. Horns honking. Cops everywhere. People were racing through the streets. I saw one guy lie down in front of a car as the furious driver got out and started pounding him trying to drag him out of the way. The sight took on a surreal, almost cinematic quality when someone stuck speakers in their window and blasted Jefferson Airplane's "Volunteers." We eventually hit the streets, though the thought of lying down in front of a car just didn't compute. We checked out the chaos, then, at the suggestion of two cops, took a bus out of town.

In all, an estimated 12,000 to 15,000 people descended on the city. 7,000 were arrested, then taken to a Washington Redskins practice field by bus and eventually allowed to pay $10 for their freedom. An estimated 150 were injured. Lots of excitement, but the war machine was not shut down.

I also went to Harrisburg, PA in 1972, in support of the Harrisburg 7 — a group of Catholic nuns and priests, including Father Philip Berrigan — who were about to go on trial for conspiracy to raid federal offices, bomb steam tunnels, and kidnap National Security Advisor Henry Kissinger. This was yet another in a series of high-profile trials, including the Chicago 7 and the Catonsville 9, that grew out of the anti-war movement.

I'm not sure how trumped up the charges were, or whether the defendants knew what they were going to do with Kissinger once they threw him in the trunk of a car and drove him out to the woods. At least with snatching a kid there's the assumption that his parents want him back. Given Nixon's anti-Semitism and ultimate loyalty to no one but himself, even if Kissinger's ear showed up in a box I'm not sure he would've succumbed to any demands.

There were speeches by politicians, marches, banners, floats, signs, music, and tons of solidarity. No riot cops. No tear gas. It was an effective demonstration of non-violent resistance. Then everyone went home. Still, the protests accomplished the goal of keeping opposition to the war in the news, and the subsequent trials kept the movement fueled with folk heroes and stories of resistance against a repressive administration.

While there was talk of solidarity and some overblown rhetoric about fighting the power structure, some of the analogies to protesting apartheid in South Africa, or to resistance efforts against other fascist states were more rhetorical than factual. There were endless debates about whether it was possible to work within the system or if it was inherently corrupt and could only be changed through violent resistance, which laid the groundwork for groups like the Weather Underground.

Still, it was all revolt in the context of a freedom we took for granted, because that is what you should be able to do in a free society. Despite the "my country, love it or leave it" sentiments, people knew they were free to protest—to write and say anything against the administration without worrying about being jailed or murdered. We may have been facing off against a government that attacked the press, but they didn't shut down newspapers and arrest or murder journalists. Protesters ended up spending a few uncomfortable hours in a football stadium. They didn't end up as dead bodies piled underneath it.

The guy I saw lie down in front of a commuter's car was obviously filled with revolutionary zeal, putting his body on the line for the cause, though he wasn't exactly a Buddhist monk dousing himself in gasoline and self-immolating. With few exceptions, you weren't taking your life in your hands. The rhetoric of the anti-war movement had the music and flavor of revolution but not the stakes. Leaders from the party in power didn't declare martial law.

We've been spoiled in this country. We've never had to deal with actual dictatorship. Actual censorship. Actual tyranny. We've never had to go out on the street and stand in front of a convoy of tanks, like that guy in Tiananmen Square. When we protest, it's with the confidence that the law protects dissent and, with some exceptions, we won't get shot or disappeared.

We've never really had to put our asses on the line like people in Eastern Europe who fought for freedom against

Soviet oppression. We get a self-important thrill out of using that kind of language because it makes us feel righteous and noble. Like we're toughing it out. But we're really not.

Maybe I'm being too critical. It won't be the first time. It might just be a defense mechanism and a resistance to over-romanticizing being part of a protest movement. It was necessary then, as it is now. Things can reach a point where the lack of public outcry can be taken as an acceptance of the status quo. And the status quo is unacceptable. As in the '60s, there's a need for a focused, sustained movement with clear goals, powerful symbols, and a coherent strategy.

MODERN
REVOLUTION

The post-inauguration demonstrations were powerful expressions of outrage at the election of our first fake president. Millions of people around the world declaring, "We're not going to take it." My favorite visual was from a rally in Mexico City that *MSNBC* aired on a loop, featuring someone proudly holding a sign reading "*Chinga tu Madre*, Trump." English translation: "Fuck your mother, Trump." With all the modern focus on diversity, it seemed there was no one at *MSNBC* who spoke Spanish. Or maybe there was. Still, the marches were a much-needed save shot for those overdosing from the Trump victory.

Like Nixon, Trump inspires protest, anger, and outrage. And he has a face built for caricature. It's no accident that two Nixon veterans were instrumental in his rise to power. There are also similarities in temperament: Deep insecurities, contempt for enemies, and the survival instincts of a rattlesnake.

It was important that people flooded airports or stormed town halls, expressing their outrage in reaction to the travel ban and GOP efforts to repeal the ACA, but there's still no single, coordinated anti-Trump mass movement. One reason may be that there are not only stylistic but substantive differences between then and now. If you were outraged in the '60s, you had no choice but to hit the streets. Now, we have the means of resistance at our fingertips, which could end up being self-defeating. Why go outside when you can register your dissent via an ironic tweet, adding your voice to the general inter-noise.

There's also no Vietnam War to galvanize resistance. No bodies arriving home in flag-draped coffins. No combat footage on the news.

The country is still in terrorist fear mode, so we're not up in arms over Afghanistan, even though, after 16 years, there seems to be no real clarity about the military or political mission, other than if we pull out the Taliban takes over and turns the country back into a terrorist summer camp.

Occupy Wall Street may have gotten some press coverage, but it fell victim to messaging overreach. A ragtag bunch of hipsters doing some urban camping wasn't going to bring the capitalist system to its knees.

While sporadic rallies have their power, there needs to be a unified anti-Trump resistance movement: If ICE agents rampage through neighborhoods, ripping people away from their families. If there's a move to repeal *Roe v. Wade*, or weaken it state by state. If more states enact harsh voter restriction measures. If there are moves to change the fundamental structure of Social Security and Medicare, while gutting Medicaid and other social safety programs that have sustained people for generations. If Trump supporters come to realize they were sold a fantasy of a new industrial revolution that is just not happening. All those affected need to come together in a single campaign. One with a strong, simple message communicated via powerful symbols.

The '60s peace sign was a unifying symbol of resistance. It had broad meaning, as well as political, social and even religious significance. You could read anything into it: outrage or hope. There's no modern anti-Trump counterpart. While the post-inauguration day marches carried a powerful message, the pussy hats—not so much. Though in an aerial shot they communicated solidarity, up close, they looked kind of stupid, like the hat grandma knit for your birthday.

Frankly, if you're going to use the word "pussy" as an organizing symbol you're going to instantly distract half the protesters by putting the wrong image in their heads. I mean, it was the reason half the guys I marched with went to demonstrations in the first place.

The message of the hat is also, to employ a term from TV writing rooms, a thinker. In that context, it referred to a joke that didn't land immediately, but needed the audience to make several connections to get, by which time the moment had passed.

The pussy hats don't carry the strength of the "fist in the gyno symbol" feminist sign. That was more direct, more defiant, more powerful. This one needs a re-think. When it comes to mass protest, irony needs to take a back seat to power. We need some simple anti-Trump visual. I'm not sure the turd emoji in a circle with a line through it is going to cut it. Someone in the graphics department needs to get on this.

The anti-Trump protest movement needs to utilize a combination of old school and new age communication. Marshall McLuhan's "the medium is the message" still holds true. Print brought us in-depth stories and analysis of events. It was the medium that published The Pentagon Papers, and broke Watergate. TV brought home the Vietnam War with a visceral impact that print could never achieve, though photojournalists captured moments that not only communicated the spirit of the times but carried a transcendent message about human behavior: A young girl crying out in anguish at Kent State as she knelt over the dead body of her classmate. (Jeffrey Miller—the guy from my home town.) A young, naked Vietnamese girl running on a dirt road screaming in agony from a napalm attack. The South Vietnamese Chief of National Police shooting a Viet-Cong operative in the head.

But we now have the advantage of social media. This revolution won't just be televised; it will be Tweeted, Instagrammed, Snapchatted and live-streamed. Visuals get around the world in real time.

The immediacy of events adds to their power. The message isn't subject to editing, or censorship, or producers who decide what's news, or how much of it to show. It's not a matter of where specific cameras are pointed. There are thousands of cameras working independently and simultaneously. In this case, the narcissism of the social media age is secondary to the power of transmitting events live. Phone cameras can be even more potent weapons if people stopped taking selfies long enough to turn their focus to capturing the actual moment. It's not about *you* being there. It's about *everyone* being there.

There's also a difference in the news cycle, both positive and negative. Daily newspapers and *The Six O'Clock News* were our basic sources of information. But there was an emotional predictability to it. The most horrific events were transmitted by sober broadcasters who provided an overall sense of stability. As well, you could prepare for the time you'd be informed, adjusting your drug or alcohol intake, accordingly.

Now we're hit with a constant stream of information, images and opinion, the effect of which can lead to over-stimulation, along with the pressure of feeling that you have to absorb it all. It can reach a point where it becomes so overwhelming the natural reaction is to shut down. The upside is more content and more immediacy. The downside can be informational overload.

Trump's skill may be in drawing supporters to his rallies, but his Achilles' heel is that he can also draw crowds of those who revile him. That's why there should be fewer but larger demonstrations. Not that these are mutually exclusive but the bigger the crowds, the more universal the symbols, the more undeniable the message.

There probably won't be riots or trials to motivate people to hit the streets. The Nixon administration's combative rhetoric about protesters, as well as pictures of cops in riot gear beating demonstrators galvanized the movement. Given Trump's notoriously thin skin, his inclination would be to react similarly, though he might also be clever enough to judo demonstrations with statements about our wonderful Constitution and the right of Americans to peacefully assemble and protest.

And since the ultimate goal of a resistance movement has to be voting this guy out, Congress needs to do its part. If Democrats aren't already drawing straws to see who gets to yell "You lie!" at the first State of the Union they're missing a moment. Of course, if they shouted it in unison it would make a powerful statement while protecting any one member from individual reprisals.

We may once again be in a battle for the soul of the country as primal as the Civil War and as volatile as the Sixties. It will be waged on several battlegrounds: the street, the media and in the American mind, which is under an unprecedented attack by a relentless barrage of misinformation and lies. Trump seems to understand not only the fleeting nature of news, but how to use disinformation as a weapon. In this case, the only way to fight back is by staying informed.

CHAPTER NINE

DIGGING FOR THE TRUTH IN THE FOG OF NEWS

"The lie can be maintained only for such time as the State can shield the people from the political, economic and/or military consequences of the lie. It thus becomes vitally important for the State to use all of its powers to repress dissent, for the truth is the mortal enemy of the lie, and thus by extension, the truth is the greatest enemy of the State."

Joseph Goebbels

There's no need to belabor the point that the cable news media fucked up. Although now that Trump's tiny fingers are within reach of the nuclear codes, and each day puts the planet at risk of annihilation, hopefully, in our final moments, as the missiles pass each other like strangers in the night on their respective paths to Moscow and Washington, someone will have the presence of mind to launch a droid into space with a message from Earth to whatever life form may eventually discover it. And that message should be: "The cable news media fucked up."

But that's all in the past. It's history. Forgive and forget. I have no choice. I can't quit them. Now that we're living in Trump World I need a touchstone with reality, a way of confirming my own reactions to the daily stream of lies and bullshit pouring out of this administration. I spend hours each day checking news/opinion sites, reading articles, scrolling through Twitter, and listening to podcasts. I even try to work in the occasional book. I'm hooked on my screens and I'm rarely unplugged. But I still need to tie off and get my cable news fix.

I watch *MSNBC*. Yes, it's a liberal cliché. I don't care. They provide information along with thoughtful analysis. They give airtime to print journalists, giving their stories a wider audience, while broadening the scope of the conversation by incorporating ideas and opinions from across the political spectrum. And, for the most part, they've banned the more ridiculous Trumpsplainers.

From Chris Matthews' passion, to Chris Hayes' intelligence, Rachel Maddow's careful analysis, and Lawrence O'Donnell's intolerance for lies, they're consistent in separating fact from fiction and digging for the truth. I also have a news crush on Joy Reid.

Based on some recent conservative hires I've read there's a move to tack toward the center, though I hope they don't fall prey to sacrificing content for broader appeal and ratings. My message to management is simple: if you expect me to suffer through the incessant stream of incontinence, catheter and boner pill ads, without taking it personally, don't screw with the line-up.

I will check out *CNN*, as back up. I have Fareed Zakaria's podcast on my rotation. And Jake Tapper and Jim Acosta have displayed a refreshing, take-no-shit attitude in response to the administration's doubletalk, misdirection, and outright lies. Though it seems the channel is also trying to be all things to all people by employing many of Trump's idiot apologists. In early February, they gave elfin bald-headed Klingon dipshit Stephen Miller air time to hawk the ridiculous claim of voter fraud in New Hampshire, in which he stated that busloads of illegal voters snuck into the state to swing the results, insisting that these were "facts" and "inarguable." They also seem to think the public is informed by letting the lefties and righties sit at a long table and shout it out. If they're going to turn the channel into the news version of the Roman Colosseum, at least throw a lion into the mix.

I don't watch *Fox*, because I have an education.

Still, cable news occasionally falls back into old habits. Like reporting the Trump tweets. We've even inherited a new opening line for a broadcast: "Donald Trump tweeted…" This allows him to virtually hijack the news cycle. Now that he's president he knows he can tweet anything that crawls into his head on the assumption that the media will follow it down the rabbit hole.

(Given the fact that the tweets often show up in the morning I'm guessing he's seized by the impulse while he's on the can, where all good ideas start. Presidential multi-tasking. You're welcome for the image.)

It's become an unfortunate aspect of this presidency that his tweets become news simply because he sent them. The error is in reporting their content without examining and exposing their intent. Most news shows treated the "Obama wiretapped me" tweet as worthy of analysis and serious consideration. But there are only two takeaways from the tweet: he was either using it to deflect media attention or he's out of his fucking mind.

Let's say it's the former and its purpose was misdirection. If so, it worked. The Russia-gate story took a momentary back seat as the "wiretapping" allegation took stage. Even after Comey stated to the House Intelligence Committee in March that he "had no information to back up the president's wiretapping tweets," Sean Spicer held fast to the alternative narrative. Then, when it appeared to run out of gas, the administration tried to breathe new life into it by stating the surveillance had been secretly contracted to British Intelligence. An allegation the Brits lambasted while insisting on an apology.

(There are 196 countries in the world, including Taiwan. Given Trump's love of deflection, that leaves 194 intelligence services to blame. That should carry him through re-election.)

Trump managed to insert the lie into the conversation to the point that the head of the FBI had to testify to Congress that there was no proof to back it up. But the moment the media or anyone in government even entertains the allegation, they've allowed bullshit into the conversation and taken another trip through the Looking Glass.

So if you're in the truth business how do you deal with a pathological liar? How do you report the truth in a post-truth world? Perhaps, given that the president has already declared the press "the enemy of the American people," you start by knowing your enemy.

The next time the President tweets about being bugged don't take it literally, or seriously. Take it tactically. Don't analyze the accusation, explaining that if Obama went to a FISA court and got a warrant to "wiretap" Trump or his people, it must have been based on hard evidence. Don't discuss whether it makes sense for his spokes-idiots to suggest that Congress should investigate. Examine the strategy behind the accusation. Think about what he wants you to think, and why. Get inside his head.

It's not surprising that during the campaign he attacked journalists, even putting their lives at risk. Now he's attacking journalism. He branded the news the same way he branded his opponents, the intelligence community or the CBO. These weren't thoughts or opinions. They were weapons.

Slamming major media outlets as "fake news" was not based on his disrespect for the press. It was about inoculating himself against future revelations in the Russia story. Roger Stone, and the late Roger Ailes were Trump advisors. Both were Nixon vets. Declaring the press "the enemy of the American people" was lifted straight from the Nixon playbook. (Maybe it's just me but every time I see Stone, the same question springs to mind: "What did Nixon's dog's dick taste like?")

Don't analyze his crazy shit in terms of whether it's rational, possible or legal. As Kellyanne Conway said, she's "not in the job of having evidence." That's true. She's in the job of poisoning our discourse by injecting disinformation into the public bloodstream. She's the Nurse Ratched of politics.

There is a presumption of honesty and sanity one should expect from a president, and Trump knows that. Don't let him use it. Don't examine his comments for accuracy or ideological consistency. Look at them as a paradigm of his thought process. Trump always reveals himself if you listen.

Think back to when Chris Matthews questioned him about whether he thought abortion was a crime and if women should be punished. Trump took a beat then landed on "Yes, there has to be some form of punishment."

People were so outraged by the comment that they missed the meaning. Even more horrifying than what he said was the beat he took before he said it, as he calculated his response. That interview was during the campaign and he knew he couldn't piss off evangelicals, so he went with "punishment." This was one of Matthews' best moments because he refused to let the candidate off the hook, and pressed him for a response. But then he focused on the content of the response and missed the meaning of the telltale beat, which was that Trump wasn't expressing his core beliefs. He was saying what he thought he had to in that moment. Even on a subject as important as abortion, the statement was purely tactical.

Look back at his floating opinions on torture. During the campaign he barked about bringing back waterboarding. The tough guy posturing worked with his supporters, based on the assumption that life is an action movie, where the evil terrorist knows the details of the imminent attack on the football stadium but the hapless interrogators are bound by the stupid law that says they can't torture the shit out of the guy and save all those drunken fans.

So, did he know at that time whether torture has ever resulted in gaining actionable intelligence? Did he know that while it was against the Geneva Conventions it was, in effect, legalized during the Bush Administration by changing the designation of prisoners to "enemy combatants?" Of course he didn't. Nor did he care. At that moment, he was just doing his act. But that was just Act One.

During the campaign Trump railed against the "dishonest, failing *New York Times*," but then suddenly arranged a post-election meeting at their offices, part of which was aired on *The Times'* podcast—*The Run-Up*. At that meeting he stated he was re-thinking his position on torture based on a conversation with one of his military advisors who told him he could get more information from a suspect with a pack of cigarettes and a beer.

Putting aside the notion that a devout Muslim would suddenly turn over the attack plans if given a Bud Light and a pack of Marlboros—vices they traditionally eschew—was the takeaway that Trump was changing his position on torture? No. He said that to *The Times'* editors because it made him seem more reasonable in that moment. And that was the goal. Along with the psychological sidebar that, as a Queens-born Manhattan *arriviste*, Trump harbors a deep-seated insecurity when it comes to the *Times*. He's a *New York Post* guy. But he secretly and desperately craves the *Times'* approval.

The other interesting aspect of the *Times'* meeting was his manner. He was soft-spoken, friendly, even charming. A marked departure from the combative tone he took during the election. And his hosts were non-confrontational, as he assumed they would be. After all, who attacks a guest in their home? Trump was completely disarming, which is an interesting word. It means warm and friendly, but it also carries the connotation of "dis-arming" your enemy by taking away his weapons. He accomplished both in that moment, which was his intention.

Not surprisingly, in late January Trump was back to being pro-torture, telling a crowd at one of his rallies that he'd spoken with "major people," and that "We've got to fight fire with fire." So, is he pro-torture or anti-torture? Neither. He was, is, and will always be about saying what is politically expedient.

Another revealing aspect of his rhetorical style is his use of hyperbole. This was evident in an Oval Office interview with *The New York Times* in early April. When asked if Susan Rice committed a crime by unmasking the names of people caught up in surveillance, he took his characteristic beat, and replied, "Do I think? Yes, I think." Then, feeling emboldened, he added, "It's such an important story for our country and the world. It is one of the big stories of our time."

No, it wasn't. It was just another fake story he was allowed to run with. And once he saw daylight, he ran with it. He might as well have added that it was right up there with the Lindbergh baby kidnapping, Watergate, and the Crucifixion. The reporters, who have done excellent coverage on Trump's campaign and his presidency, listened cordially, though they had every right to smack him in the face with a dead fish and say, "Ok, now, just stop it!"

(In late June, *The Times* used a full page to detail every lie Trump told since he took office. In an unprecedented act of transgender journalism the Gray Lady has finally grown a pair of balls.)

Though sometimes the bullshit doesn't fly and the president gets frustrated. In an early May Oval Office interview with *CBS News'* John Dickerson, the anchor pressed

Trump for details to back up his wiretapping claim. Trump launched into his typical rhetoric, stating "Surveillance of our citizens, I think that is a very big topic, and it's a topic that should be number one, and we should find out what the hell is going on." When Dickerson pressed him for clarity, Trump continued to tap dance, trying to use his usual gibberish to weasel his way out, but it wasn't working. He finally became frustrated and abruptly ended the interview.

Again, it wasn't just the content of the exchange; it was the pathology at work underneath it. Trump agreed to the interview, but still thought he could get away with evasion. He knew he'd get hit with direct questions but continued to run his game. A game he continues to play.

There's also a stylistic element to his lying, one very similar to that of his idol in Moscow, in which he casually posits alt-theories on a given phenomenon. Trump's claim during the first debate that the DNC hacker could've been some 400-pound guy sitting in his bedroom was near identical to Putin's remark in a June 2017 "interview" with Megyn Kelly, in which he stated the hacking could have been the work of Russian patriots who woke up one morning and decided to break in to the computers of a American political party during a presidential election. Each was a complete absurdity delivered with an attitude of total certainty.

Trump not only plays with content, he plays for time. That was the strategy behind his pushback during the campaign on the story about his wife's citizenship documents. He claimed she'd be holding a press conference "in a couple weeks" to deal with it in person. That was in August 2016. Anyone remember the press conference? Lawrence O'Donnell was the only one who stayed on it, but even he let it go because it became old news. As Trump knew it would.

He used the same dodge in his March sit-down with *Fox News'* Tucker Carlson on the "wiretapping" story when he said, "in a few weeks I'm going to release more information." This accomplished several things. It implied there was information in existence that would back up his claim. It also allowed him to keep the story alive despite mounting evidence that it was a lie.

Of course, some will call him a hypocrite, citing his inconsistency on most any issue, but this is meaningless. It's not about hypocrisy. Or ideas. Ideological inconsistency is not an attack against someone who has no ideology. Catching him in a contradiction isn't the end of the argument because he's not playing by the normal rules of human discourse. He's playing a game in a parallel universe. His agenda is to put alt-facts into the air, say them as often as possible, defend them as rigorously as possible and make it to the end of the segment, or the news cycle.

Look at his behavior after the Comey firing. When it became clear that the former FBI Director made notes of their conversations, Trump tweeted: "James Comey better hope that there are no 'tapes' of our conversations before he starts leaking to the press!" In true form, the media went into instant freak-out mode over whether there might actually be tapes. After Comey's testimony, an ABC reporter asked Trump if he'd testify under oath about his version of those discussions. His defiant response: "One hundred percent."

Are there tapes? Of course not—as he finally admitted. Will he ever testify under oath? Never. Each statement was about affecting the demeanor and tone of an honest man. For all the media salivating over the prospect of tapes and the notion of who was telling the truth, they completely missed the point. With Trump, it's never about content. It's always about perception.

It was one thing when the lies were coming from a candidate. Now they're coming from the president. It's no longer about campaign rhetoric or scoring debate points. It's about policy and people's lives. Given that the stakes have been raised, the media has to up its game. They not only have to provide information, they need to combat disinformation. These are the new info wars. In fighting them, they may have to take a more aggressive stance, becoming motherfuckers for truth.

Jorge Ramos had it right back in August 2015 when he got in Trump's face, insisting the candidate confirm whether he was really going to deport eleven million people. His persistence got him thrown out, insulted, and almost assaulted. And that became the story. That may become necessary.

Of course, it plays into the administration narrative that the press is being combative and that they're anti-Trump. Playing the victim works for him. But the media has to call him on it. This isn't surrendering objectivity; it's reclaiming journalistic responsibility in covering someone who's declared you the enemy.

In a post-election meeting, reporters and TV executives were invited to Trump Tower and supposedly beaten up by the president-elect over their campaign coverage, but not one of them thought to record it and leak it anonymously.

When the boy king Jared Kushner is tasked with re-shaping the federal government and bringing peace to the Middle East, don't focus on his vast new range of responsibilities. Focus on the fact that he has no history of public service, is a spoiled, career fuck-up, may have some shady business dealings of his own, and that handing that much power to a political neophyte because he's your son-in-law is banana republic shit and the act of a paranoid megalomaniac. John Oliver did a brilliant piece on this in late April. Why must comedy shows be the ones pointing out the obvious?

(Obviously, Trump thinks Kushner's the right choice to broker a peace deal because he's Jewish. Perhaps no one's told him there have been a few Jews over there trying to deal with the problem for around the last 65 years, and they still haven't cracked it. Though if Kushner gets pulled into the Russia investigation he might have to put his peacemaking responsibilities on hold.)

When Sean Spicer points to two stacks of paper on a table and tries to explain the relative value of the two health care bills by claiming the smaller pile means the bill contains less government, call him out. This is legislation affecting the lives of millions of people and one-sixth of the American economy, not a diet plate. It's ridiculous, so ridicule it, preferably in the moment.

When any press secretary tries to filibuster a press conference or offer doublespeak in response to direct questions, reporters need to call them out on their tactics, and fight back. Or turn around and walk out, en masse, to make a statement. In June, *CNN*'s Jim Acosta reached a point of exasperation over administration evasion and stonewalling, saying, "it feels like we're being slowly but surely dragged into what is a new normal in this country where the President of the United States is allowed to insulate himself from answering hard questions."

When they try to use photo ops to change the story, call them out. Toward the end of March, the House Russian-collusion investigation had ground to a halt. Nunes' mysterious White House meeting pulled momentary focus, then Trump staged yet another "big meeting" photo op, this one on the opioid epidemic. He put on his "presidential" face, conveying the impression that he not only understood the problem but was going to do something about it. Then Dopey Spice held a press conference, reading tales of addiction from his notes.

The story wasn't opioid addiction. The story was misdirection. The proof is in the Republican health care bill, in that it removes the government mandate for covering mental health and substance abuse, affecting around 1.3 million people who have been treated under Medicaid expansion. Factor in the Sessions Justice Department's return to the days of the drug wars and mandatory minimum sentences, and the mendacity behind the bullshit photo op becomes even clearer.

And please stop looking for the special moment of Trump's Cinderella-like presidential metamorphosis. *CNN* flogged this meme after his February 2017 address to Congress in which he cynically used the tears of a war widow as a political stunt. But that didn't stop *CNN*'s Van Jones from declaring "He became president in that moment. Period." No, he tricked your ass in that moment. Period.

Nor did the decision to launch cruise missiles against Syria elevate him to presidential status. It's not that Trump suddenly sat up in his chair, squared his shoulders, and realized that he had to live up to the responsibility of being president. It was that he suddenly looked around at a roomful of people waiting for an order from their Commander-in-Chief and thought, "Shit. I'm the president." Then he fired missiles at an airfield in a move that simultaneously provided emotional catharsis, registered outrage, and had no strategic military impact. The missiles were a momentary distraction. They were not, as Brian Williams stated, perverting the meaning of a line in a Leonard Cohen song, examples of "the beauty of our weapons."

And to all reporters and TV hosts, if you interview a politician who spouts talking points, and you don't call them out in the moment by debunking bullshit with facts, you're not delivering news. You're facilitating the spread of propaganda.

Donald Trump lies more often than he breathes, which makes it hard to believe a single thing he says. It is clear, however, that he's saying it. From there the question becomes: why? What's the angle? What's the hook? What's the con? Journalists should apply Occam's Razor—the philosophical principle that the simplest explanation, involving the fewest number of assumptions, is usually the best. In Trump's case the best explanation revolves around what lie he's telling, and why. As he said to John Dickerson "I don't stand by anything." In that one moment he revealed who he is and how he thinks. They need to start believing him. The one thing Trump is always honest about is his dishonesty.

Journalists need to take this into account in their coverage. But the media becoming more emboldened is only half the battle. The other half is people staying informed, which doesn't mean passively accepting whatever appears on your screen, or the interpretations you're given. We live in an informational haze between news, fake news, alternative facts, disinformation, misinformation, and lies. It's no longer possible to just sit back and absorb information. Ultimately, we have to be our own news aggregators.

INFORM
YOURSELF

The human brain works by filtering an infinite amount of stimuli and framing reality in a way that allows us to function. Imagine all the visuals you sift through, along with the mental connections you have to make, to perform a simple activity like driving a car. Reality pared down to basics. One acid trip can show you what reality can look like when that filter is temporarily disabled. It can either lead to euphoria or psychosis. That's why driving while tripping is counter-intuitive and not recommended.

Taking a drug is a voluntary experience, a conscious attempt at mind-expansion or maybe just a more playful experience of life. But what happens when that filter comes under attack resulting in disorientation and the sense that reality no longer exists? That's what happened during this election.

Trump rode in on a wave of Soviet-style propaganda that was unprecedented in an American presidential election. It wasn't just talking points or friendly facts designed to influence public opinion. This was a new style of mind-fuck. Like carbon dioxide or methane, disinformation is odorless and colorless, and can render you stupid because you don't even know it's there. And it worked because no one was ready for it.

We arm ourselves against intruders who try to break into our homes but we willingly open the gates to our minds every time we turn on the TV or laptop, or check our phones. To guard ourselves against it, we need to take a more active role in the search for truth.

It's not just a matter of tuning in a show, going on Facebook or checking your Twitter feed. It's about finding sources you trust—news shows, podcasts, websites—then sifting your way through fact and opinion and forming your own conclusions. It's about fighting your way to the truth.

CONSIDER THE SOURCE

Soon after Trump tweeted about being "wiretapped" by President Obama, I read a story on a news site about the person who may have been the source of the accusation. The piece included attacks between the writer and others in the intelligence community in which they blasted each other's reputation and veracity. When I got to the end I realized something: someone coming at this cold would have no way of knowing what was true or whom to trust.

Lunatic conspiracy theories used to be easy to recognize because they came from an easily identifiable source, usually some fat, man-titted mouth-breather, spouting hate speech for money or maybe just raging at imaginary demons. (Maybe they're pissed because girls don't like them. Or had shitty childhoods. Who cares? Their motivations are between them and their shrinks, or their confessors. To me, they're beyond redemption. I only wish there were a heaven just so Jesus could kick the shit out of them.)

But now we furiously dart back and forth between news, social media, texts, and emails to the point that we lose our ability to filter them. We've screwed ourselves with our own technology by creating a brave new world of informational relativism, in which all ideas have equal validity, as long as they're on our screens.

So how do we process everything that's thrown at us? Ironically, in a 21st Century info world, traditional journalistic standards can still apply: Who, what, when, where, and why. Who's saying it? What's their agenda and ideological bent? Do you recognize the source? Does the message feel slanted? Is it coming at a time when you have to act, like right before an election? Where is it appearing? Has it been slipped into your Facebook page or Twitter feed? How are they using language? Does it seem more intended to provoke than inform? What do you think they want you to think? If you find yourself seized with the irresistible urge to click, maybe stop and think before you go down the rabbit hole.

KNOW THE
TRICKS

Another defense is recognizing the tricks people employ to convince you that what they're saying is true. Fortunately, they often expose themselves by their own tactics. When someone tries to make a case that what they're saying is the "absolute truth" and "inarguable," instantly mistrust it. When someone, like a president says "believe me" or "trust me" know it's a sales trick to gain your confidence. When Trump spokespersons drop in "these are facts" and "no one disputes them" know that you're being worked.

When they race through a statement, dropping in loaded phrases so quickly that it's almost impossible to follow, be suspicious. Consider Kellyanne Conway's "Bowling Green Massacre." Look at the video on *YouTube*. Notice her combative tone. How she absolutely refuses to accept the idea of the question asked by Chris Matthews. She quickly pivots away by changing the subject, tosses in the "Bowling Green Massacre" then, without missing a beat, races through it, adding "which nobody reports on."

This is the tactic. Speaking so fast makes it easier to drop in the lie and move on before it can be challenged. In this case, Matthews busted her and it was debunked to the point of becoming laughable, along with her "alternative facts" neologism. The gaffes momentarily knocked her back but they didn't knock her out. After the liberation of Washington she may have her head shaved and be forced to march down Pennsylvania Avenue wearing a sign around her neck reading "collaborator." Or maybe, given this media landscape, she'll end up with her own cooking show. But right now she's still setting off smoke bombs.

Meanwhile, Sean Spicer frantically clings to life trying to do Trump but he doesn't have the skills. He's dinner theater Trump—a fool on a fool's errand. If the president were photographed running naked in the Rose Garden lighting his farts, Spicer would claim his boss was making a statement on the importance of natural gas. He also can't shake the look of impending doom on his face. He knows Big Brother is always watching.

But there's also a danger in assuming it's just a matter of recognizing the liars. You have to know the sound of the lies, the talking points, and weasel words. "Access" to health care instead of affordable care. The Obamacare "death spiral." Phrases like "free market solutions" or equating Medicaid with Welfare all carry a political agenda imbedded in the language. (If private insurance was so fantastic, why did 20 million people sign up under the ACA?) And instantly mistrust anyone name-dropping "the American people." That is the H-bomb of bullshit.

We also have to become attuned to politicians adjusting their language. Like when Paul Ryan talks about Mexico "contributing" to the wall instead of paying for it. These sneaky little word shifts are ways of hiding the truth. When did "pay for" turn into "contribute to?" And frankly, stop asking who's going to pay for, to quote former Mexican President Vicente Fox, some "fucking wall" and ask whether a wall is a real solution to a real problem or a fake solution to a problem that has been oversimplified for our consumption.

Trump's entire campaign was grounded in idiotic oversimplifications. ISIS will be quickly defeated. Crime will magically disappear. A great wall will be built. Health care will be fantastic. When complex issues are presented in such childish terms, be very afraid, or at least very skeptical.

DON'T TRUST STATS

In my previous book I cited Steven Colbert's "truthiness" and offered a corollary — "factitious" — describing numbers that are employed in the service of lies. Don't accept an argument at face value just because it comes disguised with statistics or poll numbers. People are easily dazzled by anyone tossing around a few stats. It makes them sound authoritative.

I just saw a former Congressman on a political talk show dropping in some poll results to back up his argument. He slipped them in as objective facts but wasn't busted in the moment. I knew the source was a poll that skewed Republican. I'd seen others use the same numbers on other shows so I instantly knew it was bullshit. But the host didn't. Neither did other members of the panel.

During the Gorsuch confirmation, Mitch McConnell went on *Meet the Press with Chuck Todd*, aka Sleepy Eyes. (Personally, I don't find his eyes sleepy at all. They're a little narrow, yet also kind and sympathetic, and seem to reveal the soul of someone who's seen too much of the dark side of life. Maybe that's just me.)

When Todd brought up Democrats' frustrations over the Judge Garland nomination McConnell backed up his refusal to even give Garland a hearing by stating it had been eighty years since a Court vacancy was filled by an outgoing president during an election year. Todd went back and forth, but that comment remained in the air, unchecked. A quick trip to *Politico.com* revealed that three Supreme Court seats were filled within the previous eighty years, under the same circumstances, and an additional three earlier in the twentieth century.

Since Todd was discussing the subject, he should have been aware of the talking point. He wasn't, so McConnell got away with it. This is this is how lies get injected into the conversational bloodstream.

BEWARE OF OPTICS

One of the Trump's favorite stunts is "meeting with experts" — same table, different day, different subject. Whether it's coal mining, health care, or women in business, the idea is to put out a visual that says he's sitting down with important people to discuss important problems. He squints his eyes and puts on his serious "thinking" face. Then he issues the same clunky statement to the effect of "These are the best people. We're going to do great things. Very great things." Then he dismisses the press. And if someone tries to sneak in an actual question, he burps up a smile, along with a dismissive "thank you." It's the same image every time, which should expose the strategy behind it.

Even if we become attuned to the sound of bullshit we're more vulnerable to images because their meaning seems self-evident. For all Trump's efforts to enlarge the crowd size at his inauguration versus that of President Obama's, he was knocked back by the side-by-side visuals of the two events. Moments like that are reassuring based on the assumption that pictures don't lie. But they do lie. In fact, a picture can be worth a thousand lies.

Think back to Trump's raging February 17th press conference, featuring a clueless interchange with Washington Bureau Chief for *American Urban Radio Networks*' April Ryan. When she asked the president if he planned on meeting with the CBC, his initial reaction was embarrassment, as he obviously didn't know the CBC was the Congressional Black Caucus. The moment became even more awkward when he belligerently defied Ryan to set up the meeting, asking if she knew them and if they were friends of hers. This was the same press conference in which he went after an Orthodox Jewish reporter for having the audacity to ask an "unfriendly" question about recent outbreaks of anti-Semitism in the U.S.

The optics sucked. He couldn't have looked any more racist than if he'd been wearing a hood and carrying a burning cross. But when the story began to play against him, he did damage control a few days later via a staged a photo op at the African American History museum, where he denounced both anti-Semitism and racism—a virtual exculpatory two-fer. Next to him, trotted out for the visual, was Ben Carson, in all his soporific glory. And floating in the background, protecting the moment from any embarrassing questions—Omarosa—his Black fixer.

This kind of clunky stunt reveals the simplistic level of their thinking. It also reveals their contempt for the public in that they assume this shit works. We can't just listen to the words. We have to look at the pictures and consider the nature of the event, and the agenda behind it.

BE SKEPTICAL,
BUT KEEP AN
OPEN MIND

We've officially broken into separate ideological and informational bunkers, only peeking up to hurl snark grenades at each other. (Has anyone ever been rushed to the Emergency Room with a Twitter burn?)

When you're under information attack, sometimes the only way to keep your sanity is to crawl in a foxhole, keep your head down, and shut off your mind. But that doesn't lead to knowledge. It's important to occasionally venture outside and see if you're missing anything; to know what people on the other side are thinking and why.

This comes into play in the hate-speech/free speech debate. I understand the arguments, and the passions, though in the end I come down on the side of free speech. Not just based on the First Amendment, but also as a way of looking at a phenomenon from a sociological point of view. While it's not intolerance to be intolerant of intolerance, closing off your mind won't neutralize certain opinions or make them disappear. Better to examine them up close and think about whether they have any validity, or at least understand why they might still have power with some people.

One would think that the more information sources available to us, the harder it would be to propagandize. But the opposite seems to be true. Our ears aren't attuned to listen for lies. And they're coming at us more furiously than ever, like a volley of arrows. If even one gets through you're wounded, or dead.

We're also not trained in critical thinking. We tend to absorb information passively. If pressed, we often can't say why we think what we think. And we get stubborn when pressed to back up our precious opinions though, in many cases opinions are what people have because they don't know, don't understand or decide to ignore some of the facts. The nature of our public debate doesn't help. Most discussions of serious issues are framed by the left/right arguments, but they rarely get down to the level of first principles, in which people are forced to examine the philosophical assumptions underlying their opinions.

Throwing your sense of reality into question is part of the intellectual process and can often lead to insights or creative breakthroughs. Although in this media climate it carries infinitely more risk. Accepting intellectual relativism can lead to the false equivalency of all opinions and ultimately to confusion instead of clarity. This is the delicate line we have to walk in order to find the truth, which necessitates holding on to the notion of truth itself, whether as some Platonic ideal or just as a guiding light.

Staying informed is the most important weapon in protecting yourself against propaganda. Truth moves people to action and resistance. To quote George Clinton, "Free your mind, and your ass will follow."

CHAPTER TEN

THE
2020
ELECTION

GET
READY
TO
RUMBLE!

*"'The first campaign is over. The
second has begun today. I shall lead it.'
Indeed, he campaigned as vigorously as before.
Chartering a Junkers passenger plane, he flew
from one end of Germany to the other – a novelty
in electioneering at the time – addressing three or
four big rallies a day in as many cities. Shrewdly,
he altered his tactics to attract more votes. In the
first campaign he had harped on the misery of the
people, the impotence of the Republic. Now he
depicted a happy future for all Germans if he were
elected: jobs for the workers, higher prices for the farmers,
more business for the businessmen,
a big Army for the militarists."*

William S. Shirer
The Rise and Fall of the Third Reich

"I will accept the results of the election. If I win."
Donald J. Trump

Trump will never be the President of the United States. He'll always just be the asshole who won the election. At this point, the goal is to stop him from doing it again. Toward that end, there are five takeaways from the 2016 election.

First: Trump threw out the rules. The Trump campaign wasn't about knocking on doors. It was about knocking them down. He branded his primary opponents, sticking them in a box from which they couldn't escape. Then he boxed in Hillary using the same tactics. Then he took on reality, reducing complex issues to simplistic categories, employing slogans and inflammatory rhetoric to whip up the crowds. "Drain the swamp!" "Build the wall!" "Repeal Obamacare!" Trump was selling the same "hope and change" that Obama ran on in 2008, though instead of communicating an optimistic vision for the future, he railed against the horrors of a mythical dystopian present.

Second: It shouldn't have even been close. Given his heinous behavior and vile statements, it should have been a blowout. That's not about him. That's about us. This election was a national freak-out. His crowds bought his shit because it re-empowered them in a world they felt was passing them by.

He targeted common enemies as the cause of their problems — Hillary, NATFA, TPP, Muslims, the press. Then he fobbed himself off as the solution. "I, alone, can fix it." A rich con artist branded himself as a populist man of the people. It was a bizarre irony that he burped up some empty words about anti-Semitism during his Congressional address in response to an increasing number of anti-Semitic hate crimes that were inspired by the tone of his campaign.

He played off people's socioeconomic fears, employing the gut-level identity politics used by dictators in the past and nationalists in the present. Even if his solutions were fact-averse, nobody cared. It wasn't about the facts. It was about the feeling that he was going to make their lives better.

Third: Democrats didn't get it. So they didn't know how to fight. "When they go low we go high" was a positive affirmation of the fundamental goodness and decency of the

America people. And it didn't work. Turns out we're not that good, and we're not that decent. It might as well have been "when they go low, we get high." It was high-minded, tactically impotent and ultimately useless.

People mocked his rallies, his supporters, even the stupid MAGA hats. But they were brilliant symbols employed by a guy with a visceral understanding of the power of symbols. And the parody versions Democrats whipped up didn't work. In fact, they were counter-productive. It didn't matter if you could make out the ironic message printed on it. Make America Hate Again. Yes, very clever. Biting satire. Also, totally irrelevant because the hat still looked like the original. The power was in the visual. Anyone close enough to discern the irony on your hat would also be close enough to punch you in the face.

That one simple point could be at the root of Democrats' ignorance about Republicans. The worst thing you can call a Democrat is inconsistent in their position or, horror of horrors, a hypocrite. The worst thing you can call a Republican is out of power. And all the lofty ideas in the world don't mean shit if you're out of power.

And that's the fourth lesson: Trump went dark, even though he didn't have to. It's not like the angry racist vote would've gone to Hillary. Like those people thought, "You know, I'd like to vote for Trump, but I'm just not hearing the racism." He went dark because that's who he is. And if that's how dark he went to get power, imagine how dark he'll go to keep it. He may not have a conceptual understanding of The Shock Doctrine, but he has a gut-level sense of the disorienting effect a war, terrorist attack, or economic crisis has on people, and how to take political advantage of it. I doubt he's seen *Wag the Dog*, but it's the theory underlying his every thought, statement, or tweet.

Which leads to lesson number five: Trump didn't bring a gun to a knife fight. He brought a gun to a chess match. And the upcoming elections are going to get even dirtier than 2016. By 2020, Trump may have already issued an Executive Order directing that the Democratic Party rename itself The Anti-American Job-Killing Jesus-Hating Gun-Snatching Welfare-Loving Baby-Killer Party. He may have also outlawed the press, and federal judges, and burned down Capitol Hill. Voting while non-white could be a felony.

Democrats still don't seem to get who and what they're up against. Since the election, they've been wearing their regret like a hair shirt. They talk about doing better next time — knocking on doors, going district by district, reaching out to voters they failed to connect with. They look to Michigan, Wisconsin, and Pennsylvania, trying to figure out how to win over non-college educated white people while energizing supporters who may not have turned out in big enough numbers.

In April 2017, DNC Chairman Tom Perez and Bernie Sanders went on their Magical Democracy Tour, intended to fire up the base. Based on the one interview I saw, it seems the strategy is to get back to basics while making a stand on the moral high ground. Oh, please, not the moral high ground. We'll be double-fucked. This is no time for decency, humility or high-mindedness.

In early May, Hillary came out of her emotional exile and announced the formation of a political group to fund organizations engaged in resisting Trump's agenda. The tentative name for the group: Onward Together — a reference to her campaign slogan: Stronger Together. Great idea. Horrible name. It stunk of righteousness, and weakness. Why not just call it, "Thank you, sir, may I have another?!" The name needs a serious re-think. Maybe something along the lines of "The People Are Coming For You, Asshole."

Just like the 9/11 hijackers what Trump did was the unthinkable. And the upcoming elections could yield the same result unless Democrats figure out their message and how to clearly and powerfully communicate it to traditional Republican voters who may be having buyer's remorse.

Democrats also have to stop pandering. It's annoying. And elitist. I don't think Trump supporters are looking to engage in a meaningful dialogue in which we can celebrate our diversity in a spirit of mutual respect. I've been trolled a few times on Twitter. I didn't get the sense that anyone was looking for hugs from the "libtards."

Oh, and lose the self-righteous Facebook posts. "My great-grand-niece is one-and-a-half years old and I shudder to think of the world she'll grow up in." Who cares? She's one and a half. She can't even wipe her ass and she doesn't have to look for a job. This isn't about her future. It's about our present. Which is all Trump voters cared about: Fuck climate change. I need a job, now. And frankly, it's hard to counter that. Climate change isn't sending threatening letters to shut off the lights if you don't pay the electric bill. Democrats need to get that. They also need to sell the idea that the renewable energy industry is the future. It's not a job-killer. It's a job-creator. If they're not figuring out how to incorporate the idea that "Democrats Mean Business" into the platform, they're already committing political suicide.

And don't assume that after four years of Trump, American life will be so self-evidently bleak that people will finally wake up and embrace liberalism, ushering in a brave new world of free college, universal health care, and a unicorn in every garage. Whether the results in the congressional elections in Montana and Georgia reflected any anti-Trump blowback, it's dangerous to assume it will necessarily be there in four years and that his support will wane. "We lost by less!" is not a powerful rallying cry.

Democrats have to stop thinking about politics as a debating society. This is a street fight. They have to make the case to Trump's people that they were conned. Which won't be easy. Like any mark in an elaborate con, it's embarrassing to admit you were naïve enough to fall for it. It's human nature to feel foolish. Yet, it's also human nature to want payback. Voters who flipped can be flipped back.

In this effort, Trump's own tactics need to be used against him. He needs to be re-branded to those people who put their faith in him as their savior. Forget those who voted for him because of his racism. They're beyond reach or redemption. They just have to get old and die. He has to be re-branded to those who voted for him in spite of it. People who were desperate enough to overlook his obvious faults and vote for someone who promised to fix their lives. The message is simple: He lied to you to get your votes. And now you're suffering.

Think of him as the *Star Wars* Death Star. The only way to take him out is to blow up his power source.

THE
REBRANDING
OF THE
PRESIDENT

Trump has spent decades creating his brand. He knows its power, which is why he viciously repels anything that might tarnish it. No other politician could have survived Pussygate. Deny 'til you die. Put out female surrogates to show you're not a threat. Threaten lawsuits. Feign outrage and indignation. Play the victim. Then stage a rally with friendly supporters, and roll up in your plane. It was pure theatre. But the optics were powerful.

But it's one thing to run for office as the outsider railing against the status quo. The game changes when you become the status quo. And while he's employing the same tactics against his new enemies — the press, the intelligence community, the former FBI Director, even the former president — he now has to own his shit. Trump is stuck with himself.

Despite his claim that he would be "so presidential," it's just not playing. He's already demonstrated a basic inability to grasp the enormity of his responsibilities. He even admits he thought the job would be easier, and had no idea policy was so complicated. It's a testament to Trump's arrogance and his disdain for people that he thinks he can fake the most important job in the world. Though I don't think he was planning on winning, let alone governing. If he wasn't a clear and present danger to the planet and everyone on it, I'd almost feel sorry for him. He must be freaking out. How ironic that the most powerful person in the world feels so vulnerable.

Trump knows it only takes one accusation to stick for the whole stack of bullshit to come tumbling down. That's why when someone nails him, like Peter Alexander did at his February press conference, calling him on his "greatest electoral victory" lie, he immediately scrambles, trying to pivot his way out. If the media fact checks him later, he simply insists that they got it wrong and stalls until he can change the subject, or until his critics collapse from exasperation, or move on to the next story.

Meanwhile, Russia-gate remains in the air, like a layer of the carbon dioxide he's declared a non-existent threat to the planet. Call it political climate change. And unlike actual climate change, he can't deny its existence.

But it's not enough to wait for him to get busted. As vulnerable as he is, he's already demonstrated an uncanny ability to weasel out of trouble. But he might not be able to escape if the lies and scandals begin to feed the political narrative that he's an ignorant, dangerously incompetent, lying fake who's hell-bent on dismantling a democratic system of government that has sustained us for over 240 years. A clear and present danger to the country — exactly the kind of demagogue American democracy was meant to repel. Trump must be re-branded as "the enemy of the American people."

Toward that end, there needs to be a constant call for his impeachment, not because it's possible, given Republican control of Congress, but because it's a powerful weapon. Like birtherism, the power is in the attack. It tarnishes his brand and puts him on the defensive. The more time he has to spend pushing back, the more vulnerable he is. It took decades to effectively brand Hillary as dishonest, but once it stuck, Republicans worked it like a boxer jabbing at his opponent's open cut. Benghazi! Emails! She's dishonest! Secretive! A liar! It all fed the same theme.

Attack his business dealings, past and present. Keep the Emoluments Clause in the conversation, along with the fact that he never placed his business in a blind trust, and that he's very likely monetizing the presidency. He's an aspiring American Putin. Or his puppet. Trump's business dealings could eventually be the smoking gun in the Russia investigations.

Keep the sexual harassment allegations alive. What happened to all the women who accused him? He was going to sue all of them after the election.

Attack the lies about his education. Call for his Fordham and University of Pennsylvania transcripts. For all his name-dropping about going to the best schools, he attended Fordham University then transferred to the University of Pennsylvania, where he took some courses at the Wharton School of Business and received a B.A. Not an MBA. Some say the only reason he got in was that his daddy donated money to the school. I'm not saying that. But some people are. And no one who was there at the time seems to remember him. So it's a mystery he should clear up by releasing all his college transcripts. Which I'm sure he will. Right after he releases his tax returns.

He needs to be pounded with waves of negative attack ads, like the bombing of German gun batteries at Normandy in preparation for the allied landing. No more glossy soft-filter ads with warm-sounding voice-overs and noble, uplifting messages. The more apocalyptic the better, like the Daisy Girl spot from the 1964 election. The ads need to be run in every state he won, starting now.

Even though re-taking the House in 2018 is the immediate goal, it's not just a matter of focusing on the dynamics of the specific races and the merits of the respective candidates. Re-branding Trump re-brands the party that elected him, and continues to work with him to enact policies that will make life worse for most Americans. Like taking health insurance away from 20 million people, and pulling out of the Paris Climate Accords. The anti-Trump message is an anti-Republican message. Tie them together and they all become vulnerable which, of course, is Republicans' greatest fear. Along with having the leader of their party become a laughingstock.

THE
MOCKING
OF THE
PRESIDENT

American political humor over the last century has ranged from the lighthearted jokes of Will Rogers and gentle needling of Bob Hope, to the slightly more acerbic Johnny Carson, to the more biting social commentary of comics like Mort Sahl, Dick Gregory, Jon Stewart, and Bill Maher. Politicians on the business end of the jokes either laughed along or sucked it up and took it, smiling to convey the impression that they were good sports. It is and always has been part of the cost of being in power. The more volatile the times the more thin-skinned and erratic our leaders, the more the tone shifted from light-hearted entertainment to political weapon, and even a means of dissent.

Occasionally, politicians appeared on the very shows that mocked them, a way of defusing the attack by showing they could take it and laugh along. Nixon did it. Sarah Palin took a shot at it. As did Trump. Though it didn't stick. Trump seethed during the 2011 White House Correspondents' Association dinner, and has since registered his displeasure at being lampooned on *SNL*, though he doesn't seem to get that the more he reacts, the more it reveals his insecurities, and the more mockable he becomes. His reaction becomes part of the story, making him look even more petty. On one level he may even realize it, but he's so psychologically damaged that he's powerless against himself. He probably doesn't understand why he can't jail Alec Baldwin and shut down the show. Well, at least he can't, yet. (Hopefully no one will tell him that *The Smothers Brothers* got yanked off *CBS* in the late '60s, the result of striking a nerve with their anti-war commentary.)

Comedy may have once been an amusing sideshow but it's now taken on an unprecedented power in our political dialogue. The more autocratic the regime, the more self-important and pretentious the politicians, the more humor has surfaced as a political weapon. And Trump is such an easy target. A tangerine, raccoon-eyed Piñata, who gets consistently beaten by John Oliver, Samantha Bee, Trevor Noah, Seth Meyers, Jimmy Kimmel, and Steven Colbert. Unfortunately, no candy spills out.

In a scathing monologue in May, Colbert referred to the president's mouth, saying its only value was as "Vladimir Putin's cock-holster." While I cringed at the image, what I loved even more than the joke was the outrage in Colbert's delivery. He knew he was stepping over the line and didn't care. The underlying message was: you deserve this. Think about it: Trump pushed a guy who teaches Sunday school to this level of anger.

SNL is riding a wave of popularity and political relevance it hasn't seen since Tina Fey. Melissa McCarthy is surreal as Sean Spicer. The harder she hits, the more she scowls, the funnier and more powerful it gets. Though with the rumors of Spicer's demise getting stronger, they may both be out of a job. And then there's Alec Baldwin's Trump. He brilliantly brands the guy as a clueless, childish, imbecile who's completely out of his league.

Comics and political TV shows are often the strongest voices for debunking bullshit or screaming truth to power. At times, they've even been advocates for change, like with Jon Stewart's public shaming of those in Congress who were blocking the Zadroga Act. Their popularity is also the direct result of a fragmented news environment and news organizations falling prey to ratings pressure. It's ironic that *The Daily Show's* popularity was based on lampooning the anemic performance of news channels yet, on occasion, became a more trusted source of information than the actual news.

Real Time with Bill Maher is still the gold standard of comedy and intelligent political discourse. And W. Kamau Bell's *United Shades of America* has found a sweet spot as a hybrid of *The Daily Show* and *60 Minutes,* using humor to expose the some of the darker recesses of the American mind.

There's a catharsis in humor. It reinforces the knowledge that we're living in the same reality. It's a survival mechanism, a way to cling to sanity. Yet, it's dangerous to assume that jokes, alone, will make Trump's weaknesses self-evident to those who need to see them. It didn't work during the primaries, or in the general election. It turns out no politician is actually "devastated" by an article or "destroyed" by a comedy show impersonation. But it's crucial to keep hammering him, as just another weapon in the war.

Unless Trump literally exposes himself during the State of the Union—a move Kellyanne Conway would probably spin as another example of the president's unique way of communicating with his supporters—the only way we'll ever rid ourselves of this guy will be to deconstruct the persona he's created and vote him out of office, which requires turning many who voted for him.

But, they won't necessarily be turned by the "liberal" media. The Russian pee tape could run on a loop, and it still might not resonate with the people who need to hear it. Trump voters may not trust *CNN, MSNBC, The New York Times,* or *The Washington Post,* but they may listen to their own. As impotent as it feels to write this, conservatives may just be the saviors of American democracy.

THE
FRAGGING
OF THE
PRESIDENT

"Donald Trump's repeated lack of respect for the truth may put him in jeopardy of being viewed as 'a fake president'." That may sound like a comment from the liberal media but it's from a March 2017 editorial in *The Wall Street Journal.*

We've had the making, selling, and branding of the president. Now we can add the fragging of the president. "Fragging" was a term that arose out of the Vietnam War, referring to soldiers who were so afraid of their platoon leader's erratic, dangerous behavior, they'd roll a fragmentation grenade at his feet and blow him up, faking a battlefield death to save themselves.

Despite the Republican orthodoxy in Reagan's so-called 11th commandment, that of never speaking ill of other party members, many conservatives are lining up to take their shots. It doesn't matter whether their criticism is based on embarrassment at the man who's become their standard-bearer, or the concomitant fear that he could put a stain on the party resulting in an electoral backlash, their motivations are secondary to their actions.

And no, I'm not referring to *Fox News.* Despite sporadic outbreaks of journalism, they're guilty of laying the intellectual and emotional groundwork that resulted in President Trump. They don't even get to visit the high road. (There's some weird dynamic at work on *Fox and Friends*: Two schmucks on a couch with a woman who seems to find them entertaining. Maybe it's a subliminal message that pretty girls like conservative dorks. Opinion journalism with a sidebar of masturbatory fantasy.)

Nor am I referring to the cadres of angry, right wing fembots doing their version of "daddy didn't love me so now I'm taking my anger out on the world." Ok, maybe that's sexist. I'll put gender aside and say that they're just as hateful as their male counterparts and few seem to be showing any genuine signs of regret.

I'm talking about those in the media who may have the credibility to reach people who need to be reached. Megyn Kelly's now on *NBC*, though it remains to be seen if she lost her conservative cred by taking on Trump's misogyny during the primaries. (She may have lost all journalistic cred after a softball interview with Vladimir Putin, followed up by a sit-down with evolutionary throwback, Alex Jones. Though the real blame should be on the network for using these grotesque stunts to launch her on the network. If the intention is to whitewash her *Fox* past, that's not going to cut it.)

Nicole Wallace and Steve Schmidt have been on the Sarah Palin Atonement Tour on *MSNBC* offering insights as well as appropriate outrage from a conservative point of view. So have Michael Steele, Stuart Stevens, Rick Wilson, Charlie Sykes and Joe Scarborough. Mike Murphy seemed to disappear after the election but I'm waiting to see if he resurfaces.

CNN features a gaggle of conservative voices, though it seems they've just leased out the channel to anyone with an opinion. Like a hair salon with a "station available" sign in the window, they'll take in anyone who has a steady client base.

While some commentators remain measured in their comments, others seem ready to lose it. Ana Navarro looks like she could leap the White House fence, scale the building, kick in the Oval Office doors and gut punch the president. Hopefully, she'll bring a camera crew.

And somewhere in the media wilderness there's even nutty Glenn Beck. During the Obama years Beck did his loopy patriot routine on *Fox,* occasionally breaking down and sobbing, "I fear for my country!" Well, now he's got a fucking reason.

Conservative editorial writers have also come out against Trump. William Kristol, George Will, David Frum, David Brooks, Jennifer Rubin, and Ross Douthat most notable among them. Even some members of Congress, like Lindsey Graham and John McCain, are occasionally breaking ranks, though it's ironic that McCain is the one who gave us Palin, who helped set the ideological table for Trump. Still, maybe this election has been the catalyst for them to rediscover their inner patriot.

But before delivering another blistering takedown, or writing another scathing editorial about how the man in the White House doesn't represent real conservative values, some need to stop and reflect on their culpability in unleashing this evil bastard into our world in the first place. Where was all this patriotism over the last eight years?

Trump can sling the talking point that he inherited "a mess." The world is always a mess. But if "mess" accurately describes the state of the world in 2016, then in 2009 President Obama inherited a world-shaking, economy crashing clusterfuck. And his reward for fixing it was eight years of disrespect.

Whether it was political calculation or residual racism, Republicans lined up behind a strategy of obstruction. They fought every effort to bail the country out of a depression caused by Republican policies, then criticized the recovery for being too slow.

Few conservatives called Trump out on his birtherism. Boehner's catty "I take the president at his word that he's a Christian" dodge was so slimy I'm surprised he didn't slither out of his suit when he said it. The fact that Joe Wilson's "You lie!" insult was never slapped back with appropriate outrage meant it had Republicans' tacit approval. Some even participated when Tea Partiers marched in D.C. in their stupid hats and buckle shoes screaming about the tyrant in the White House.

It wasn't just the tonnage of opposition, but the tone and level of hysteria. Obama's a Socialist! A communist! A tyrant! A dictator! Although the reference to Claude Raines' speech in *Casablanca*, "I am shocked, shocked to find that gambling is going on in here," is overused, the hypocrisy in play is appropriate. Eight years of politically motivated, angry rhetoric created an atmosphere of hatred and mistrust that infected the country and bequeathed us the asshole now in charge.

And for those who might equate the anger directed at Obama with that now directed at Trump, the anti-Obama anger was based on what he represented socially, and politically. The anti-Trump sentiments come from what he's said and done.

We may have philosophical differences on the role of government, tax rates, corporate regulation, and so-called entitlements, but at least there's general agreement on the idea that the President of the United States ought to have some measure of intelligence, a basic knowledge of world affairs, a sense of history, and a decency and dignity befitting the office.

Conservatives will be important voices in changing the conversation over the next several years. Journalists, opinion writers, and Republican strategists, even some members of Congress, may be the only ones who can convey an anti-Trump message with credibility. They can't all be marginalized as RINOS. They can help sell the idea that we've crossed a dangerous line, one that is becoming more evident with each new revelation in the Russia investigation.

Despite administration pushback, it's all sounding eerily familiar— denials, firings, stonewalling—but with the added Trumpian touch of misdirection and counter-narratives designed to deflect media and public attention.

Again, the Nixon parallels are becoming more obvious. It's no coincidence that "impeachment" is in the air. And, just like Nixon, Trump may end up screwing himself. Not only because of what he did, but based on who he is.

WATERGATE
AS
PSYCHOLOGICAL
PARADIGM

It's already a cliché to talk about the cliché of comparing the Trump campaign team's alleged collusion with the Russians to Watergate. But it fits. The stars of Watergate are all over TV: Woodward and Bernstein, Nixon's White House counsel John Dean, former prosecutor Richard Ben-Veniste, former member of the House Judiciary Committee Elizabeth Holzman.

Even the language is resurfacing. "What did the president know and when did he know it." Or more likely in this case: "What did the president lie about not knowing, and when did he lie about not knowing it." There are the non-denial denials, along with White House spokespersons distancing the president from his former associates. Paul Manafort? The guy who ran the campaign for five months? Barely knew him.

We've had politicians who've been under investigation for shady deals, con games, tax evasion, sexual impropriety, kickbacks, bribery, cover-ups, and lies, but we've yet to have the whole complement of nastiness in one person who happens to be the president. And who may also be guilty of treason, as defined in the Constitution as giving "aid and comfort to the enemy." I'm not sure about the "aid" part but the love letters to Putin during the campaign certainly looked comforting.

This behavior was bizarre for any presidential candidate, let alone a Republican. Hating on the old Soviet Union or Putin's Russia has always been a no-brainer for Republicans. It's page one of the freshman orientation handbook, right next to lowering taxes and pissing on the poor. It might have carried some plausibility coming from someone who billed himself as a political philosopher advocating a world view based on casting off the shackles of

Cold War thinking and forming new alliances in the quest for peace in the 21st century. But Trump is not a thinker. He's not a visionary. He can barely see past his next Happy Meal. So what was it about?

In hindsight, his "if you're listening" shout-out to Russian hackers to uncover Hillary's 33,000 missing emails seems less like a snarky comment and more of a cheeky way of saying he knew exactly what was going on. This was the arrogance of power and the rush the criminal gets in taunting his adversaries — the thrill of saying something publically while privately knowing the truth. Despite public denials, the same phenomenon seemed to be in play with Roger Stone's comment that it would soon be "Podesta's turn in the barrel," which came just days before the scandal broke. Also suspiciously similar was Giuliani's alluding to the campaign having "tricks up their sleeve." Even Trump's denials were too clever by half. Saying he had no dealings "in Russia" didn't mean he had no dealings "with Russians."

Though it's too soon to know whether this will take him down, it already has the feel, the words, the music, and even the stink of Watergate.

Lies. Contact between the Trump campaign and the Russians was initially downplayed by Republicans as inconsequential. But the stink of guilt worsened when the late December revelations of Flynn's conversations with the Russian ambassador were fobbed off as the two wishing each other Merry Christmas. When President Obama finally slapped the Russians with sanctions, and Putin responded by inviting the children of embassy staff to a Kremlin holiday party, all I could think was "My God, Putin's going to eat them!"

None of it made sense. Not the events. Not the cover stories. Each day it seemed more likely there was collusion between the Trump campaign and Russian intelligence, which is probably the first time the words "Trump" and "intelligence" have been used in the same sentence.

Then factor in Carter Page's stunning on-air admission

to Chris Hayes. His initial denials sounded like he'd never even heard of Russia, let alone the ambassador. And he'd certainly never met him. That suddenly changed to "Ok, I may have, accidentally, bumped into someone at the Republican convention who may have been the Russian ambassador. I couldn't quite tell from the accent and the fact that he reeked of vodka if he was, in fact, Russian, but either way we certainly never spoke. Ok, we might have had a conversation, however brief and irrelevant, but just about the weather and nothing to do with the election. Ok, it may have come up once or twice, but nothing illegal went on because that was the only time I met him! Except for the other time. Just stop grilling me and leave me alone!"

This guy looked so guilty, I expected him to confess to killing Kennedy. And why go on TV knowing you have something to hide? Just hide it by not going on TV. It was a perverse attempt at covering your ass by exposing it. Months later he made a return appearance on the show, still walking that same line. Of course he may be completely innocent. Just a patsy caught up in a larger investigation. There were certainly minor players in Watergate who were momentarily dragged into the spotlight.

Send in the surrogates. As far back as December, Trump and his minions were already obfuscating. Representative Trent Franks went on *MSNBC*, slamming the Obama administration for trying to "delegitimize the election," and fobbing it off as "leaks from unnamed sources." If he were tap-dancing any more, he would've had a cane and a tophat.

Presiding over the March 20th appearance of FBI Director Comey and NSA head Admiral Mike Rogers in front of House Intelligence Committee, Chairman Devon Nunes pledged to investigate the Russia connection "no matter where it took him." It turns out it took him right to the White House the next day to alert them to some new "revelations," something he didn't feel he could share with members of his own committee, or the public. He steadfastly refused to admit any wrongdoing and insisted that he wouldn't step down. Then he stepped down. Maybe calling Nunes the Chairman of the Intelligence Committee was like one of those high school nicknames, like when you called the fat kid, "slim."

Non-denial denials. "Nothing to see." "A witch hunt." "McCarthyism." "Phony baloney garbage." "It's the media's fault!" "We're innocent." "Hillary and Susan Rice are guilty! And British Intelligence! Investigate them! Not us!" It's all reminiscent of Nixon-era pushback.

It was fascinating to watch Sean Spicer deliver the daily talking points, frantically grabbing for weasel words in response to direct questions. That is, when he wasn't playing hide-and-seek with the press by ducking into the shrubbery. Meanwhile, the administration and its congressional surrogates tried to make the ridiculous argument that the problem was the leaking of information, not the information, itself.

Then there was Trump's February press conference in which he conducted himself with all the grace and self-control of King Kong climbing the Empire State Building. Referring to the media as "horrible people" and purveyors of "fake news." Spitting out raging, self-righteous responses to questions he wasn't asked. Attacking the intelligence community by saying he was going to bring in a billionaire investor to look into it — a guy with no government experience who ran an investment fund called Cerberus Capital. Cerberus is the Greek mythological creature guarding the gates of hell. He should fit right in. Or he would have, if anyone heard anything about him since. From there Trump struck back by insisting that the leaks were real but the news was fake, it was everyone else's fault, and the dog ate his homework.

He was snarling, snorting. Doing his tough guy routine, with that angry, Lhasa Apso under-bite. This would have been bizarre behavior from an NFL lineman with a traumatic brain injury. Then I remembered this was the leader of the free world. And when he defended his new, Russian reach-around policy on the grounds that "nuclear holocaust would be like no other" all I could do was curl up in a fetal ball, and rhythmically rock back and forth, comforting myself with the thought that at least being vaporized will be quick.

Firings. By February, underlings were already waking up to find themselves thrown under the proverbial bus. From "General Flynn has my complete confidence" to "I've asked for his resignation." By the way, if transcripts exist of FBI wiretaps of Flynn's conversations wouldn't his syntax make his intentions clear? If he said, "The president elect has instructed me to tell you not to worry about sanctions" then he obviously didn't go rogue.

And of course, there was the May firing of FBI Director James Comey, based on an ever-shifting set of reasons, where the president and his spokespeople couldn't even get their cover stories straight.

After his odd response to a question he wasn't asked during his Senate confirmation hearings, Southern Muppet Jeff Sessions recused himself from the investigation. I would think a newly confirmed Attorney General would at least have time to stick a family picture on his desk before having to recuse himself from an investigation of his boss.

In June he appeared before the Senate Intelligence Committee to answer questions about his alleged meetings with the Russians, along with any conversations he may have had with the president on the matter. Turns out he never met any Russians, though maybe he did, but he didn't talk to the president about it, unless he did, in which case he couldn't talk about whatever it was they did or didn't talk about.

The cover-up. "It's not the crime, it's the cover-up." No, it's the crime *and* the cover-up. The stink of the cover-up is what leads to the uncovering of the crime and often puts those involved in the classic double-bind Michael Corleone faced in *Godfather II*: you're either guilty of the crime, or of perjury for lying about it under oath. Maybe they should put the whole team together at the White House and have a movie night.

At some point, it's a matter of tonnage. Goofy Spice's marginalizing of Paul Manafort as someone who just dropped by the campaign. Flynn's lying and firing, along with his taking money from the Turkish government and not disclosing it. Sessions' stonewalling. Carter Page, Michael Cohen and Jared Kushner allegedly all had connections and/or business with the Russians, or met with the Russian ambassador at least once. Then there's Trump's arm-twisting Comey to back off the investigation, then firing him when he wouldn't play along, leading to a he said/he said public stand-off. Followed by threats to fire the special counsel.

At some point, it's more than just a chorus of lies. It's a bullshit symphony. Do they have to put on Cossack outfits, slam Stoli shots and dance the kazatsky before people draw the obvious conclusions? The allegations are penetrating the outer circle of associates and reaching people inside the administration. Many are already lawyering up, including Trump, perhaps based on multiple accounts of asking members of the intelligence community to push back against the FBI investigation.

It's also interesting how many in the media parroted the "Flynn lied to Pence" story, accepting that framing of events. How about the possibility that Trump and his campaign managers and advisors, who had contacts in Russia, were all in on it, and Pence was either aware of it or was out of the loop because he was just a squeaky clean Christian, cast to take the stink off a crooked candidate. (While he made his Faustian bargain, it would be ironic if Trump is eventually booted and Pence takes over. One wonders how much shit he's already taken and if he'd pop an LBJ-like boner the second he sat behind the big desk.)

In Watergate it was "follow the money." With Trump it's follow the noise. And maybe the rubles. As of this writing there's no definitive proof to back up claims against the president of collusion with the Russians to influence the election or of obstructing justice. All I know is what people are saying. And people are saying that he's guilty as shit. That he reeks of guilt. He stinks of it. Though I seriously doubt he cooked up the scheme, as he doesn't know fuck-all about hacking. He practically just learned the word.

But no matter how you break it down, these things seem clear: If Trump was directly involved, then he's guilty and has to go. We'll skip the treason part. Just resign. If he didn't know what his campaign staff was up to, then he hired a team of incompetent renegades and was oblivious to their actions. And most are still with him, which is a national security risk. So, he has to go.

He's obviously not sticking by Flynn, Kushner or anyone else out of loyalty, but out of self-preservation. And he's not giving an inch. He continues to fight each new revelation with non-denial denials, staged counter-events, counter narratives, and private attorneys, while trying to maintain the illusion of innocence.

He must be the world's shittiest poker player because his tells are everywhere. Watch his face when he responds to a question about the scandal, or any question he doesn't want to answer. He takes a beat, looks down, squints his eyes, and scowls. It must be tough to keep that many lies in the air at once with all those reporters firing questions and throwing all your past statements in your face. But when you light that many fires, you can't be surprised when they start burning out of control. And you can't prepare for everything. Shit unravels in unexpected ways.

Look at Watergate, not as historical precedent, but as an example of chaos theory. It was the 1972 election and even though Nixon was 30 points up in the polls he was still paranoid enough to fear he could lose to McGovern; hence, the DNC break-in.

But then the five burglars were stumbled on by a night watchman, and arrested. The event was played down, relegated to the level of a "third-rate burglary." Then, the *Washington* Post reported a story about payoffs to the defendants, using cash that was connected to the Committee to Re-Elect the President (CREEP). Still more pushback, famously by press secretary Ron Ziegler, who stood at the podium wearing a similar condescending sneer, defiantly accusing *The Post* of "shabby journalism" and "character assassination."

With each new revelation, the scandal got closer to the president: Denials, firings, special prosecutors, and bi-partisan congressional hearings. John Dean's testimony. The revelation of an Oval Office recording system. The tapes were subpoenaed. Nixon stonewalled, insisting the special prosecutor be fired. Two Attorneys General refused, leading to the Saturday Night Massacre. A third, Supreme Court wannabe Robert Bork, did the dirty deed. Finally the Court ordered Nixon to turn over the tapes. The noose tightened. Finally Republicans went to the president and told him he needed to resign for the good of the country. And he did.

For all his faults and dirty tricks, Nixon was still an attorney, and tethered to the law, and the Constitution. He was able to look past the moment to his place in history and the prospect of rehabilitating his image, which to some extent, he was able to do. In time, people referred to him as an elder statesman.

Maybe the enormity of it all crashed in on him and he disintegrated like Bogart's Captain Queeg at the end of *The Caine Mutiny*, where his paranoid ravings lead to a quiet moment of clarity in which he came to the realization that he'd lost his moral center and cracked.

But even if the investigations continue to close in on Trump, he'll probably never have that introspective moment. That would require a level of self-awareness and an inner decency he doesn't seem to possess.

There was no straight line from the plan to break into the DNC to Nixon's resignation. All the best-laid plans don't mean shit in a world where a night watchman's flashlight can change the course of history. But even if chaos theory doesn't get him, there's also Watergate as behavioral paradigm.

The epithet "Tricky Dick" stuck to Nixon because it arose from the man himself. The same holds true for Trump. If this scandal doesn't sink him, his pathology might. This is Watergate as morality play, Shakespeare or Greek tragedy.

Trump may be paranoid enough to think that the world is out to get him, but the sheer number of scandals that have surrounded him didn't come out of nowhere. He's in a world of his own making.

There is an arrogance that can come with reaching a position of power. You feel untouchable. But that same feeling can lead some people to take that one step too far. Your own nature can turn around and smack you down. Call it hubris, karma, poetic justice or screwing with the gods. Like Icarus, Trump may end up flying too close to the sun. And considering the man is made of butter, that endeavor is doomed to failure.

He also reveals himself by those he puts around him. When you engage in dirty business, you tend to surround yourself with unscrupulous people. You may think it protects you but it can also render you uniquely vulnerable.

While in moments of triumph, there's the secret delight in pulling off a crime—like that moment in *Reservoir Dogs* after the heist—the inherent danger is that if shit goes wrong, everyone will look out for themselves, which means no one's looking out for you. Those in the inner circle are privy to the boss' secrets. At some point loyalty fades away and self-preservation kicks in. Someone will cop a plea.

The other variable is congressional loyalty. They had a power-gasm over his election. They've let him slide on the putting his business into a blind trust and releasing his taxes. Most are still cynically playing the odds. When Trump took a break from the tweetstorms and conspiracy theories long enough to get the AHCA though the House, Republicans eventually got on board. They even participated in a celebratory photo-op. They'll do the same if McConnell manages to power it through the Senate.

For all their religious moralizing, they wouldn't give a shit if Trump ran a string of call girls out of the west wing as long as they got to cut taxes and ban abortion. Their obstructionist behavior during the Obama years proved that, despite the revisionist hagiography of Barry Goldwater, the "conscience of a conservative" might be an oxymoron. But there could be limits to the patience of a conservative. Particularly if their 2018 polling shows Trump is beginning to harm the brand.

When she tucks him in bed at night, Kellyanne should read to him from Julius Caesar. If Trump turns into a political liability the Tuesday Group and the Freedom Caucus will sell him out in a New York minute.

And even if Pence somehow became implicated they've got Paul Ryan. It's like Russian nesting dolls of evil. As long as they get to take the highway to dystopia they really don't care who's driving the bus.

ROCK THE VOTE

The Republican takeaway from their 2012 election loss was supposedly about reaching out to black and Latino voters. And they did. But not in that warm, fuzzy, old-timey Christian values, big tent kind of way. The reach-out was about doing everything they could to stop them from registering and voting.

The catalyst for the idea of voter fraud was the cartoonish 2009 Acorn video, and while the scandal only got real traction on *Fox*, it was completely successful in planting the idea of voter fraud in the public mind. Trump took it one ominous step further by encouraging "election monitors" to go to Philadelphia to ensure that people weren't voting illegally. Right. Like truckloads of Trumpaloompas with shotguns, wearing deputy voter badges, were going to hit the inner city and start randomly checking people's IDs.

This was never real. Nor was Trump's wild accusation about 3 million illegal voters in California, and busloads of Democrats sneaking into New Hampshire. The media assumed he was just a lunatic obsessing about crowd sizes but didn't consider he might have also been a devious prick who was setting the rhetorical table for future voter restriction efforts.

Looking at it in this context it's hardly a coincidence he was laser-focused on deportation. It had nothing to do with removing rapists and murderers. It was about getting rid of potential Democratic voters. The road to citizenship is also the road to the voting booth. And people tend to vote for those who made it possible for them to become citizens.

The 2013 gutting of a key provision in the Voting Rights Act opened the door for states to engage in the very activities the law was put in place to prevent. Per a *New York Times'* article, by early November 2016, 32 states had some form of voter ID laws.

In May 2017, Trump signed an Executive Order appointing voter-hating Kansas Secretary of State Kris Kobach to co-chair a commission, with Vice President Pence, designed to study and investigate voter fraud. This was never about voter fraud. The fraud was the commission itself. It's voter suppression in preparation for 2018 and 2020.

In my previous book I wrote: "You can't run for the presidency by alienating women, African-Americans, Latinos, Asians, Muslims and frankly, anyone with a barely functioning cerebral cortex." Well, it turns out not only can you run for the presidency, you can win it. Even though, according to the U.S. Census Bureau, Caucasians will be in the minority by 2044 that doesn't necessarily mean they'll be the voting minority. Only 60% of eligible voters voted in the last election.

Republicans only have to defend 8 Senate seats in the midterms, and many Democrats are up for re-election in traditionally red states. Though retaking the House is more promising. Democrats need 24 seats to flip control, though it's hardly a cakewalk.

According to *The Washington Post*, Republicans control 69 of 99 state legislative chambers and 33 governorships. They have total control of 25 states, and partial control of 20. Republican state legislators will have the power to gerrymander districts in 2020 to their hearts' content while trying to pass stricter voter ID laws.

Angry white people may be a dying breed, but future elections may not rest on how prolifically they can replicate. It may just be a matter of kneecapping your opponents to level the playing field. Just deport, disenfranchise, or scare the shit out of as many voters as you can in order to counteract the changing demographic. In the dark arts of politics, it's not just a matter of identifying who's voting, but of targeting those you want to stop from voting.

If it turns out that the Russians actually found a way to hack voting machines in rust belt states and orchestrate a Trump victory, then we're all screwed because nothing is safe and our elections are a sham. But short of screwing with the actual voting machines, the GOP will be pulling all-nighters to figure out how to screw with who gets into them.

To combat these efforts, Democrats have to intensify voter registration particularly in swing states and in those districts that could flip, while fighting voter restriction efforts in the courts. Like the North Carolina bill that got shot down in a lower court for "targeting African-American voters with almost surgical precision."

This is just one more battle in a multi-front war. It's not just a matter of rebranding Trump, framing Republican ideology, money, advertising, or getting out the vote. None of this will mean anything if it's not in the service of communicating a clear, economic message via people who can sell it and connect with voters, emotionally. It's personality, politics and policy. It's not just a matter of flipping the House or the Senate. It's about flipping the script.

FLIP THE SCRIPT

The echo hadn't rung out on Trump's "American carnage" inaugural address before Democrats started queuing up for 2020. The contenders are already out on the public highway. I have a very simple calculus when it comes to figuring out who's running: If they're on the talkers or political podcasts, they're running. If they've written a book that has "America" "hope" or "vision" in the title, they're running. If they smile and toss off a coquettish laugh, saying it's way too early to even think about running, they're running. If they soberly state that they're happy doing the job the people of their state elected them to do and just want to do whatever they can to help the party, they're running. Oh, and if they insist in no uncertain terms they're not running, they're running.

Democrats already have a list of hot, young draft picks. Gavin Newsome, Julian Castro, Tim Ryan, Cory Booker, Kamala Harris, Jason Kander, Deval Patrick, Eric Garcetti. All smart, experienced and telegenic. And not all white men. They're virtual Trump antibodies. Congressmen Adam Schiff and Eric Swalwell have been making their bones as spokespersons for the House Intelligence Committee, and as frequent cable commentators. There's nothing like a good investigation to raise your political profile. Even if Russia-gate doesn't end up taking down Trump, it could be the carcass they feed off.

Elizabeth Warren could galvanize women just by reminding them of Mitch McConnell's demeaning "She was warned. She was given an explanation. Nevertheless she persisted" crack, when she tried to read Coretta Scott's King letter into the record during the Sessions' confirmation hearings. This was one step away from "Woman, shut up and sit down."

(McConnell's decision was baffling. For a politician that shrewd, the more calculating move would have been to allow her to read it into the record, and then move on. Why create an event that could be used as ammunition against you when it's so much slicker to judo it?)

Others like Amy Klobuchar and 2016 also-ran Martin O'Malley are already testing the waters in Iowa and New Hampshire. Though I still think Sherrod Brown is the guy to reach rust belt voters either as the head of the ticket, or as VP.

And before we completely descend into the celebritization of politics can we please reset the boundaries. Theoretically, anyone in this great land of ours can become president, but that doesn't mean anyone should. You don't get to be the president because you played one on TV. This is real life, not Governing With The Stars.

And let's also dispense with the myth of the outsider who's going to come in and clean up Washington. A president with no government experience is as useful as a pilot who's never flown a plane or a surgeon who's never been to med school. The fact that people buy this bullshit idea is living proof that some Americans are stupid enough to believe anything.

Many Democrats still haven't let go of the Bernie lament. In hindsight, maybe they were right. There's nothing worse than losing a 2-person race. And she lost. But should that be the 2020 takeaway? Go more progressive? Run younger Bernies? Or actual Bernie? Or Joe Biden? After four years of Trump abuse, we may yearn for some grandfatherly comfort. (I'm assuming Hillary's done. Even though Reagan took a few shots before he hit it in 1980, if she announced another run I think the entire Democratic base would leap out of their yoga pants, grab pitchforks and storm the town square.)

Maybe the party elders will become the spiritual leaders of a new movement, standing behind younger Democrats to fire up the base and get out the vote. Though I'm not sure how far left that movement will be. The nation may never embrace progressive ideals. I'm not sure we're mature enough to handle the concept of higher taxes in exchange for more services. Socialism is still the kiss of death, even though most Americans have no clue what it means or that to some degree, they already have it.

It may also be a mistake to assume that Democrats will be running against Trump. The Russia investigation could still yield revelations that are so self-evidently crooked or treasonous that congressional Republicans will be compelled to impeach him. Or Putin could wake one morning and decide he's bored with sleeping with their superior Russian hookers and feel it might be fun to throw the American government into further chaos by having Julian Assange release the pee tape.

That would leave us President Pence, one of the great minds of the 1950s, and a guy deeply in need of a charisma transplant. And that could lead to a 2020 primary challenge. Several Republicans seem to be raising their national profiles. There's Nebraska Senator Ben Sasse. Former Florida Congressman David Jolly. Obviously Paul Ryan's not done. Nor is Scott Walker. Or John Kasich.

Evan McMullin ran as an Independent in 2016, obviously in preparation for 2020. He's a strong conservative voice, with a CIA background. He's also a Mormon, but seemingly not an ideologue. Sort of the hipster Mitt Romney. He could be an intriguing choice for Republicans.

Ordinarily you could just file all this speculation under the heading of premature election, particularly when we're still working on surviving the results of the last one. But the media can barely contain their 2020 fever. They're like teenagers who just lost their virginity. They're all excited and can't wait to go again.

However, if Trump is still in office and we don't experience another major terrorist attack, in which case we'll become obsessed with national defense, he'll have to run on his own record, and the results of his policies.

The social contract underlying both the New Deal and Great Society have withstood a relentless pounding by Republicans over the last several decades and now they're feeling empowered enough to finish the job. As bluntly stated by Trump OMB Director, Mick Mulvaney — a guy who acts like his hobbies are bar fights and haunting the dreams of young children — "We're not doing that anymore." It's supply side economics, with a side of 'roid rage.

But if factories don't magically sprout up, and jobs don't return, people may begin to feel betrayed. Most people can't wrap their minds around climate change because it's not something tangible in their lives, but they may react when they lose their health care or free birth control. Clean water is just a liberal talking point until flammable, carcinogenic brown shit starts pouring out of the faucet.

Should Elizabeth Warren or Bernie Sanders decide to run, I would support them wholeheartedly, as I agree with their vision of how life ought to be. But if it's just going to be high ideals with no details and no balls then we could be headed for another November ass-kicking. Frankly, the only sight more revolting than watching Trump get elected would be watching him get re-elected. (Remember Bush 2004? That seemed impossible, too.) To me, there is only one 2020 agenda for any patriotic, sensible American, left, right or center — VOTE TRUMP OUT!

With that goal in mind, I have a modest proposal: Instead of the two parties going through the traditional internecine battles between their respective moderate and extreme wings, form a bi-partisan ticket — some combination of a Republican, Democrat or Independent. Call it the New Patriot party. The Coalition for a New America. Call it the Vote the Crazy Motherfucker Out Party. Who cares? Just vote the crazy motherfucker out.

It's a message that might just resonate with voters. It could siphon off Republicans with buyer's remorse while giving Trump supporters a face-saving option. Extremists on the right could yell RINO until their heads exploded but the attack might lose its power. After four years of Trump, reasonable people on either side might just be looking for salvation. And sanity. Ideological purity is meaningless if you're out of power.

Politically, it would freak the shit out of Trump. Imagine him trying to fight a dual-front war. It didn't work for Hitler. It wouldn't work for him. He wouldn't know whom to tweet against.

It could also work as a pragmatic solution to Washington gridlock. Of course it would necessitate politicians getting beyond partisan politics. "Let's compromise" hardly qualifies as a rallying cry. Progressives would have to let go of their platform of "Utopia or Die," and get past the "narcissism of small differences." And those on the right might have to back off the war on Planned Parenthood. It's just sex and human reproduction. It won't hurt you.

It would also help if the old South would actually just die, and not rise again, zombielike, from the grave. Not the people, the mentality. We need to bury this part of our past and salt the earth so it doesn't grow again. Younger generations have been raised in a different media environment. The culture has changed. Hopefully race hate isn't hereditary, like a genetic predisposition for diabetes. Maybe they just need some encouragement. Or therapy. In the '60s, Freedom Riders got on buses and went down South to register voters. Why not send teams of therapists to work on their anger issues? Psychological freedom riders. I wonder if they'd be welcomed with the same kind of Southern hospitality.

There are legitimate conversations about our social responsibility to each other and how that should be reflected in the role of the federal government. But when politicians on either side namedrop "the American people" to justify their policies, they're simply revealing a value judgment on American life. One side thinks we live in a society where if you do well, you can kick in a little more to lift other people up, creating a world in which everyone feels like they have a shot. This gives rise to a strong middle class in which people feel they can climb as far up the economic ladder as their talents and hard work can take them. Of course, we use the economic ladder as the measure of success, but that's how we define happiness, which is another conversation.

To those on the other side, this is simply "income redistribution" and creates a nanny state by giving lazy people welfare for life. They think we live in a cashocracy, where they've made their money with their hard work and anyone else should be able to do the same, regardless of their individual abilities, background or life circumstances. After all, America is the land of opportunity. Why should they have to pay to give anyone a chance they didn't have? These people tend to universalize their own experience, assuming what's true for them is true for everyone.

You either get what society thinks you deserve by virtue of being a citizen, or you simply get what you can pay for. Historically, we've only made progress in this country by striking a balance between working in a capitalist system and living in a democratic society. Though our most powerful American symbol is still the flag, not the ATM.

Imperfect times necessitate imperfect solutions. A united front against Trump would promote a message of true bi-partisanship. Ultimately, people crave balance and stasis. If life in Trump World gets too dark, people might be willing to reach across the aisle and go a little parliamentary by forming a coalition ticket. This could provide some genuine leg tingle for voters weary of partisan politics. As much as we love our contests and our winners and losers, if American life becomes a zero sum game, ultimately nobody wins.

Of course, I have no illusions that this will ever happen. Both the hard-core right and progressive left are way too dug in. It's about power and ideological purity. In some ways we're still fighting The Civil War. Our times could be summed up in the famous line from the 1967 movie, *Cool Hand Luke*: "What we got here is failure to communicate."

Democrats have to be ready for a streetfight. And until they prove they are, please stop sending me fund-raising emails. You're starting to sound like some guy outside a 7/11, barking "Gimme a dollar!" First get your shit together. Then hit me up for cash.

     We also can't assume the metrics of the last election will be the same in another four years. We have no idea what the country, the world, or the political landscape will look like.

CHAPTER ELEVEN

THE
2020
ZEITGEIST

AMERICA
SHINING CITY ON A HILL
OR
TRUMPIAN DYSTOPIA?

*We assume Orwell's 1984 dystopian nightmare
can't happen here, yet we've been narcotized into
a more Orwellian somnambulism. We're inebriated on
our own mythology, priapic at our military supremacy,
and malleable via our iconic imagery, whether it's
Jesus or the flag. Jacked up on Adderall, Red Bull,
and patriotism, we only unite in war, tragedy, and
the Super Bowl. We've become style over substance,
image over reality, propaganda over truth, and
symbol over meaning… Sadly, as we devolve from
Democracy to Idiocracy, America may become the
first world power to crumble under the weight
of its own stupidity.*

*Welcome to Dumbfuckistan: The Dumbed-Down,
Disinformed, Dysfunctional,
Disunited States of America*

Zeitgeist — the spirit of the times. One of those utilitarian German words that blend unrelated concepts into an expressive verbal strudel. Like *weltanschauung* (world view), *weltschmerz* (world-weariness) or even *fremdenfeindlichkeit* (fear of foreigners).

I've never had the urge to study German, especially not with French seductively taunting me. It would be like wanting to master armpit farts before learning classical piano. Still, there's something about this moment in history that brings the few German words I know to mind. I'm stuck somewhere between the hysteria of likening the current political situation to the rise of the Third Reich, and the assumption that, of course, it can't happen here.

While we've had our flirtations with right wing demagogues — McCarthy, Goldwater, Wallace — ultimately our fundamental decency kicked in and we rejected them. But with Trump, we've come dangerously close to growing our very own American dictator. And unlike the German version, this wasn't a reaction to economic hard times. We weren't in a depression. I think it was the emotional blowback from the election of the first African-American president and changes in the social and demographic fabric of the country.

When you consider that Hillary won the popular vote, most Americans felt the country was basically headed in the right direction. Not that life was ideal. It's never ideal. Someone's always pissed off about something, whether it's jobs, income inequality, gun violence, abortion, taxes or transgender people peeing wherever they like. There's nothing we love more than being pissed off about something.

Presidential elections reflect the spirit of the times and the mood of the country as we careen back and forth between hope and fear. Just looking back at my own boomer lifetime: Eisenhower offered stability to people exhausted by war. JFK symbolized hope for a new generation. LBJ calmed a nation still in shock from the JFK assassination and was a voice of sanity in contrast to Goldwater and his nuke-happy running mate. Nixon ran on "law and order" in a time of anti-war protests, riots, and social revolution. (John Ehrlichman, Nixon's counsel and Assistant for Domestic Affairs, later admitted they were intentionally playing the race card.) Carter represented a post-Watergate, cleansing return to our ideals. Reagan sold national pride to people tired of introspection, inflation and our impotence in resolving the Iran hostage crisis. Bush 1 — well, we just punted on that one. Clinton was the boomer JFK. Then Bush 2 narrowly rode in on a return to old-time values, thanks to Al Gore distancing himself from Clinton's record.

(You could play alternative history and posit that even if Gore prevailed in 2000, 9/11 might've happened anyway and Republicans would have seized on it, hammering Democrats for being soft on defense and possibly winning the White House in 2004, essentially delaying the start of the Iraq War by a year or so.)

Obama promised a return to competence and stability after 9/11, a disastrous Iraq War, and near economic collapse, while also symbolizing social progress as the first African-American president — literal hope and change. But his victory kicked off a right wing freak-out. JFK's declaration in his 1960 inaugural address that "the torch has been passed to a new generation" was a message of hope for the future. Obama's election resulted in that torch being picked up by a mob of angry Republican villagers as they rampaged into town shrieking about socialism.

And this led to Trump. People flocked to hear him sell a return to the halcyon days of American industrial might and national pride — Nixonian fear-mongering with a touch of neo-Reaganism.

As he said during the campaign, "We're going to win so much, you may even get tired of winning. You're gonna say, 'please, please, it's too much winning. We can't take it anymore. Mr. President, it's too much.' And I'll say 'no, it isn't. We have to keep winning. We have to win more!'"

Well, so far, not so much winning. Trump came out of the box stepping on his own dick: A dystopian inaugural address, followed by ravings about crowd sizes. Two botched Muslim bans shot down in the courts. A brewing scandal involving collusion with a hostile foreign power during the election. If it's not actual treason, it's treason-ish. One cabinet secretary gone, and an Attorney General "misspeaking" to Congress and subsequently recusing himself from the Russia investigation. Ridiculous wiretapping accusations against his predecessor. Demonizing the press and intelligence communities. Press conferences ranging from ignorant to racist to deranged. And threatening North Korea with nuclear war.

(From a purely political standpoint, I think he blew it by not coming out with a WPA-style infrastructure bill funded by repatriating corporate money stashed overseas. This would have put Democrats in the schizophrenic position of having to vote against jobs, which could have sent them deeper into the political wilderness. He could have even stuck the money for his stupid wall in there instead of trying to jam it into a budget fight as a dim-witted negotiating ploy. Of course, with the specter of obstruction of justice charges looming over Trump, his people are making noises about $1 trillion in infrastructure spending. All the Kings Horses…)

Trump may be evidencing himself as a total disaster. But unless there's another terrorist attack, which could send us into survival mode, Americans tend to vote their economic self-interest. Even though Trump's proposed budget amounts to a virtual drone strike on the poor and middle class, for argument's sake, suppose his policies magically lead to economic growth.

Let's say a combination of low corporate taxes and de-regulation kickstarts the engine of capitalism and a new prosperity sweeps the nation. There are more jobs than people. Factories are turning out stuff we didn't even know we needed. Even in the crime-ravaged inner cities gang kids are beating their Glocks into skateboards so they can ride them to their brand new, Jesus-themed charter schools. And we're all living in McMansions and driving Humvees, since it turned out they didn't harm the environment because climate change actually was a Chinese hoax, so the polar ice caps re-iced, and the bears were happily fishing again instead of helplessly floating out to sea.

Let's say ISIS has been wiped off the face of the Earth because he actually "bombed the shit out of them." And the ones he didn't blow up buckled under the threat of his gangsta commander-in-chief rap, or fell under the sway of his capitalist charm, and abandoned their jihadi ways to take construction jobs building Trump golf courses. Meanwhile, we built so many nukes the Russians and North Koreans went limp. Oh, and despite his complete lack of foreign policy experience, Jared Kushner used his boyish charm to bring peace to the Middle East.

Let's say every American citizen was armed, but no one was angry, and we reclaimed our might as the industrial capital of the world. And life was nothing but beer, sex, and football, as a feeling of hope and peace spread across the land. Even with less tax money coming in, he just put the recovery on the credit card and kick the deficit can down the road. People only thought they cared about the deficit when the Republican talking point was about "mortgaging our children's future." If people are working, no one will care. Raising the deficit didn't tarnish the Reagan hagiography.

Let's say he's not a consummate bullshit artist who's on a power trip that would make Hitler look like a Buddhist. Trump could go down in history for actually doing great things. Big things. Fantastic things. So fantastic. And amazing. If that happened, I'd be the first to agree with the Reverend Franklin Graham (son of the miraculously still not dead Reverend Billy Graham, advisor to presidents and one the great religious hucksters of all time) when he said "It wasn't the Russians who intervened in the election, it was God." I'd agree that the Republican Sky Daddy looked down from the clouds, pointed a giant finger at the pussy-grabber, and bellowed "Him! He is the anointed one!" Then wise men came out of the east guided by a shining star to his humble birthplace in Queens N.Y., bearing gold-plated toilets to lay at his feet.

However, if that doesn't happen, he'll have no excuses. Just like with Nixon's petulant goodbye to the press after losing the 1962 California Governor's race, he won't have Obama to kick around anymore. You have to give Republicans credit. For eight years it was two degrees of Obama-bashing. They could blame the rain on Obama, unless there was a draught, in which case they'd blame the lack of rain on him. But if times are bad, the blame game will become inoperative.

Trump may have campaigned on the re-empowerment of angry, white America, but if their lives go down the shitter, their love may turn out to be purely transactional. And Democrats will have to make sure he owns it. He likes putting his name on things. He can put his name on 2020. Call it Trump World.

He may be so power drunk that he's underestimating the potential blowback from his policies: If he signs a mutant health care bill that kicks millions off their insurance, there will be a backlash. If there are more police shootings because the Attorney General made it tougher to prosecute bad cops, it will lead to more confrontation and violence. If he screws with net neutrality, he'll instantly feel the wrath of millennials. Changing the structure of Social Security and Medicare will provoke strong reactions from an aging boomer generation.

It doesn't matter that during the campaign he said, "I'm going to protect and save your Social Security and your Medicare." People interpreted that to mean he was going to leave those existing structures in place. But if you hold that statement up to the light, it might not mean what you think it means.

"I will protect and save" could easily be restated as "the Social Security trust fund is running out of money so the only way to *save* it is to privatize it. And the only way to *protect* Medicare is through block grants to the states to allow them to administer it, as they're more in touch with the specific needs of their people." That could result in states making harsh cuts.

Imagine if he succeeds in privatization just as George Bush tried after being re-elected in 2004. Then imagine if the Social Security trust fund was in the stock market during the 2008 crash. Though maybe if the war on terror gets too costly, and if Social Security goes bust, we could save a fortune on bombs <u>and</u> entitlements by dropping old people from planes. It's win-win.

And that's assuming he won't plunge us into a war. Given his desire for a massive increase in the defense budget, and his lust for "winning wars" again, he's already revealed himself as a classic, trigger-happy chickenhawk. It's not exactly comforting that the most sobering military influence on him is a guy nicknamed "Mad Dog."

Trump likes playing army. He likes saluting when he gets off the helicopter. It's like he's in military school all over again, but with live ammo. He may not be satisfied with just putting on the American version of those nutty North Korean missile parades, with soldiers marching in jerky lockstep, followed by caravans of tanks; basically, dicks on wheels.

(You know that in his spare time he poses in the mirror wearing his soldier suit and RayBans. I bet Ivanka's already working on a line of Daddy Dictator Couture to hawk on her website.)

Like many his age, Trump's stuck in that Manichean World War II mentality of the good guys against the bad guys, with troops coming home to march in ticker-tape victory parades. The mission-creep lessons of Vietnam, Iraq and Afghanistan seem lost on him, along with the fact that overwhelming military power doesn't guarantee victory, especially not on a conventional battlefield.

He'd probably prefer a Gulf War-type, mechanized, telegenic battle where superior firepower wins out. Something branded and stage-managed, with a snappy name like Desert Storm. (It was obvious they'd learned the media lessons of Vietnam. There were no bodies being carried off the battlefield. No flag-draped coffins and somber funerals. The media was embedded, and the message was controlled. They even cast it well. General "Stormin' Norman" Schwarzkopf was the perfect host for the last of our modern battles.)

Trump's already in a nuclear dick measuring contest with Kim Jung-un, though he's just working his tough guy negotiating ploy, thinking it will make the other guy blink. He thinks he's being clever, but his bluster reveals the simplicity of his thinking.

He always comes out with the same opening gambit, which may work when you're trying to acquire land to build a casino. But this is nuclear poker. If the North Korean boy king is willing to commit national suicide, that could be his ace in the hole.

Then there's the fight against terrorism at home. It's indicative of Trump's schizophrenic campaign rhetoric that he was hawking militarism, while simultaneously pushing isolationism. Nation-building has been an ill-conceived failure with horrific consequences. But equally misguided is the simplistic notion that retreating behind real or virtual border walls will keep us safe. 9/11 proved that the world has a way of reaching out and remind us it's there. If this is Trump World 2020, he'll have a tough time lying about his record, let alone running on it.

Of course, none of these things may happen so dramatically. Trump may have evidenced himself as a neophyte when it comes to governing, but like the creature in *Alien*, he may have the ability to learn. He could graduate from grabbing power to figuring out how to wield it more subtly. Or he could just get out of the way and let Republicans work on the gradual "deconstruction of the administrative state."

The price of our 2016 American freak-out was our national soul. Hopefully we didn't sell it. Maybe we just took a reverse mortgage on it. Whether Trump turns out to be just a psychotic episode in American history or the wave of the future remains to be seen. Only time, world events, and whether he survives the Russia-gate investigations will tell. In the meantime, the question becomes not only how to fight it, but how to survive it.

CHAPTER TWELVE

DON'T GIVE IN TO CYNICISM OR DESPAIR

"We must accept finite disappointment, but never lose infinite hope."

Martin Luther King, Jr.

In August 2016, a photograph of a dazed, bloody Syrian boy sitting in the back of an ambulance captured international attention. That was after the picture of a drowned 3-year-old Syrian boy lying on a beach captured international attention. Since then the horrifying images of children suffering from a sarin gas attack, courtesy of their own government, not only captured international attention but compelled the president to reverse his policy of non-intervention and launch a retaliatory missile strike.

In relating the story to *Fox Business Network's* Maria Bartiromo, Trump noted that the information about the attack was relayed to Chinese President Xi Jinping while they were eating "the most beautiful piece of chocolate cake you've ever seen."

What the fuck is the matter with this person?! If you were telling this story, would you really feel compelled to include the cake part? That's like telling someone their loved one was kidnapped by a serial killer, dragged into a dank basement, murdered in cold blood, and then eaten… with a zesty Sriracha sauce.

And it's not like he was relating the story with any degree of irony, noting the juxtaposition between the deadly violence of the missile attack and the life-affirming sweetness of the cake. Then he said he'd bombed Iraq instead of Syria. When reality surpasses parody and satire, and even black humor seems tame, what world are we in? And are we doomed to live there?

Several months into his term a poll showed that over 90% of Trump voters were still happy with their choice. Only some felt like they got drunk and woke up married to a hooker then realized they had to bring her home for Thanksgiving. (Movie idea: A young conservative gets drunk, wakes up married to a hooker and realizes he has to bring her home for Thanksgiving. Title: "Ho For The Holidays.")

Even if the Russia story becomes an all-consuming shit-cloud, the Republican House probably won't move to impeach. And even if, in two years, a Democratic House filed articles of impeachment, the Senate would never convict. And I doubt Trump will ever resign. Despite cries that he's done; he's never done. The guy loves fighting, hates losing, and lives for revenge. Cockroach that he is, so far he's proven he can survive most anything.

Meanwhile, the GOP agenda remains slowly on the march, as Republicans reshape America in their own, dark image. In my previous book I sarcastically suggested that if some states really wanted to secede from Obama's America they could get the fuck out. We'd build a wall and fence them out. A bit snarky, I admit. Well now the tables have turned and blue states are talking secession.

So, maybe we'll go. As long as we're building a great big, beautiful wall along our southern border, we could build another one down from Canada, sectioning off California, Oregon, and Washington. Califoregonington. Maybe the two walls could meet, albeit perpendicularly, with a special door that allowed immigrants into the new America West. We'll keep Hawaii since it's already on our side. And west coast economies are thriving. You can hang on to Kansas. It's a Republican Petri Dish disaster anyway.

Obviously, that's not happening so we're stuck together. So are those of us unhappy with this president just screwed? Who knows? He may have taken an oath to "preserve, protect, and defend the Constitution" but that doesn't mean it meant anything beyond the words he had to say in a ceremony.

He's basically playing at being president. He doesn't like governing. He resents the idea of separation of powers, gets angry at being cock-blocked by Congress, but loves Executive Orders because ruling by fiat reflects his temperament. He hates the First Amendment but loves the Second Amendment, and who knows if he'll come to develop an affection for the Fifth Amendment, like his good friend, Michael Flynn.

In the meantime, the future of the planet could simply come down to what Trump wants—the fate of the world hanging in the balance of an unbalanced mind. So, what does he want? Immortality? He's already been elected president. His portrait will eventually hang in the White House, a level of fame far eclipsing having your name on a golf course, fake university or slab of beautifully marbled meat. He'll eventually have a presidential library, though it'll be gold-plated, with a crappy gift shop and no books.

I'm sure he dreams about having his face carved on Mt. Rushmore, maybe sandblasting over Washington, Jefferson, Lincoln, and Roosevelt. Or maybe he'll build his own golden tribute to immortality in Washington, something blending the dignity of the Lincoln Memorial and the tumescence of the Washington Monument. Then all the schoolkids could take field trips to D.C. and bitch about how tiring it was to climb to the top of Trump's dick.

Or maybe he's envisioning a Trump presidential dynasty, modeled on the succession of Kim Il-sung, Kim Jung-il and Kim Jung-un. He's politically marooned the two imbecile sons to either running his business, or pretending to run it, while they jet around the world murdering exotic animals. Maybe he's setting us up for the other two—Ivanka/Jared 2024. Though frankly, if we do get stuck with a Kim Dynasty, I'd prefer one in the lineage of Kardashian and Kanye. He seems a tad less crazy than Trump.

Though if he is after immortality, his victory could turn out to be more of a curse than a blessing, the result of putting himself in a position where the Peter Principle bites him in the ass. He may have actually lied his way up to the level of his incompetence. As much as he craves fame, he could end up with infamy. Number one on the Top Ten List of Great American Fuck-Ups.

If all he wants is to steal billions in a Putin-style kleptocracy, he can have at it. Just don't kill us. If there's a terrorist attack, we can only hope he doesn't go right for the nukes. Maybe Ivanka can explain to him that money will lose its value if we're all dead.

So until he reveals himself, how do we deal with it?

Tracking the daily shit show has become exhausting. We're being hit with an unprecedented level of misinformation, the point of which is to beat people into submission—mentally, physically, and emotionally. To confuse and disorient us to the point where facts are subjective, truth is relative, and meaning doesn't exist.

Even though the media has learned its Trump-coverage lessons, some have occasionally slipped back into old habits. When Trump couldn't find anyone to lavish praise on him for his first 100 days in office, he praised himself by staging one of his masturbatory rallies in Harrisburg, Pennsylvania. And on the same day as the annual White House Correspondents' Association Dinner, the venue that launched him into our lives in 2011. The one he was too much of a pussy to attend this time.

I didn't watch the rally, as one of my survival tactics is to moderate my Trump intake. I can absorb it in small doses, usually filtered, but I can't drink it straight. So in an effort to depressurize, I turned on the TV to search for a baseball game, but before I could switch to *ESPN,* there it was—the stupid, fucking rally. On *MSNBC.* Same crowd. Same signs. Same MAGA hats. Same stupid shtick.

And there he was, grinning like an imbecile while barfing up his self-aggrandizing, perverted version of history. And once again, it aired uninterrupted, with the graphic: Breaking News! And illustrated with a rolling series of quotes from his speech. There were no studio cutaways. No commentary. No context. I kept it on as long as I could, with the sound on mute, just to see if they'd break in. They didn't.

At some point I couldn't even stand the visual of this preening cow carcass working the crowd so I hit the "guide" button and my TV spontaneously switched to a movie: *Judgment at Nuremberg.* I decided to take that as a sign that at least DirecTV believes that goodness triumphs over evil. Whether it actually does remains to be seen.

So, until then, how do we cope? In difficult times we tend to cling to our myths. We have faith in our American institutions and the comforting feeling that our democracy will protect us. It's an integral part of our American mindset, and our popular culture to think that scandals always come out. That the bad guys always get busted, the good guys always win, and the integrity of the system is restored.

We take heart in the *Mr. Smith Goes to Washington* mythology that good always triumphs, but it doesn't. We only think it does, which reflects both our strength as a nation, and our naiveté as a people. There's no historical record of the lying, cheating, and stealing that politicians have gotten away with over the years because they never got busted. We never hear about the backroom deals that stayed hidden in the back room. There have been successful payoffs in exchange for favors. We like to think that crime doesn't pay but, in truth, crime probably pays very well.

So where do we look for hope? Human nature? I don't know. Sometimes I look at history and wonder where we get the balls to refer to what we've got going on here as civilization. We all go through life in the 100 or so years we get. My century was ushered in with the post-WWII age, through Korea, Vietnam, 9/11, Iraq and Afghanistan. We also managed to work in a Cold War, during which the U.S. and U.S.S.R. compiled tens of thousands of nuclear warheads and the only deterrent to one side annihilating the other was our "mutually assured destruction," shorthanded into the Strangelovian acronym MAD. And it was madness.

We've managed to inflict an unspeakable amount of carnage on one another in a seemingly endless series of wars and conflicts, either between nations or within them. Paradoxically, the only thing occasionally preventing people from killing each other has been the autocratic rule of a dictator, yet his removal has often left a power vacuum resulting in civil war. Even when a movement like the Arab Spring offered momentary hope somehow the country got sucked back into the totalitarian vortex. We've even managed to pervert our religious traditions into excuses for murder.

Our ability to create more sophisticated weapons of

mass destruction has brought us the era of drone war — war as video game. We've even invented the phrase "collateral damage" to disinfect the fact that on occasion, civilians get killed. The horror that is Syria is a perfect paradigm for the state of the world, and the impotence of civilized people to do anything to stop it.

According to former Director of the National Security Council, the late Zbigniew Brzezinski, in a book entitled *Out of Control: Global Turmoil on the Eve of the 21st Century* in the previous century alone we managed to kill between 167 and 175 million people. When you filter out all the times, places, and players, and the direct and indirect causes, all this homicidal mania turns into one giant human clusterfuck.

I'm not sure what evidence there is that the 21st century will bring out our better angels instead of our inner demons. At this moment, there are about 57 wars on 5 continents, mostly the result of repressive dictatorships, oligarchies, and kleptocracies, as well as terrorists, drug gangs, and long-standing civil wars.

And the irony is that most of the tools for these conflicts have been manufactured by the U.S., England, France, Russia, China, and Germany — more or less the "civilized world." So, in the broadest sense, we're not actually killing each other, we're killing ourselves. We're actually committing global suicide by manufacturing the implements of our own destruction.

Who knows if the fault lies in our stars or in ourselves. Maybe civilization is heading for an inevitable showdown between an American jihadist hell-bent on starting a holy war with the east and Middle East fanatics working toward a holy war with the west. Both sides could get their wish and blow up the world, and it will actually end with a bang, with each side uttering the final, pathetic whimper "you started it." A fitting epitaph for the human race.

Still, there has to be some happy medium between "don't worry, be happy" and "we're all going to die." Maintaining a healthy skepticism is a survival mechanism. But loss of hope can descend into apathy, nihilism, and ultimately into fatalism. Which doesn't seem like the best way to live. The only constant in life is change. And living in a state of fear can be paralyzing. To paraphrase Heraclitus: you can't drown in the same river twice.

I like to think that the arc of the moral universe bends toward justice. The same could be said for the arc of American history. It also bends toward reason, and sanity. But it's a slow, slow bend. And each step forward seems to lead to a backlash. It takes decades for new ideas to permeate society and be accepted as the new normal. It also requires generations to die out without leaving a slime trail of hatred behind them.

Ultimately, American democracy may only be as vital as the most hopeful among us, and as weak as the most cynical. As Yale professor Timothy Snyder noted on *Real Time with Bill Maher:* our institutions won't save us; we have to save the institutions. Whether this election turns out to be a pendulum swing or a descent into madness may be up to us.

Optimism may not be the logical takeaway from modern life or human behavior but it may be our only salvation. We have to hold on to our ideals, not because they reflect our current reality, but because they become a self-fulfilling existential choice. Ultimately, you create the world based on how you believe it should be.

(I realize that teeters dangerously close to sounding like one of those inspirational quotes people stick on Facebook with sunsets in the background, all to create the impression that they have deep thoughts. That's why I tend to avoid expressions of hope. It's hard to make the case without sounding hacky.)

At this point, it would be easy to drag out the well-known quote from "The Diary of Anne Frank."

> *"In spite of everything, I still believe that*
> *people are really good at heart.*
> *I simply can't build up my hopes on a*

foundation consisting of confusion,
misery, and death. I see the world
gradually being turned into a wilderness,
I hear the ever-approaching thunder which
will destroy us, too, I can feel the suffering of
millions and yet, if I look up to the heavens,
I think that it will all come right, that this
cruelty too will end, and that peace
and tranquility will return again.

C'mon, it's the optimist's mic drop. How could you stay cynical with those words staring you in the face? I mean if a young girl could find hope with Nazis thumping up the stairs, then no one's got the right to bitch or drown in self-pity. But it's also too manipulative.

Right after the election I downloaded two books. The first was William S. Shirer's *The Rise and Fall of the Third Reich.* I'm still slogging through it. Knowing how it turns out takes some of the curse off it, but it's still scary as shit. I just felt a need to look for historical parallels.

(Anyone who reacted to Trump's "I alone can fix it" convention speech, not just for its megalomania, but for the unusual phrasing, might want to check out the speech Hitler made to his supporters after his release from prison. He said, "I alone lead the movement." Seems Melania wasn't the only one plagiarizing. Though, if you're going to steal, steal from the best.)

It's a sad fact of life that human beings are susceptible to the impulses of a dictator. Economic desperation, anger, changing times—when these conditions conspire, people don't think rationally, they react emotionally. This opens the door for tyrants who find convenient scapegoats and promise easy solutions. By reducing the complexities of life to simple categories, they take advantage of people's frustrations and use them as a steppingstone to power.

And even though the daily insanity has occasionally driven me to a point where I'm ready to blow my brains out, metaphorically speaking, I managed to find an unexpected source of optimism, ironically from a guy who actually blew his brains out. Hunter S. Thompson. Specifically, his masterwork on American politics: *Fear and Loathing on the Campaign Trail – 1972*. That was the other book I read.

Despite the surly, drunken cynicism that flavored most every page, somehow a feeling of optimism rose out of it. At heart, this guy was a patriot. (This may just be my misreading but I'm going with it.) While covering the 1972 election, he wrote:

"The tragedy of all this is that George McGovern,
for all his mistakes and all his imprecise
talk about 'new politics' and 'honesty in government'
is one of the few men who've run for
President of the United States in this
century who really understands what a
fantastic monument to all the best instincts
of the human race this country might have been
if we could have kept it out of the hands of
greedy little hustlers like Richard Nixon."

We've now got ourselves another greedy little hustler who rose to power by playing to the worst in us instead of inspiring the best in us. But the genius of democracy is that it's a safeguard against authoritarianism.

We survived Hitler, Nixon, and Cheney. If we don't blow ourselves up, there's a good chance we'll survive Trump. And while all the references to dictatorships and the Trumpocalypse may seem like hysterical over-reactions, I'd rather overreact and be relieved than assume the best and be shocked.

Meanwhile I'll be checking out real estate in some of our picturesque, small American towns. I'm assuming the North Koreans won't waste a nuke on Middle America. I've also renewed my passport in the event that being an ex-pat becomes a viable alternative. I probably won't leave, but fantasizing about it is an effective coping mechanism and an emotional safety valve.

So, that's it. I'm done ranting here, though I'll probably keep it up in another forum. There's not much to do but write, talk to people, stay informed, attend the occasional rally, vote, drink some wine, take a pill, try not to get too down, stock up on canned goods, and hold fast to loved ones, wherever they are. I may even try meditating, or an occasional walk in the woods.

I'll close it out with the words of the great CBS journalist Edward R. Murrow, who helped take down another power-mad American politician: "Goodnight. And good luck."

IAN GURVITZ
BIOGRAPHY

I am a native New Yorker who has lived in Los Angeles for the last 30 years, working as a television writer. I've written several books: *Hello, Lied the Agent,"* a journal about TV development; *Deconstructing God – A Heretic's Case for Religion"* and *Welcome to Dumbfuckistan – The Dumbed-Down, Disinformed, Dysfunctional, Disunited States of America.* I also published a book of drawings — *Talking Heads*, and wrote and directed an indie film, *L.A. Blues.*

I've written on politics and religion for *The Huffington Post*, and *Attn.com.*, and contributed pieces on various subjects to the *L.A. Times*, and *Creative Screenwriting* Magazine.

I can be found on social media, should anyone want to engage in a meaningful dialogue. If any trolls want to get into it I've already been hit a few times. I'm going to take the high road and interpret ((( ))) as hugs. If anyone's still not mollified, there's not much I can do but offer a pre-emptive, heartfelt fuck off. Sorry, I meant ((( ))).